Disconnected

Disconnected

Haves and Have-Nots in the Information Age

WILLIAM WRESCH

RUTGERS UNIVERSITY PRESS
New Brunswick, New Jersey

Library of Congress Cataloging-in-Publication Data

Wresch, William, 1947–
    Disconnected : haves and have-nots in the information age / William B.
Wresch.
       p.   cm.
    Includes bibliographical references and index.
    ISBN 0-8135-2369-9 (alk. paper). — ISBN 0-8135-2370-2 (pbk. : alk.
paper)
    1. Information technology.   2. Information technology—Social aspects.
3. Information society. I. Title.
T58.5.W74   1996
306.4'2—dc20   96-22375
                                                         CIP

British Cataloging-in-Publication information available

Manufactured in the United States of America

Dedicated to David Lush, a journalist whose integrity, courage, and effort is an example to all of us

Contents

Preface

There's an old joke about a farmer who can't get a mule to budge. No matter what he tries, the mule just won't move. Finally, another farmer walks up, surveys the situation, and offers to solve the problem. He reaches into the back of a wagon, pulls out a two-by-four, and hits the mule hard on the side of the head. The mule immediately begins following orders. The man with the two-by-four turns to the mule's owner and says, "A mule will do anything you want, but first you have to get his attention."

This book is the result of my being hit by a two-by-four. It shouldn't have been necessary to get my attention. My Ph.D. dissertation was on human information processing. I head a university Computer Information Systems program. I have directed Total Quality Management teams and preached the importance of information gathering. I sat through meetings of a Governor's Task Force in Accountability and saw the continued need for information in the public sector. I have spent the last two decades as a living, breathing citizen of the information age, but I just wasn't seeing it.

I got my two-by-four in Africa. The U.S. government sponsors the Fulbright Exchange Program, which goes back fifty years to the effort after the Second World War to help rebuild European universities. The program worked, and we have been sending American professors all over the world ever since (we also bring lots of professors and graduate students here). I was selected to teach for a year in the Computer Science Department of the newly established University of Namibia. My family and I arrived in Windhoek, Namibia, in September 1993.

Namibia is a country in transition. One of the last colonies in Africa, it was taken by the Germans in 1884 and run with singular brutality until 1915, when the South Africans took over. For the next seventy-five years whites ruled. The brutality of the South African regime has been described in many books, and we had an opportunity to study the country's sad history before we arrived. We knew we were going to a country that had been through hell. We also knew we were going to a country that was making every effort to move beyond its history to an era of reconciliation, democracy, and opportunity.

But the past doesn't just go away—not in three years of independence. We discovered political problems as people slowly adjusted to majority rule, economic problems as tax policies were changed to benefit the poor, educational problems as attention was finally paid to the needs of black children. These were all problems people expected and were responding to.

My two-by-four came from a different direction. It began moving in my direction when I began asking questions. I spent roughly two months visiting corporate centers near the university. Windhoek, the capital of Namibia, is a modern city of 150,000 and the home to a number of fairly large businesses, all of which have sophisticated computer installations. Since I was to help design the computer curriculum at the university, I thought a good first step would be to visit these information-systems managers and find out what equipment, what development tools, and what design methodology they used. Essentially I wanted to know what my students would have to know to find jobs.

But I was curious and went a little further. Since these managers were working in a fairly remote corner of Africa, I was interested in their training. Computing is a field that keeps you humble. Whatever you knew last week is basically useless this week. How did these people stay up-to-date? What were their sources of information? It turned out they had easy access to some information and no access to other information. They were constantly in touch with people and resources in South Africa, Europe, and the United States, but knew almost nothing about other African states. I met only one manager who had visited another African country (other than South Africa) to learn how his peers in that country handled information. I found that very curious.

But the two-by-four struck with a vengeance when I took my next step. After I had my interviews with information-systems managers I felt I knew what the University of Namibia needed to do to meet their needs. But a university in the developing world has other responsibilities as well. Was there anything it could do, I wondered, about Namibia's huge unemployment problem? Every street corner in downtown Windhoek has dozens of men standing, waiting all day, every day, hoping for a day's work. I began interviewing these men. These conversations quickly became agony for me, for the men, and for my translator, Szacky Nuujoma, but we persisted. What I learned didn't make me feel very good.

Szacky and I began by getting background information on the men—what kinds of jobs they were able to get, how often they worked, what they were paid, where they lived, how they lived. We learned these men thought a good week was one in which they earned forty-five Namibian dollars (about twelve U.S. dollars). Since the cost of living in Windhoek is similar to that of a city in the

United States, they were all slowly starving. Often they went for weeks without any work. They talked of nothing but getting a day's employment, they dreamt of nothing else, they were obsessed with getting work.

Since the primary struggle of their lives was to find work, I asked how they found out about jobs. I used many of the same questions I had used with the corporate managers, only instead of asking how they found out about computer innovations, I asked how they found out about jobs. The answers were astonishing. It quickly became apparent that these men had no resources. Read the want ads in the paper? Many couldn't read; none could afford a paper. Watch the business news on TV? They didn't have electricity, much less TVs—besides, TV is broadcast in English, the official, but largely unknown, national language. Get help from churches, clubs, sports groups? These men were from a northern tribe, the Owambos. They had no connections to local groups. Anyway, with six or even seven days a week spent on the corners waiting for work, when did they have time to form alliances?

Any information source I asked them about came up dry. They were aliens in Windhoek, immigrants in their own country. There were few resources in Namibia to help men such as these, but what there were, these men would never know about. They were cut off from everything. The worst aspect of their situation was that there was little chance it would ever change. There was no hope.

This series of interviews left me shaken. I gave each man a little bit of money for his time, shook his hand, and then watched him walk back out to his corner. I now understood the gulf that existed between these men and those who drove by them.

It was about that this time that I also encountered the first people who wanted to enlarge that gulf. Oddly enough the encounter occurred at the U.S. embassy. A group of business people from California was visiting Namibia, and both the embassy and the Namibian government were excited about starting business connections between the two countries. The reception was a busy affair, with the main hall of the embassy full of people meeting, talking, exchanging business cards.

The press had been invited, and someone I knew from the local chamber of commerce introduced me to the business reporter from one of the local weeklies. The paper was notorious for its reactionary editorial policy, but they had sent a reporter and I tried to be courteous. It turned out that the reporter was very happy to talk to me, and we spent quite a bit of time together. Curiously, he never approached any of the California delegation, even though they were all around him. After a while he left. As near as I could tell, he never spoke with a Californian, and when I picked up the paper on Sunday there wasn't a word about the trade delegation, even though such delegations are rare. When

I tried to understand his behavior, I realized the reception invitations had identified the group as business people from California. It was only after he arrived that the reporter discovered with the rest of us that the entire delegation was African American. These weren't the kind of people he had expected to meet. They weren't people he wanted to meet. They weren't people he was prepared to write about. They weren't people he wanted his readers to know about. That Americans of African descent might own businesses, that they might be successful enough to afford the costs of world travel, that they might want to establish business relations with black Namibians—this was not something his paper would ever report.

Now the two-by-four had gotten my attention. I ached for the men who baked in the tropical sun day after day with no idea of how to get off the corner, for the managers who were blind to the rest of Africa, for citizens who were being sold a prepackaged view of the world by a newspaper that printed all the news that fit their prejudices. Gradually I began to take a new look at the information age—a much less complacent look.

Most worrisome for me was that as I looked for solutions, they seemed less and less technological. It would have been easy if I could have just said, "Import the latest Intel chips and Novell networks and everything will be fine." Actually, Namibia already had a significant technological base. Windhoek alone had thirty PC vendors. A week after Intel's Pentium chip was commercially available, there were Pentium computers in Namibia. The technology was there. It might not be available in every corner of the country, but it was in the country.

Technology didn't explain the problem. Something was at work in Namibia, something I would study in depth over the next nine months. Those studies would lead me back to the United States for a fresh look at our own information handling—the procedures and approaches that make us a model for the world, and the procedures and approaches that make us a planetwide laughingstock. This book is essentially a very lengthy report on that research.

This book is divided into five parts. The introduction, which serves as an executive summary, stands by itself. It presents my main arguments and key points. Chapters 1 to 5 cover principal information sources. Obviously, we all receive information from many sources, and any attempt to group or categorize those sources is personal and arbitrary. My hope is not that everyone will agree with my five labels or groups, but that these groups seem useful in describing our everyday experience.

The next three chapters, 6 to 8, describe information movement. For information to be useful to me, I have to be able to get to it. Much of the excitement about current technological developments is based on the hope that we will now have easier and faster access to information. And technology is helping. But we have to be realistic about both technology and other forces in the world.

Chapters 9 to 11 address an even more vexing problem. What if I manage to get the information and then can't understand it? What if the real problem is me? After eleven chapters of problems, it is only fair to finish with a chapter on solutions. There are some, and they are often no more complicated than being honest with one another.

Let me close this preface with thanks. The Fulbright Exchange Program sent me to Africa to lecture and so started me thinking on this topic of information access. Needless to say, they aren't responsible for any conclusions I have formed during my time in Namibia, or for any errors in my judgment. Helen Picard, the United States Information Service representative in Namibia, represents our country admirably, and helped me and my family frequently during our stay. The ambassador, Marshall MacCallie, and his wife Amee, were also a constant help. As an American, I felt reassured by the MacCallies and by the rest of our embassy staff—we are, in fact, putting our best foot forward in Africa.

The University of Namibia, only founded in 1993, was an excellent host. The senior university management had far better things to do with their time than solve my problems, but they were always there when I needed them. Also of great help was David Lush. Author of *Last Steps to Uhuru*, an excellent book about the independence of Namibia, David is brave, insightful, and knows half the people in Africa. He guided my research on the media, fed me document after document, and introduced me to his peers around southern Africa. If this book has anything useful to say about the media, it is because of David.

Another special source was Charles Chipango, a government expert in rural development. I got lucky when he chose to take my computer science class. What I know about the Bushman situation in Tsumkwe comes largely from him. He took me around and showed me the areas outsiders never see. I wish those places weren't there, and I have some regrets about seeing what I saw, but Charles made sure I saw the truth.

Additionally, Michael Gent was important to this project. A management professor also in Namibia on a Fulbright, he was our next-door neighbor and my mentor on business. When the subject of management came up, he was always ready with a book or an anecdote. His students at Canisius are lucky to have him.

If this book turns out to be useful, thank these individuals who helped. Karen Reeds was an active and enthusiastic editor. Shyamala Reddy had the courage to look at an early version of this book and offered very helpful suggestions while passing up limitless opportunities to criticize the many rough spots she found.

Neil Postman offered encouragement and helpful suggestions. I was honored that he took the time to help with this project.

If this book turns out to be wrong, blame me. Part of me hopes this book *is* wrong. I would like to think things are better than what I found and that there are fewer barriers than I identified. I would like to think the information highway will have an off ramp at every country and at every home. Maybe it will just take a little longer. It's a nice thought. Sometimes nice thoughts are true. Sometimes.

Disconnected

Information Rich, Information Poor

Theo Schoeman washes his BMW at 5:00 A.M. He is out early in part to beat the heat. While Windhoek, Namibia, sits at fifty-six hundred feet, its elevation can only partially offset the effects of the tropical sun that will rise by 6:30 and take afternoon temperatures into the nineties. Mostly Schoeman is up early because he faces a very full day. President of the family business, Schoeman Computers, he has an endless stream of business information he must absorb. Besides his e-mail connections to the business centers of Europe, he also receives CD-ROMs with thousands of business and technical articles from periodicals around the world. If he can get to his desk by six, he should be able to read his latest CDs for two hours before his employees arrive and the daily routine of meetings and phone calls start.

But not all of his connections are electronic. Fluent in English, German, and Afrikaans, he travels at least once each year to trade shows in Germany and the United States. He has a regular buyer in California who does direct purchasing for him, shipped out on a regular flight each Friday. They converse daily either via phone or via electronic mail. A lifelong Namibian, he has a wide circle of friends, but he supplements that circle with formal relationships he has cultivated over the years. When people in the technology field started talking about forming a group, he helped found the Namibian Information Technology Association (NITA). When the government civil service formed a Data Services Division, he began having regular meetings with its head and supplied her with free training sessions for her new employees.

In many ways Theo Schoeman could be the ideal "Information Man." When people describe the future, he is much of what they hope for—educated, affluent, well traveled. It would be nice to think that most of the world's people will live like Theo sometime soon. But before we get too excited about that future, there are a few additional things we should know about Theo Schoeman's day. After his twelve or fourteen hours at the office, Schoeman will come home. He may put a movie into his VCR, but it won't be a Namibian movie—there is no such thing. He might curl up with a Namibian book, but he won't do it very often—only about half a dozen are published each year. He could turn on the tube, but all he will see on it is American reruns and government propaganda. He might pick up the phone and direct dial dozens of friends in the United States or Germany, but he couldn't call more than a handful of people outside the capital city in his own country. In other words, Schoeman has amazing access to some kinds of information, no access at all to others—either the information doesn't exist or he can't get to it. There are barriers and blind spots in his world. Even the best and the brightest face limits.

Across town is Negumbo Johannes—everyone's nightmare about the information age. Johannes wakes every morning at six. He sleeps on the floor of a friend's house in Wanaheda. The house is a concrete block rectangle about the size of a one-car garage in the United States. Wanaheda is on the northern outskirts of Windhoek, north because that is where blacks were allowed to live under South African rule. His street is gravel. Water and electricity are planned, but neither has arrived yet. Johannes drinks a glass of water from the bucket on the table and goes next door to meet Filippus Erastus, a friend from his village along the Angolan border. Together they start the one-hour walk that takes them to downtown Windhoek.

Johannes and Erastus are day laborers. Men in their early twenties, they attended five or six years of school in their village and then spent the rest of their youth herding cattle for their family. At sixteen or seventeen they each had younger brothers who could take over the herd, so they started looking for something better. In the north there is nothing. Two or three times a year they went in to Oshikati, the main city of the north, to sell cattle or visit friends. The city is big, but there is little manufacturing, just small retail outlets and a few slaughterhouses. There are no jobs. Under South African rule members of their tribe were forbidden to travel or move to the southern parts of Namibia, but with independence in 1990 all restrictions were dropped. Some of their friends moved to Windhoek. That is where the money was. That is where the jobs were. Johannes and Erastus followed.

They did not find jobs. Windhoek, at 150,000 people, is far larger than Oshikati, and there is some manufacturing there, but not nearly enough to employ the thousands who stream in from the outer reaches of the country. Johannes tried. In his first weeks he walked to every business in the city. Each has a sign mounted by the employees' entrance—No Work it says in three languages. Several times he has used the entrance anyway, only to be chased away before he could even ask for a job. There is no work.

So he and his friends from the north stand on various corners in the downtown area. They arrive by seven and stand until four. On a good day a construction foreman will pull a pickup truck up to the corner. Johannes and all the other men—maybe twenty or thirty—will run to the truck. Some will jump in the back hoping they will be selected. Usually the foreman will order them back out and query each man individually about previous jobs he has done. Johannes will stand and describe work he has done and try to meet the man's eyes as long as he can. Sometimes he is chosen; sometimes he is not. When he is not, he never knows why. He is just ordered away. If he is chosen, he jumps into the back of the truck with the other lucky men.

On the job site, he does whatever he is told. Sometimes it is concrete work, building the walls of new houses. Sometimes it is loading or unloading trucks. Often it is digging foundations or trenches for water or electricity. On rare occasions his boss will give him a small lunch. Usually he works through the day on an empty stomach. At five the foreman will pay the men. It will be some amount between fifteen and twenty-five Namibian dollars (four to seven U.S. dollars). He takes whatever he is given without complaint, for any comments may mean he is never hired again. The foreman may drive the men up to Wanaheda or may let them walk.

Most days Johannes just stands on his corner waiting for work. He talks to the other men about places they may have recently worked, rumors they have heard about jobs. They get no lunch. They have no bathrooms. They debate whether to stay on the corner or move to another corner. Eventually the day passes and Johannes starts the hour-long walk home. He will fix some sort of dinner, his one meal of the day. He will pass the evening talking to his neighbors. The next day he will be back on the corner. In the past, he and his friends spent six days a week waiting for work and played soccer on Sunday. Recently some of the men have started spending Sunday on the corner too. Johannes hasn't yet, but since he is being hired fewer and fewer days each week (three days of work is an exceptional week), he is debating standing Sundays too. It would be a desperate thing to do, ending any break from the monotony of the corner, any break from the tropical sun, any break from the embarrassment of standing so visibly unemployed in a city where many drive Mercedes.

Negumbo Johannes leads a life of brutal poverty. He has no money, he has no skills, he has very little hope. His life has become almost an obsession with finding a job. He talks about it all day and dreams about it at night. His mental health is almost as precarious as his physical health. What he does not know is that his situation is getting worse. The information age has arrived in Africa and new systems are being established. Those systems totally exclude him.

Consider, if you will, Johannes's job search. Public information vehicles are available in Namibia that might tell him about economic trends and job opportunities. But he is excluded from virtually all of them. Newspapers cost N\$ 1.50—10 percent of his daily wage on days when he has a wage. So he doesn't buy them. Television is broadcast by the state, but few of his neighbors have a TV, and broadcasts are in English, a language he doesn't know. Radio has one channel broadcasting in Oshiwambo, his only source of news. Professional information excludes him because he has no profession. Namibia has professional societies to help their members stay current, and to help their members find work, but he will never be a member. Organizational information bypasses him as well. None of his employers take the time to inform him of their future directions, their future prospects. He will only be there a day—why should they waste time talking to him? His personal information is virtually nonexistent. He has no connections to church or sports or social groups that might give him job tips. His school friends are as desperate as he is. He has traveled nowhere but Windhoek and his village in the north, so he knows nothing of the world. The only language he speaks is his tribal language, a language few speak in Windhoek or elsewhere in the world. As for the great wired future, he will never in his life see a computer, much less use one to communicate or learn.

Both Theo Schoeman and Negumbo Johannes have much to tell us about our age. One is information rich, the other information poor. The gulf between them seems infinite. They might as well be living on separate planets. Yet even the rich man has problems. The information available to him is not nearly as unlimited as might seem the case. Faxes and modems may carry information, but they do not guarantee that information will exist to carry. Cyberspace is populated with numerous black holes—information vacuums that are largely ignored. As for Negumbo Johannes, he just wants to know who might give him a laboring job the next day, and he can't find anyone who will even talk to him. If this is the information age, what age is *he* in?

There may be miracles happening all around us—masses of optical fiber, four-hundred-channel TV, satellite uplinks, a World Wide Web of resources there at the click of a button. But Schoeman and Johannes remind us that, as is usually the case, there is much more to the story. For information rich and poor alike, there are problems. To understand those problems, and then to solve them, we must begin by looking at unexamined assumptions.

Unexamined Assumptions

One of the most basic models of the communication process begins with a simple triangle: sender, message, receiver. Somebody has to talk, something has to be said, somebody has to listen. If we map that model onto an overview of information handling, we could say information has to be generated, it has to be transmitted, and it has to be understood.

Nothing could be simpler. Except we make assumptions about each step in the process. We assume masses of information are being generated, more information every day, more than the world has ever seen before. That's not exactly wrong, but it's not totally right, either. Too much information is unavailable, even to the information rich like Theo Schoeman. We're missing something.

Similarly, we assume that information transmission problems are now a thing of the past. After all, we have optical fiber and satellite delivery systems. But is that all it really takes? If laying fiber means information now flows everywhere, what is Negumbo Johannes's problem?

And what about us as information receivers? Even if untold quantities of new information were suddenly available and delivered free to our door, would we know what to do with it? Where is the evidence to support *that* assumption?

The central point of this book is that we haven't asked enough about the basics. If information is doubling every three or five or seven or ten years, where has all that information gone? Is the world really awash in information? And if it is, is that the end to all the world's problems? We are counting articles and pointing to large numbers, but not looking closely enough at the information being generated. We are talking about bandwidth as a solution to information flow without looking carefully enough at how information really moves from one place to another—and why it often cannot move at all. And we are arrogant about our own abilities to handle information despite endless examples of our frailties.

If we are going to take advantage of developments in information access, we have to begin by being honest about the kind of information that is available, the ability of information to move, and our own ability to process it. We will take a quick overview of those three areas in this chapter, and then spend the rest of the book examining them in detail.

HOW MUCH INFORMATION IS THERE?

Over the past decade or two we have been told there is an information explosion going on. We are told we now live in the information age. John Naisbitt summed up much of this sentiment in his massive best seller, *Megatrends* (1982).

His first trend: "Although we continue to think we live in an industrial society, we have in fact changed to an economy based on the creation and distribution of information" (1). He goes on to say that "more than 60 percent of us work with information as programmers, teachers, clerks, secretaries, accountants, stockbrokers, managers, insurance people, bureaucrats, lawyers, bankers, and technicians" (14). As support for his assertions, Naisbitt cites the following figures: (1) Between six and seven thousand scientific articles are written each day; (2) scientific and technical information now increases 13 percent per year, which means it doubles every 5.5 years; and (3) the rate will soon jump to perhaps 40 percent per year because of new, more powerful information systems, and an increasing population of scientists (24).

More recently it is Alvin Toffler who has commanded our attention with his series of books describing the changes being brought to our world by new information systems. His descriptions of the information flowing through an ordinary grocery store shows all of us the practical business implications of information systems. His *Powershift* (1990) is a careful case-by-case description of how the availability of information is changing power relationships among individuals, organizations, and nations. He sums up much of the impact this way: "We are creating new networks of knowledge . . . linking concepts in startling ways . . . building up amazing hierarchies of inference . . . spawning new theories, hypotheses, and images, based on novel assumptions, new languages, codes, and logics. Businesses, governments, and individuals are collecting and storing more sheer data than any previous generation in history" (85).

It is not too surprising that given this mountain of new data, we are already hearing from counselors telling us how to handle the stress such information is bringing us. In his popular book *Information Anxiety* (1989), Richard Saul Wurman describes sixteen warning signs of this new malady. Among his signs: (1) Feeling guilty about that ever-higher stack of periodicals waiting to be read; (2) feeling depressed because you don't know what all the buttons are on your VCR; (3) thinking the person next to you understands everything you don't; and (4) reacting emotionally to information you don't really understand—such as not knowing what the Dow Jones really is but panicking when you hear that it has dropped five hundred points (36).

All these authors seem to answer the question, How much information is there? They tell us simply that there is far more than there was before, that the amount is ever increasing, and that it is already more than many of us can handle. Are they right? Without question there is more information available to us than there has been in the past. At least there is more of certain *kinds* of information. There is clearly more scientific information available: we can see the results in new manufacturing processes, new medical treatments, and even in the genetically altered food we eat. But what about other kinds of information? Does Dan Rather tell us twice as much each night as he did five years ago? Does your local paper have twice as much news? Does it even still exist? Does your employer tell you twice as much about your company's progress? Does the company down the block tell you anything about its activities? The World Wide Web has infinitely more information than five years ago, since it did not exist five years ago, but what kind of information is on the Web? What kind of information is not?

DEFINING INFORMATION

If we want to start discussions of an information explosion, and define this as the information age, it would be helpful if we would begin by defining the term *information*. Toffler defines information as "data that have been fitted into categories and classification schemes or other patterns" (18). That's not a bad beginning. It implies that information is something that has been worked on—"fitted" into patterns or other larger structures. But it is still vague. For instance, it does not tell us where we might go looking for information, or what forms we might find it in.

Michael Buckland (1991) at the School of Library and Information Studies at the University of California–Berkeley takes a look at the forms of information. He focuses on "information-as-thing." This is a very practical approach for a librarian to take. In essence he asks, Where is this stuff and how much room will it occupy? His answer is that information comes as

1. data—records that can be stored on a computer;
2. text and documents—papers, letters, books—that may be on paper, microfilm, or in electronic form;
3. spoken language in any medium;
4. objects—dinosaur bones, rock collections, and skeletons;
5. records of events—photos, news reports, and memoirs.

Such a definition is both insightful and practical. It reminds us that information can come in many forms. The weakness of Buckland's definition is its neutrality. It does not help us later, when we try to determine why there seems to be limitless information in some areas and no information in others.

This book tries a different approach. My assumption is that information is not a neutral object to be discovered and counted, like atoms or zebras, but an expression shaped from the very beginning by the creators of that information. In short, information comes from somebody, and that somebody determines from the beginning how much information there will be, what form it will take, and even if it will exist at all. If you want to understand information, go to its source.

How many sources are there? In one sense there are billions—each of us who has ever occupied our planet. For the sake of brevity, though, we will look at just five sources: public information, personal information, organizational information, professional information, and commercial information. These five do not exhaust all the information sources we may encounter, but they represent major sources. By examining each, we will see how much information is really out there, what form it takes, and how good it is.

PUBLIC INFORMATION. In our rush to examine all the new opportunities made available by technology, we often forget that much of the information people have still comes from very traditional sources—television, movies, radio, newspapers, and books. It is true digital information is supplementing and even supplanting these earlier forms, but it hasn't totally replaced them and won't anytime soon.

But while these traditional sources of information are still important, they are not always accessible. For instance, CNN is nice, but to see it you not only need a television, you need an electrical outlet to plug the TV into. That may not be a problem in the United States, where we have 850 TV sets per 1,000 population, but it is a problem in countries such as Bangladesh (5 TVs per 1,000) and Kenya (9 TVs per 1,000). Books are still a critical resource for information, but some countries have virtually no publishing industry. The entire continent of Africa, for example, produces just 2 percent of the world's book titles.

Besides availability, there is the question of origination. There are lots of movies circulating through the world, but they come from very few countries. Developing nations occasionally complain about this cultural dependence, and even formed the New World Information and Communications Order, but there is no sign of real change here. In the meantime, not only do some countries struggle under the weight of foreign cultures, but exporting countries such as ours have almost no opportunity to hear other voices or see other perspectives. The information flow is all one way.

PERSONAL INFORMATION. "It's not what you know, it's who you know" is cynical, but it is accurate. It might be even more accurate if rephrased: who you know determines what you know. The value of personal contacts may be more difficult to calculate than the number of scientific articles published or the bandwidth of optical-fiber telecommunications networks, but it can be seen in the success rate in job-seekers' networks and in the conscious effort being placed on creating mentorships, especially for women and minorities. All of us also have an anecdote about an opportunity that came our way or a problem we were able to solve because we know someone. It seems a truism that successful people just have a bigger Rolodex than others.

While personal information access is a central process for many people, it poses several problems. The first is the possibility of conscious abuse. Many women's network were set up specifically as a response to the perception that "old boy" networks were creating an unfair advantage for men—men talked to each other, helped each other, in ways that were closed to women.

A second problem is less visible, but may in fact be a more difficult problem to overcome. The problem is cultural. Some cultures interact, others are more aloof. College calculus may serve as the best, if most unlikely, example here. Uri Triesmann tried to determine why Asian students at the University of California–Berkeley were able to pass calculus while black students almost always failed. Both groups had been stars in high school—getting into Berkeley isn't easy—yet blacks just could not pass the course. Some might respond to those results with racial slurs or attacks on affirmative action. Triesmann moved into the dorms and studied how both groups spent their days. What he discovered is that Asian students began each quarter by setting up study groups. These were not just groups for grinds—they had their pizzas and social evenings, too, but most of their time together was for studying. Blacks had social groups too, but these groups were strictly social. When it came time to study, each black student went back to his dorm room, closed the door, and studied alone. That was their culture, and it was a cultural trait that was destroying them.

Cultures of isolation aren't the only problems of personal information channels. Since these channels are largely invisible, they can be filled with myths, lies, and hatreds. Few outsiders even know what is being said, nor do they have opportunities to correct even the most egregious errors. Yet error-prone or not, these are channels that supply much of the world's information.

ORGANIZATIONAL INFORMATION. Whether organizations are businesses, universities, or government agencies, they seem to be conflicted over information. Internally, organizations seem more willing to share information with members and employees. Externally, organizations seem unwilling to tell the world what is going on, and seem very willing to lie.

Internal organizational communication is based around an ideal and a reality. The ideal is that organizations function best when employees know what is going on. Maybe they have been asked an opinion, maybe they have played a role in forming policy, maybe not. But at least they know what the organization is trying to do. The reality is that information flows within a context. We can put in new e-mail systems and create a system that is theoretically capable of letting each and every worker have electronic access to the CEO. But that does not mean the CEO will ever read the e-mail coming in. Nor does it mean that all workers will be thrilled with new opportunities to communicate with an organization to which they may have, at best, a tangential relationship.

An area of information flow that may be even more challenging is the new flows being created between organizations. Electronic data interchange (EDI) systems connect companies and government agencies in ways never attempted before. The computer systems needed for this new interchange may be daunting, but they are nothing compared to the ethical and legal challenges on the horizon.

Then there is the question of how organizations communicate with the rest of the world. Whether the organizations are public or private, large corporations or small proprietorships, information is withheld from outsiders as a routine measure.

PROFESSIONAL INFORMATION. A major source of information is professional bodies, of which there are many. In the United States the last decade or so has seen a major growth in the number of these bodies (u.s. census 1993:787):

Professional Bodies	*1980*	*1992*
Scientific, technical, and engineering associations	1,039	1,365
Trade, business, and commercial associations	3,118	3,851
Health and medical associations	1,413	2,290

With more than seven thousand professional associations in existence in 1992, it would appear every occupational group or subspecialty had some organization they could contact to push their professional interests or communicate professional information. How much information do these associations generate? One calculation says there have now been a million papers published in the mathematics field, half within just the last ten years.

Without question, professions are producing in volume. The problem is whether the large number masks areas of information that are being left empty. Professions tend to have specific biases—who they will let in, who they will listen to, what they will say to the public, and how they will relate to each other. Each bias curbs the kind of information professions produce and the kind of information available to members of the profession.

COMMERCIAL INFORMATION. Information can be sold. We are used to credit bureaus selling information about our purchasing and payment histories. Now those bureaus are being joined by thousands of businesses whose entire inventory consists of information in a database. Their competitive edge is based solely on the size and contents of that database. Universities are entering the information business in a big way, selling not just collections of other people's information, but original research. Join any of their research consortia and you too can get the latest data months, or years, before your competition.

As this information industry matures and grows, we begin to see that it will not only be a major force in the economy—an employer of thousands, maybe tens of thousands—but it will be like any other industry. It will produce products for which there is a market. The names of the fifty most credit-worthy individuals in your zip code may be available from many sources. It may be less easy to access the phone numbers of the federal programs an immigrant may turn to for temporary help. Universities may have new sources of funds for building material science research centers. They may have less money available to pay visiting poets. The commercialization of information has commercial consequences. Profitable information is available from many sources; nonprofit information struggles to survive on handouts. Each of these five information sources shapes information, with some of the "shapes" looking more and more like distortions.

HOW ACCESSIBLE IS INFORMATION?

If the amount of information available is somewhat less than our hopes, at least now we can easily get to information, right? We have all these satellites and optical-fiber networks. Access to information is no longer supposed to be a problem. Naisbitt even divides American history along the fault line of information access: "The following year—1957—marked the beginning of the globalization of the information revolution: The Russians launched *Sputnik*, the missing technological catalyst in a growing information society. The real importance of *Sputnik* is *not* that it began the space age, but that it introduced the era of global satellite communications" (12).

With satellites in the air, information flow seems sure to follow. And any measure of data traffic makes it clear huge amounts of information are in fact moving through space. Some, Toffler among them, have looked at the data traffic and remarked on the global linkages that seem to be following: "As capital flows electronically across national borders, zipping back and forth from Zurich to Hong Kong, Hong Kong to Norway, Norway to Tokyo, Tokyo to Wall Street in milliseconds, information traces equally complex pathways. A change in U.S. T-bill rates or the yen–deutsche mark ratio is instantly known around the world, and the morning after the big event in Los Angeles, youngsters in Ho Chi Minh City discuss the latest Grammy winners. The mental borders of the state become as permeable as its financial frontiers" (364).

Toffler and the others are obviously right. Information does flow more easily to many places. Who can help but be impressed by the ability to send e-mail around the world in minutes, the chance to access libraries and databases in other nations, the transportation system that can cross continents in hours. We can get to far more information far more easily than ever before.

At least some of us can. In our excitement to explore the new opportunities before us, we may overlook a few things. For instance, we may forget to note that half the Americans living on Indian reservations have no telephones. What information will they be downloading? By concentrating on computer information, we may also forget to notice that millions of people around the globe never saw *Schindler's List*—their governments would not let them. We sometimes even ignore our own problems, information that turns out to be lies, datalines that become doorways for thieves.

Despite all the satellites we put in the sky and the cellular-phone networks we build along our interstates, there is some information we cannot get. If this really is the information age, those barriers need to be examined, and ultimately they need to be removed. We will look at three barriers—transmission problems—not because they are the only barriers information faces, but because they represent the kinds of problems that will preoccupy our efforts to make all information available to all people. These are the problems: information exiles, tyranny, and information criminals.

INFORMATION EXILES. Information is like any other commodity in that it is not evenly distributed across the world. Some people live in the midst of gold fields; many others can barely find coal. Parts of the information vacuum we instantly recognize. For example, no one expects the Bushmen of the Kalahari to walk around with cellular phones (as we will see, they have a long list of communication problems). Other isolates are less obvious. The growing army of people living in neighborhoods (or countries) too dangerous to visit certainly qualify. In either case, the number of people totally removed from the information infrastructure is huge.

What happens to these people in the information age? As subsistence farming and handicrafts persisted through the industrial age, will the disconnected carry on, barely feeding themselves, producing the primitive and quaint for middle-class coffee tables? Early indications are that the disconnected will fare far worse than their predecessors in previous revolutions. The gap between the rich and the poor, the knowing and the ignorant, will be larger, the room along the margins far smaller.

TYRANNY. While previous revolutions created classes of haves and have-nots, the information age is already showing that it will be complicated by the "wills" and "will-nots." You can bring the optical fiber to Johnny, but you can't make him connect. There are no shortages of examples to prove this assertion, but let's take one contemporary example—satellite dishes. In one week's time in late 1993, three distinct corners of the world showed just how arbitrary our species can be.

The week began in China with an announcement that the sale and manufacture of satellite dishes was now banned. Too many comrades were using the dishes to bring in "decadent" news and entertainment shows. Decadent information might lead to decadent ideas and then to decadent actions. So the government stepped in and satellite access ended.

The news from Algeria was more bizarre. Islamic fundamentalists decided it was no longer enough to cleanse Algeria of Western influences by murdering women tourists caught shopping in street malls. Now they had turned their attention to neighbors who had satellite dishes. Since the dishes were pointed toward Europe rather than Mecca, it was obvious Western ideas were entering the country. The response was attacks on dish owners.

But for pure cussedness, no one beats the South Africans. In 1993, with majority rule in the offing, the South African Broadcasting Corporation (SABC) elected a new board of directors, including blacks. The response of the Christian Right was to refuse to pay their TV license fees and to ask SABC to fix their TVs so they could no longer get public television. To these Christians it was obvious SABC was now a communist agency and would begin giving air time to blacks and other atheistic forces. They would rather have no television at all than risk the possibility of an occasional black face flickering across their living room.

China, Algeria, South Africa—all places where people are deciding whether they will or will not listen, view, read, or discuss. The same decision—to include or exclude, to listen or turn away, to read or ignore—is being made individually the world over. Rejectionists are constantly saying, "You don't look like me—I have nothing to learn from you," "You aren't my sex—I won't listen to you," "You are too old, too young, too light, too dark." If information is the currency of this age, much of our species is proud to wear rags.

INFORMATION CRIMINALS. While one group kills to keep information secret, another group uses the very technology of information to perform crimes. To remind us of the kind of people we face, let's begin with three brief horror stories—all well known, but worth repeating. Just days before he was elected president of the United States, Republicans seeking to block his election got into Bill Clinton's passport records looking for information that might be embarrassing. Here is a man only weeks from being president of the United States, yet even he is vulnerable to illegal searches.

This incident was preceded by the discovery that Internal Revenue Service agents in St. Louis were calling up tax records on their computers and looking to see how much their friends and neighbors earned. They had the time, they had the technology, they had the curiosity—they did not have the discipline, integrity, or supervision to protect honest taxpayers.

The third example is described in dramatic detail in *Cuckoo's Egg* (1990) by Clifford Stoll. Stoll describes how he tracked down communist agents who were using the Internet to break into secret military archives—essentially to spy on American military bases without ever leaving their homes in Europe. One of the scarier moments in the book is when Stoll tells the U.S. Army about the agents and they refuse to believe him. If ever there was an organization that should have some security sense . . .

Every advance in electronics means that more information can be held in more places for less money and accessed more easily. Unless criminals (and governments) can be held at bay, the very technology that transmits our new-found data stream will be so dangerous we will refuse to use it. What good is a strand of optical fiber to every door if we are too scared to plug it in?

ARE WE READY FOR INFORMATION?

What if there really is an information explosion at some point? And what if it happened at the same time that some combination of luck and technology meant that the information got to everyone effortlessly? Would we know what to do with it? There are three ways of looking at ourselves as information processors. None of the views is very attractive.

EDUCATION. Assuming we can find some way to get the optical fiber to Johnny, and assuming that Johnny won't be shot if he hooks up, what if Johnny can't read? A world of information may be physically and politically available to people, but it may be no more useful to them than a library is to illiterates. Some totalitarian governments figured this out long ago. It was the stated public policy of South Africa to limit the education of nonwhites. Dr. Hendrik Verwoerd began his stint as minister of Bantu Education with a very clear statement of policy: "When I have control of Native education I will reform it so that Natives will be taught from childhood to realize that equality with Europeans is not for them. People who believe in equality are not desirable teachers for the Natives. Education must train and teach people in accordance with their opportunities in life, according to the sphere in which they live."

That such words could be uttered in public says much about the tragedy of South Africa. Unfortunately, South Africa is not the only place where education has been used to control, to limit. Education is a weapon demagogues are ready to wield.

Even for those with some connection to basic human values, education is a problem. In the developing world, where fewer than half the citizens may make it to the sixth grade, information resources are inaccessible resources. Barely able to read, what difference does it make that they can review scientific articles from around the globe?

PSYCHOLOGY. Brilliant, well-educated, well-connected people can also miss most of what is happening in the world. In fact, it is quite likely that they will. All it requires is that they take a part of the world and explore it to the exclusion of everything else. An example often given is the railroad industry. Creating railroads is no small matter. These are complicated systems that were the technological and political extremes of their time. Leaders of the railroad industry can be forgiven for being preoccupied with getting lines built, designing locomotives that were powerful and reliable, and getting trains out on time. These were not foolish people. But they were hypnotized. By focusing exclusively on railroads they missed out on larger opportunities in transportation.

How could they and countless industries since them make such an obvious error? The information was there. Why didn't they use it? If we are to prepare for the free flow of information, one place to start working is on our own perceptions.

NOISE. Neil Postman's *Amusing Ourselves to Death* is a lengthy indictment of contemporary American culture. It takes only an hour or two of prime time television to fully agree. The print media follow suit. How could our founding fathers ever believe that the First Amendment would be used to protect the right of newspapers to print Elvis sightings, Princess Di's appointment calendar, and conversations with extraterrestrials? Were we always so silly? Will the information age cause us to finally come of age and end this terminal adolescence that seems to control the United States?

Maybe not. For one thing, the sheer volume of information involved leaves plenty of room for trivial pursuits. The typical CD-ROM drive now being built into many home computers holds 600 million bytes of information. This is in excess of three hundred thousand pages of text. After you put all the great books of antiquity (meaning any book on which the copyright has expired) on one disk, what do you put on the others? Articles about Elvis sightings, and Princess Di's activities, and . . . Suddenly the much-vaunted information highway has become silly street. Maybe that's what we want. Maybe the noise we hear is the noise we crave.

FIGHTING FOR INFORMATION

While it would be lovely if the nature of the world suddenly changed and we were all suddenly awash in information, as the examples above illustrate, we still live in a world in which information is restricted. The limits come from institutions that reveal and pursue only information that meets their needs. The limits come from tyrants who have already learned how to clamp down the Internet as effectively as they cut off satellite communication and television. The limits may be our own as we routinely ignore or distort information that does not match our prejudices. The limits are there, overwhelming satellite launches and trenches full of fiber. If we want information, we will have to fight for it.

The Stakes

Why fight? An increasingly common question is, Is all this really necessary? For the tired executive who spends all day in meetings, uses audix and e-mail by the hour, stares at endless computer printouts, and then goes home to a pile of mail and thirty channels on her cable TV, the answer might appear to be no. Another eighty or hundred channels, yet another computer network, yet another club or association, yet another conference call is like giving someone already eating three thousand calories a day another three or four thousand calories. They are just as likely to be sick as grateful. Yet like the person eating lots of food, all of it sugar and preservatives, it may well be wise for that person to take a look at the quality of her diet. She may discover that Theo Schoeman is not the only executive who has total access to some kinds of information but absolute blind spots elsewhere. Hidden by the overflowing e-mail list may be the fact that some kinds of information are absent.

If she is clever, she will survive despite the holes in her information system. Others, however, may not fare as well. For the poor, the starving, the abused, the desperate, information access may be the only hope. For these people, the stakes are life and death.

THE INVISIBLE

According to a report circulated by Human Rights Watch–Africa in early 1994, slavery still persists in Mauritania. While the practice is officially banned, Human Rights Watch believes there are over one hundred thousand slaves in the country. The government of Maaoviya Ould Sid'ahmed Taya is apparently making no effort to stop slavery or to stop cruel punishments of slaves. It is reported that the punishment for attempted escape is as follows: "The victim is seated flat with his legs spread out and buried in sand up to his waist. Coals are placed between his legs and lit, slowly burning the legs, thighs, and genitals of the victim." Because the country is so obscure, few seem aware of the atrocities being routinely committed.

The report by Human Rights Watch–Africa was picked up by the wire services and carried widely throughout Africa. There was no immediate response from Mauritania, and certainly no indication that the country had suddenly decided to free its slaves. But the publicity still mattered. To the enslaved of that nation at least the possibility of freedom now exists. As long as their treatment was unknown to the rest of the world, there was no reason why it might ever improve. True, just shining the light of day on vermin does not instantly solve the problem. When St. Louis was being gradually drowned by the Mississippi in the summer of 1993, the publicity drew thousands of spectators who stood and watched while people's homes went under. But the publicity also drew thousands of volunteers who worked in the heat and the mud to fill sandbags to save other people's homes. Both groups were out on the levees. Both groups walk the Earth. A human tragedy reduced to a five-minute segment on late-night TV may be ghastly entertainment to the twisted, but it can also be an alarm bell to the many who will risk everything to help. And there are people who will help when they know about a problem. To believe otherwise is to believe oneself a member of a very sad species.

Information makes the invisible visible. It will bring hope. Ultimately it will bring help.

THE VULNERABLE

Mary Byron lived just one day after her boyfriend was released from jail. That's how long it took him to track her down and shoot her seven times. She had no idea he was stalking her. Why should she? She thought he was in jail. "Had we known the assailant was out, our daughter would not have been working that day," says her father. "Probably not even within the state." But the police did not tell her Donovan Harris was being released from jail, even though he had hurt her before.

It isn't cheap or easy, but some communities are making more of an effort to warn past victims that their assailants are back on the streets. At a cost of fifty-five thousand dollars to start and fifty-seven thousand dollars a year to operate, Louisville, Kentucky, now has a computerized system that keeps track of prisoners as they move through the judicial system and notifies past victims if criminals are about to be released. The computer keeps calling until somebody answers, and a taped message warns victims that their accused attackers are about to be released. It has already saved the life of one woman, who ran out to get a gun when she found out her abusive husband was about to be released from jail. She returned home to find him waiting with a knife (DAVIS 1995).

Warning people that they are in danger is only part of the solution. The real solution would be to remove the danger. But until that happens, the vulnerable can be helped by at least warning them of the danger they face—giving them a better chance at life than Mary Byron had.

THE IGNORANT

In *Broca's Brain*, Carl Sagan makes an interesting point about scientific issues that are left unresolved. He says that rich people gamble their money on projects. Scientists gamble their lives. If a scientist invests years and years in a research project that goes nowhere, he has wasted a significant portion of his professional life. So he looks very carefully at areas of research, determining which has the most likely prospect. There is still a chance he will hit a dead end and have nothing to show for years of work, but he tries to improve the odds by looking before he leaps.

Scientists are not the only ones gambling their lives. Negumbo Johannes gambled when he chose to move to Windhoek. But his gamble was less informed. He knew nothing about the cities of Namibia. His trip to Windhoek was his first trip away from home. When interviewed, he said he chose Windhoek because when men returned from Windhoek around Christmas time, they were well dressed when they got off the bus. On that basis he decided everyone in Windhoek was rich and he should go there.

In the United States, young people the age of Negumbo Johannes are also making decisions, picking colleges and workplaces. Some have been groomed for the decision for years. They have parents who are knowledgeable, or older siblings, or social connections. They have a pretty clear sense of what they are getting into. Other young men and women are wandering blind. At one urban university in the Midwest there is a special program for minority students. It appears attractive, yet records show the program graduates a mere 17 percent of its students even after seven years of study. That information is publicly available, but only to those who know what to ask, and where. The rest are gambling seven years of their lives on a college degree, unaware they have only one chance in six of succeeding. Would they enter the program if they knew the odds? What other situations do they face, what other burdens do they bear, what other losses do they suffer because they never understood what they were getting into? The cost of ignorance is high. People do in fact gamble their lives on their decisions.

THE MISDIRECTED

All is not a struggle for jobs and food and safety and housing. There are still poetry and sunsets and music. There are also people who help. One of the world's blessings is the millions of these kind souls. One of the world's torments is the difficulty often encountered in using this help well. One study by the World Bank found less than one project in three was successful. Many were clearly failures, even in the early years, when they were receiving substantial funding. Others collapsed the minute external funding dried up.

Helping isn't easy. Good intentions lie in ruins worldwide. One cause is that people know too little about the problem they are trying to solve. Whether the problem is homelessness, teen pregnancy, or starvation in the Sahel, problems are always more complicated than people originally think. It is especially difficult where problems are only half-seen. Getting the necessary information may involve leaving the office to actually talk to the dirty, the sick, and the powerless, or it may take sneaking TV cameras past the local junta's soldiers, or getting the international accountants past the doctored books, or reading the books or articles some would rather censor. Learning comes before helping. But learning isn't easy.

There are some who are concerned that nations will be marched from one crisis to another by the power of TV images—governments and aid agencies putting out the fire-of-the-week based on the latest CNN broadcast. A bigger problem may be the quality of the images and the quality of other information sources. For too many of the problems of the world, the necessary information just is not coming through. We have the people and right intentions. What we often do not have is a good sense of how to use them.

So what are the stakes? For many, the stakes are life and death. The technical, personal, and social requisites to the information age are substantial and need to be recognized, but the benefits are real. Large-scale, multilevel access of information by trained citizens does not guarantee that people will suddenly drop their prejudices, stop making stupid decisions, or have the courage to act on the data before them, but it certainly gets us closer to that time than we are now. So whatever the current problems of information creation and transfer are, those problems need to be solved. Let's start by first examining the sources of information.

Part I

Problems at the Source

Chapter 1   World Media

"Baywatch" is more embarrassment than entertainment
for people there [in rural areas]. The nudity, the physical
contact . . .   —NAHUM GORELICK,
               Namibian Broadcast Company

IT'S A TUESDAY NIGHT in Africa. You happen to live in a capital city with all the perks—electricity and a television signal. So you come home from a hard day at the office and switch on the tube. Here is your evening lineup for Windhoek, Namibia:

5:00	"Sesame Street"
6:00	"Casper and Friends"
6:30	"The Rich Also Cry"
7:00	"Zoom"
7:30	"Growing Pains"
8:00	News
8:30	"Tropical Heat"
9:25	"Parliamentary Report"
9:30	"Talking Point"
10:30	Sports

Cable subscribers could supplement that lineup with "Goof Troop," "Scooby Doo," "The Flintstones," and "Garfield and Friends" as well as "The Wonder Years," "The Simpsons," and the movie *Don't Tell Mama the Babysitter's Dead.*

What a great way to spend an evening. A mongoose frolicking in the back yard, Kudu steaks on the grill, and American reruns on the tube.

Some version of this evening is occurring all around the world. In Hanoi, "Charlie's Angels" now airs six times a week (HUCKSHORN 1995). In the Crimea five hundred Russians demonstrated for a return to Russian-language dubbing of "Santa Barbara," complaining that the new Ukrainian-language version was totally unacceptable: "It's like a friend you've known for years suddenly changing her voice" (MEEK 1995). American television appears nearly everywhere.

In one sense, what is on the world's TV screens or in the papers may not seem to matter, after all, we now have electronic mail and new computer systems. Public media seem like quaint artifacts of the past. But they are very much a force of the present. While popular descriptions of life in the information age seem to dwell on state-of-the-art computer systems and communication links, it is clear that much, if not most, of the information people have comes from nothing fancier than television screens and daily newspapers. It is here that information starts, and too frequently it is here that information ends.

In looking at public information, we will examine five sources: television, movies, newspapers, radio, and books. Each source shapes what people know about the world around them. Each in its own way is obvious and simple. However, the variation in information people receive around the world is striking and hardly obvious.

Television

How important is television around the world? We know it is central to American culture, but what about the rest of the world? Available figures tell us TV is very important just about everywhere on the planet. To begin with, the United States is *not* the top nation in the world in television ownership. That honor goes to the Netherlands, with 906 TVs per 1,000 people (U.S. CENSUS 1993:856). The United States is only second, with 815 per 1,000. Still, we have a big edge over third and fourth place, Canada at 641 and Japan at 620. But in one sense, whether the number is 600 or 900 per 1,000, assuming that just a few people are willing to share their televisions with a spouse or watch with their children, most of the developed countries are saturated with televisions.

As one would expect, the developing world has far fewer TV sets. Ghana has just 15 per 1,000 population, India 32, Madagascar 20. For people in the developing world, television is not a common occurrence. But that does not mean it is unimportant, because in relative terms, it still carries significant weight. Consider the table below, which compares television ownership to newspaper circulation in the developing world (per 1,000 population) (U.S. CENSUS 1993:856):

Country	Newspaper Circulation	Television Ownership
Algeria	51	74
Bangladesh	6	5
Colombia	61	115
Egypt	57	109
Guatemala	21	52
Iraq	34	69
Kenya	15	9
Madagascar	4	20
South Africa	38	105

There are exceptions, such as Bangladesh and Kenya, but for the clear majority of developing nations, television is a far more significant source of information than newspapers. It turns out radio is even more important, but television is undoubtedly a source of significance.

Given TV's important place even in the developing world, television programming begins to matter. What are they watching on their TVs around the world? In many cases, they are watching American reruns. Old Hollywood sitcoms and daytime soaps may seem to make no sense at all across the deserts and jungles of the world, but you run into them everywhere. The American dominance of world television probably reaches its most ludicrous end in Cairo. Here, in a country where American tourists are followed by heavily armed tourist police to protect them from Muslim fundamentalists, much of Cairo spent 1993 protesting the removal of "The Bold and the Beautiful" from a daily prime time slot. Henceforth it will only be seen once weekly, its daily slot taken by "Oskin," the story of a Japanese girl who works her way from rages to riches. Given a choice between beautifully dressed, immoral American pap and long-laboring Japanese morality, Egyptians in droves are calling for American Escapism. Explained one columnist, "We have 30 million Oskins like her. We have our fill of poverty, deprivation and need" (ELTAHAWY 1994).

An interesting footnote to this example came from one South African newspaper that covered the Cairo controversy. It could not help gloating, "Egypt is way behind South Africa in the 'Bold and Beautiful' series. For example, Caroline is dead, Kirsten has left the show, and Clark has remarried." Poor, backward Egypt, it just can't keep up with South Africa on American soaps.

What is there about television that leads to such overwhelming American programming dominance? Actually, there are three forces at work: economics, international marketing, and language luck.

ECONOMICS

Forget the content of television shows for a minute—the actors, the dialogue, the setting. Think money. For established studios, television is a marvelous industry. Creating a product requires a heavy investment, but once that product is completed, it is one of the most unique products ever made—you can make copies of it for almost nothing and transport it practically for free. The product seems designed for export.

Economics works the other way for newer and less-developed television stations. Put yourself in the position of Nahum Gorelick, managing director of the Namibian Broadcast Company. He has air time to fill—about eight hours a day. He also has a limited budget. What can he use to fill his time slots? "Baywatch." Not exactly a cultural export, "Baywatch" consists mostly of people wearing very little, doing little of consequence on American beaches. Namibia has beaches, but not idle adolescents, for whom the show was written. But it is cheap. One hour costs NBC $450. Gorelick says he has received complaints about the show from rural viewers, but he has air time to fill and a limited budget.

By Gorelick's estimates, an hour of local content would cost twelve hundred dollars if it were undirected (like local soccer matches), and well over two thousand dollars if it involved actors and directors. To achieve export standards, his costs would be even higher. By one estimate, export prices represent less than 1 percent of local production costs (LENT 1993). Gorelick has a limited budget, so he goes with the cheap American product. This programming choice is repeated over and over as Gorelick and his colleagues around the world try to fill time slots. American TV may not be very good, but it is cheap.

Not all world television is American. Brazil has arrived at a compromise. In order to stay on the air twenty hours a day, TV Globo shows early morning cartoons and late-night feature films from the United States but puts their locally produced soaps—*telenovelas*—in prime time. Audiences much prefer the local shows, with one rating of American television shows by university students giving the imported shows just a 1.6 on a 10-point scale (OLIVEIRA 1993), but the cost of local production is too high and the cost of imports too low, so some American content is inevitable.

In Asia, Hollywood has an even smaller portion of the market, ranging from 5 percent in China and South Korea to 15 to 20 percent in Malaysia and the Philippines (LENT 1993). But the rules of economics have not changed. In this case, the exporter is Hong Kong, where studios are able to produce thousands of hours of programming cheaply. The Hong Kong studios have language and cultural advantages to their programming, with costs no higher than Hollywood.

But whether the exporter is Hollywood or Hong Kong, television around the world uses a great deal of foreign product—economics demand it. Can local cultures respond? One reaction is local content laws. For instance, South Africa is rewriting its broadcasting laws to demand 50 percent local content on its public television station and 30 percent local content on private TV stations (PEARCE 1995). But such laws are anachronistic in the age of satellite networks. With one satellite network setting up in neighboring Swaziland and broadcasting to all of South Africa from there, national content laws do not have any effect. Cheap imports rain in unchecked.

INTERNATIONAL MARKETING

The second reason for American dominance is marketing. For proof, there is no need to look further than MTV in Europe. Since arriving in Europe in 1990, the channel has grown threefold to 59 million households, 700,000 more than in the United States (TULLY 1994). Broadcasts are in English and are beamed across the Continent rather than to individual countries. Music tends to be American or British, but some European groups are included. MTV also broadcasts news and socially conscious programs on topics such as global warming and European immigrants.

CNN has even a bigger reach, as it demonstrated in May 1994. Putting together a global press conference simultaneously broadcast to 141 countries, CNN's International Center in Atlanta put President Bill Clinton on the air for ninety minutes to answer questions from around the world. Clinton took questions from journalists in Sarajevo, Seoul, Johannesburg, and Jerusalem (WALKER 1994). The only problem for CNN is time zones. While Clinton got prime time in the United States and the breakfast hours in Asia, his worldwide press conference hit Europe, the Middle East, and Africa in the middle of the night.

Even where American names aren't on the channel, there may be American involvement. One of the largest makers of French TV programs, Hamster Productions, is one-third owned by Capital Cities/ABC (STEVENSON 1994), and their influence is more than financial. "There is no day when we don't say, 'What would ABC have done?' " says Pierre Grimblat, president of Hamster. "They are so modern and so knowledgeable about the international destiny of television." With a European TV market estimated at 350 million people, American companies Time Warner, Turner Broadcasting, Viacom, Walt Disney, Coca Cable, US West, and NBC are all investing in Europe. Already a major influence, American presence on international television seems ready to grow. In large measure it is growing because American producers are going after international television—they market to it, they work for it, they think worldwide.

LANGUAGE LUCK

Besides cheap prices and marketing muscle, what makes the United States such an important player in world television? A good case can be made for the accident of our national language. When the British were planting their flag around the world, they left more behind than cricket and people who drive on the wrong side of the road. Learn to speak Chinese and you can speak to a billion people, but those people all live in one place. Learn to speak English and you can speak to fewer native speakers, but those natives live all over the world. Add the business and technical strength of the United States and you have a language worth learning.

American companies can trade on that advantage. Unlike their competitors in Berlin, Tokyo, or Moscow, the American product comes factory fresh with the "right" language. No costs or delays for translating, no laughable dubbing or illegible subtitles—you get good old English in the original. Of course this is also true for the people who created the language in the first place, the English. It is interesting to see how they have played to that advantage.

England, and especially the BBC, has not been sitting idly by watching the United States take over world TV. Creating a world television service in 1991, its twenty-four-hour news and information channel reaches the Pacific, the Middle East, Eastern Europe, and Canada. One jingoistic English columnist described the importance of the TV channel to England: "Where the fight was once for territory and 'zones of influence,' in future it could be for air-space" (WALDEN 1994). He went on to describe how the BBC might prevail in such a fight: "Hundreds of millions of people who have hitherto been starved of entertainment and subjected to Victorian sexual taboos, will be easy meat for the international purveyors of low pictorial diversion in all its forms, soft-porn included [read "Hollywood"] . . . as international audiences tire of pap [read "Hollywood" again] and become more educated and discriminating, the world market for more sophisticated and demanding television will grow [read "BBC"]." Does this mean "The Bold and the Beautiful" competing for air time with "Monty Python" is the moral equivalent of war? If so, we face an interesting century.

The BBC is not relying on its programming alone. It has its own technological efforts, including satellites carefully routed to cover the most customers. AsiaSat covers Turkey to Malaysia. In addition to ensuring citizens with a satellite dish can get their broadcasts, BBC World Service also has rebroadcasting agreements that cover Ghana, Botswana, Nigeria, and Kenya. Viewers need to pay a subscription fee and purchase a decoder (this instantly drops the African viewing audience to a minuscule percentage), but it is a foothold for the BBC with the "more educated and discriminating." Even where they are unable to get an audience for the full BBC service, BBC World Service has become a source for news bulletins in countries such as Swaziland.

Whether advanced technology and sophisticated programming will make the BBC a serious contender with American efforts is still in doubt. What is not in doubt is the dominance of the English language. American broadcasters may have to consider British competitors. They have nothing to fear from broadcasters in other languages. As one commentator noted, "The Anglo-Saxons will retain a global advantage as decisive in its sphere as 'the oil weapon' used to be: the English language" (WALDEN 1994).

Movies

If there is one area in which Americans hold an even greater edge, it is the movies. Not only is the dominance greater, but the attention being paid to the situation is greater. Movie people are not shy by nature, so the position of Hollywood is very visible, as is the reaction of less-successful nations. The most recent and most visible clash came during the final round of GATT negotiations. The 1993 General Agreement on Trade and Tariffs was able to come to closure only when participants agreed they could not agree on the subject of intellectual property rights. The French got much of the blame for being the main obstacle to agreement, but who could blame them? Here in the land of the Cannes Film Festival, 75 percent of the French movie market goes to American films. The French aren't fighting to become a world force in film, or even a significant exporter, they just want to increase their share of the domestic French film market from 25 to 40 percent. Hardly a lofty goal. One wonders whether French directors are more embarrassed by the puny nature of their industry's goals or by the fact that they may have to force their countrymen to watch their movies.

While the problem with the French may be the most recent clash over the international movie industry, the problem is hardly new. In his excellent history of the film industry, Ray Armes (1987) reviews the growth and conflicts of the business over the last century. It would appear there was never a time without turbulence. In the beginning, it was the French who ruled the film world. By 1908 Charles Pathé, who had industrialized film production in France, was exporting to the world. His dominance was so complete that until the First World War he was selling twice as many films in the United States as all American companies combined. After the war, and with the direction of the Motion Picture Producers and Distributors Association, U.S. filmmakers first took control of the American market and then took on the world.

American success came quickly. Already by 1925 the United States had knocked out one of its major competitors and was controlling 95 percent of the British market (in 1994 the United States still had 84 percent of the British market [ROSEN 1994]). It held 60 percent of the European market and up to 80 or 90 percent in parts of Asia and Latin America. By 1930, fully a third of Hollywood's income was coming from overseas. By the 1960s, Hollywood was getting half its income overseas.

How could anyone achieve that kind of dominance in an industry? There appear to be four factors at work: quantity, cost, distribution channels, and language.

QUANTITY

Once you have a movie theater, you need movies. A nation with movie theaters will need hundreds of films a year. To quote Armes, "A country is more than ever vulnerable to imports from abroad, unless—like present-day India—it can produce on its own the many hundreds of films needed each year to feed such exhibition outlets" (1987:41). Production of so many films requires a substantial film industry. This means a pool of talent, financing, administrative abilities, and technology. Few countries have been able accumulate the needed resources. India has been a notable success, producing 763 films in 1983. With so many local films, it can keep its theaters occupied and has less need for foreign imports.

But few countries have matched this level of production. Mexico, Brazil, and Argentina have been able to create significant industries and were all able to produce nearly one hundred films a year already in the 1950s. Even Burma, Pakistan, and South Korea could produce fifty films a year by 1955. Such quantities took significant efforts, but still left a vacuum to be filled. These countries all needed to import films. Needless to say, countries producing even fewer films had even more need for imports. Hollywood filled that need. Meanwhile, back in the United States, Hollywood production was sufficient to fill American theaters without any need for imports. Film distribution was a one-way street.

COST

For companies able to export movies, it is hard to imagine a better cost structure. Just as in television production, almost all the costs of film production go for the master negative and first print. After that, costs are almost nil. This means a company exporting films is in a marvelous position. Since its distribution and sales costs are low, it can charge very little and still make a large profit. As Armes puts it, "It was like being able to sell an imported Rolls Royce for less than the cost of the cheapest locally produced car and still make virtually a 100 percent profit" (37).

While great for the film exporter, the cost situation is less attractive to the local studio. It has to try to recover its production costs but cannot compete on price—virtually anything it wants to charge for a film the exporter can undercut. It can try to export too, and Mexico, for one, has had some success in this area, but export opportunities are limited by the distribution system.

DISTRIBUTION

Distribution of films is a significant business in its own right, and one prone to monopoly. Possibly the best example here comes from the French. Two French companies, COMACICO and SECMA, essentially controlled all of French-speaking Africa through the 1960s and 1970s. They not only controlled 60 percent of the theaters in this part of Africa but were sole suppliers to the remaining 40 percent (ARMES 1987:45). With this kind of control, they could determine which films were shown—which would be imported from France and which, if any, local films would be seen. The monopoly was finally broken in 1974 by a pan-African organization. Unfortunately for African filmmakers, this new distributor has not shown much interest in increasing the quantity of African films distributed through the area. Until distributors take such action, filmmakers are virtually helpless.

LANGUAGE

Language is the other factor affecting the distribution of movies. It was not always so. Up until the late 1920s, movies were silent. With no language, a movie made in France could be understood as easily in Moscow as in Paris. The medium was instantly international. Sound changed that. It massively increased production costs and so helped kill the industry in some poorer nations, but it also erected a barrier that protected other countries from unlimited imports. Now a movie made in France was noticeably different from a movie made in Moscow. Local films finally had one advantage.

Playing the language card, though, has its own dangers. For a filmmaker in India, for example, producing films in Hindi may give your film an advantage over competitors from America or Britain, but it also means your film cannot be exported. The language barrier works both ways—it keeps others out, but it also keeps you in. If you play the language card, you have to be willing to accept a niche market.

Even here, things get a little fuzzy. Although Hindi is spoken by millions of India's people, it is still a minority language in that country. To help expand its domestic market, Indian filmmakers arrived at an ingenious solution. They minimized language by going to song and dance movies. Such movies became so successful in India that when K. A. Abbas's Munna was produced in 1954, it was only the second movie to be made in India without any songs, since sound came to the country in 1931. While Indian producers may have taken it to an extreme, they are not the only ones to turn to musicals—Hollywood had a few to its credit as well. And musicals are not the only solution to the language problem. Hong Kong kung fu movies may go long stretches with little dialogue beyond "Ugh, Oof." Hollywood "action" movies can match that with dialogue like "I'll be back."

Of course all these "solutions" to the language problem assume filmmakers who are willing to give up dialogue as a significant part of their film. Where dialogue still matters, you have to choose between losing much of the international market, adding the extra expense (and enduring the often comic result) of dubbing, or you can try to go with an international language. Guess what language that might be. Once again English provides an edge for some filmmakers.

The result of all these forces is that some parts of the world simply are not part of the cinema world. France's Ministry of Cooperation has helped fund a number of movies in French-speaking Africa, with the result that dirt-poor Burkina Faso (formerly Upper Volta), with a total of twelve movie theaters in the country, hosts a biannual film festival, has its own film school and movie studio, and distributes movies throughout the region. But this is the exception for Africa. In the English-speaking parts of the continent, local filmmaking is almost nonexistent. Kenya has yet to produce a feature film. Ghana has a state-supported film organization but has only sporadically produced feature films. Nigeria is one of the most populous countries of Africa, yet it produces few films and has no film industry.

Often relatively small amounts of money can be a barrier. In Zimbabwe, the producers of Pfuma Yedu (Our Heritage) were able to make the film with the help of the Danish Development Agency, but then were stopped by postproduction costs, unable to come up with thirty thousand dollars to transfer the film from sixteen- to thirty-five millimeter. The film sat unseen for three years (MBASO 1993). Lack of local investment funds has blocked many other film projects before they were even started.

The result of all this is a strange mixture of voices. We hear Hollywood around the world. We hear from some filmmakers, but only in their own country. And some places in the world are totally silent, their voices not only unknown elsewhere but also unknown at home. What the artists of Zimbabwe or Kenya or Namibia or Angola may think of their lives is unknown to us, and unknown to their countrymen. They have no opportunity to express themselves through film.

Newspapers

For many people, television and movies may be nice, but newspapers are where the *real* information is. Well, maybe. It is certainly true that newspapers are a major source of information. But just how important are they? Consider one extreme example. Ethiopia sells 1 newspaper each day for every 1,000 people in the country. Twice as many people watch TV (2 per 1,000). Almost two hundred times as many Ethiopians get their news over the radio. Think this is an exception that only holds in the developing world? How about the United States? Only 1 person in 4 reads a daily paper. Four out of 5 have televisions, and the average American owns 2.1 radios (U.S. CENSUS 1993).

Newspapers are certainly an important information source, but they suffer two problems: quantity and quality. Let's begin with some of the quantity issues.

QUANTITY

Here are newspaper circulation figures for some countries around the world (per 1,000 population) (U.S. CENSUS 1993). As you can see, the range is quite dramatic:

Country	Newspaper Circulation
Algeria	51
Bulgaria	451
Cuba	124
Ethiopia	1
Hong Kong	632
India	26
Israel	261
Japan	587
Kenya	15
Mexico	127
Norway	614
Soviet Union	482
United Kingdom	395
United States	250
Zimbabwe	21

The United States is somewhere in the middle of the pack. The world's great newspaper readers seem to be the people of Hong Kong, Japan, and Scandinavia. On the other hand, the developing world reads even less than Americans. Part of this is a question of literacy, part of it a matter of money. Newspapers can be expensive, often far more as a percentage of a daily wage than they would be in the United States. Newspapers are not the medium of the poor.

QUALITY

If newspapers lag behind television and radio in circulation, they at least have the advantage of quality, don't they? Well, maybe not. Besides the fact that many stories around the world can't be covered because of censors or danger to reporters, there are two other factors that are shaping the quality of news: cost and international news flow.

COST. Reporters don't come cheap. One vision of reporting is that it is now a high-tech enterprise with reporters working computers and phones and working with huge databases, cranking out stories without effort. Even at the leading papers where technology is available, the computer work has to be followed up. Too often this means sitting in endless meetings, or waiting to talk to people, or phoning again and again. The result is that even in the best of times under the best of circumstances, reporters aren't very productive. If we were to use an industrial metaphor, while TV production may be at the pinnacle of the industrial/information enterprise, news reporters are essentially still hunters and gatherers. They handcraft each story, producing about as much each day as the average basket weaver or wood carver. They survive from a different age.

Their handcrafting does not come cheap. Neither does paper, printing presses, and all the other associated costs of newspaper production. The results became obvious in the United States in 1995 with the closure of *New York Newsday*, the *Houston Post*, and the *Baltimore Evening Sun*. Add to that eight hundred lay-offs at the *Los Angeles Times* and you get a sense for how desperate the times have become (KURTZ 1995).

What is less obvious is the impact of these financial pressures on the quality of the news. In their fight for circulation, the *Miami Herald* has said it will concentrate on the nine subjects reader surveys indicate are most popular—national and world news are not among the nine. The *Buffalo News* has moved to a front-page format focusing on three main stories. Recent leads have been O. J. Simpson remarriage rumors and coverage of the Dagwood Bumstead comic strip. A local radio ad asserts, "You can get the facts without straining your brain." How lucky for Buffalo.

More subtle is the financial impact on the news mix. Consider these costs from a small-town daily in middle America. Reporters' salaries begin at $20,000. Fifteen reporters are needed to cover local news, sports, and photography. Quick multiplication shows minimum costs of $300,000 per year for local news. Meanwhile, national and international news is coming in off the wire. Cost? For the Associated Press, $800 a week, $500 per month for *New York Times*. That totals $47,600 ($41,600 plus $6,000), or roughly the cost of two local reporters. So the big cost is local news. Small wonder that larger chains can buy up local papers, cut the local reporters, go with wire service news, and expect a 20 percent return on their investment (GLENNON 1994).

The result is sensationalism and recycled wire-service news. In some cases it is recycled sensationalism—the O. J. story of the day appearing in paper after paper in city after city. Putting out a newspaper with real news in it may never have been harder. To quote one editor, "There's a real spiritual self-doubt that I don't remember experiencing before" (KURTZ 1995:D1).

INTERNATIONAL NEWS FLOW. Every few years the subject of information flow comes up, usually accompanied by accusations of cultural imperialism. The United Nations Educational, Scientific, and Cultural Organization (UNESCO) already had one publication in 1953 calling attention to the prominence of industrialized nations in the world's news flow, and by the late 1970s there were several efforts at analysis underway, most notably Sean MacBride's commission, which produced *Many Voices, One World* (1980), a detailed analysis of information movement around the world. All of this led to calls for a New World Information and Communications Order (NWICO) with increased information rights for developing nations. The United States objected to many of the proposals in NWICO and eventually pulled out of UNESCO entirely, partially as a result of this opposition. With support for NWICO slipping, many of its proposals were dropped, but it did lead to a number of regional news agencies, such as CANA (Caribbean News Agency), PANA (Pan African News Agency), and IPS (Inter-Press Service). These regional news services were intended to break the hold of international news groups such as Reuters and AP. The new regionals have been uneven in their success, but they are still around today.

Has talk of a new world order in information changed the way news flows today? Studies can point to a few places where regional news has a larger place than in the past, but generally not much has changed. International news traffic is still dominated by Reuters and AP, and the flow is still from the industrialized world to the developing world—from rich to poor. They print far more news about the United States than we print about them.

It is usually the representatives of the developing world who complain about this news flow, concerned about how invisible they are to the rest of the world—only getting news coverage for famines, flood, or genocide—but the flow is not good for the United States and other rich nations either. For one thing, since little news flows to us with any regularity, we know little about the world. Disasters like Rwanda seem to spring at us out of nowhere, when actually the massacres there had been building for months. But a little guerilla warfare, a little political infighting, a few dozen machete deaths, none were enough to warrant space in American papers. There was no news until tens of thousands were dying. It is as though we are always walking in halfway through a play, and are then asked to make brilliant decisions about how the play should end.

Meanwhile, the information that flows from the United States to the rest of the world may not always be the information we would like to share. Consider the famous Bobbitt penis trial. As the trial played out in the United States, the *Citizen*, a daily paper in Johannesburg, South Africa, was giving the penis trial daily coverage—at a time when South Africa was just months from its first democratic elections and at a time when the country was in the midst of de facto civil war. True, the trial was on page three, with page one describing Nelson Mandela's concerns over civil war, an armed standoff at an Afrikaner radio station, and an agreement by Mandela and De Klerk on reestablishing legitimate local government. Page two was used for continuations of page one news. But the penis trial was the biggest story on page three, with a four-column head, and over twenty column inches of text. Below the trial story was an article on the arraignment of five terrorists who had fired into a Cape Town tavern (only a two-column head). Only on subsequent pages do we learn about two young people killed in feuds between ANC factions, the daring rescue of a pilot who had crashed in a small plane, the funding of a Zulu march on Pretoria that left fifteen dead, and the handover of a major South African port to Namibia. Again, this was not a slow news period, yet an American sex trial was given a major position—both space and placement in priority over a number of serious South African stories.

What is one to think of all this? At first blush it appears the dominant information of the information age is who is pregnant by whom on "The Bold and the Beautiful" and which sex crimes are being committed in which American suburbs. Or maybe all this proves is that America's role in the information age is to provide comic relief.

What could possibly explain the world's fascination with American sex crimes? Having seen endless stories about crazy Americans popping up in one African newspaper after another, I once asked an editor, "Don't you have any crazy people in Africa? Why only cover the crazy people in my country?" His response was that Africa had plenty of crazy people of its own, but: "If I want to cover them, I have to send out a reporter, he's gone all day, when he gets back I have to rewrite everything he's written, and even then I can't be sure he's gotten the names right or quoted correctly so we won't be sued. Meanwhile, sitting across the room from me the teletype keeps pounding out story after story, all accurately researched and correctly spelled. I can just slip out today's 'Crazy American' story and have ten or twelve column inches filled in five minutes" (LUSH 1994).

In one sense we are back to economics—it is cheaper to get news off the wire than to get original news. In another sense we are looking at quality—American reporters spell better than African reporters. Either way, what appears to be an international plot for "cultural imperialism" is really daily decisions made by editors around the world. Stories about Americans, crazy or otherwise, are easy to get.

The result of these factors is newspapers that are less than anyone would like. Local news seems to be slowly disappearing under financial pressure. News flow seems to be all in one direction, and the news that flows seems more suited for the *National Enquirer* than the *New York Times*. The news in newspapers seems to be less than anyone would like, and is declining in quality and quantity.

Radio

Radio is the Rodney Dangerfield of information sources. No one gives it much respect. That is a mistake. The United States may have 2.1 radios for every person in the country, but we are not the only nation with more radios than people. That list includes Australia, Canada, Denmark, the Netherlands, South Korea, and the United Kingdom. Even in the developing world radios are a common commodity. Consider these figures (per 1,000 people) (u.s. census 1993:856):

Country	Number of Radios
Algeria	233
Bolivia	599
Cuba	345
Ghana	266
Mexico	243
Nigeria	172
South Africa	326

Only in desperately poor countries such as Bangladesh and India does the ownership of radios fall below one hundred per one thousand people, and even in those countries, radio ownership is far more common than ownership of newspapers or televisions. Radio appears to be the one communication medium that is uniformly available around the world.

Radio also tends to be local. Programming does not need to be imported. There may be some music from the United States (country western is very popular in southern Africa), but local music makes it onto the radio as well, as does lots of talk.

Talk can be disastrous. Much of the tragedy of Rwanda can be traced to a radio station that broadcast calls for genocide and then urged people to flee the country. Its lies may be responsible for hundreds of thousands of deaths. Smaller crises have been caused in South Africa when right-wing groups put an illegal radio station on the air and issued calls for armed rebellion. Other problems seem to be occurring in the United States as a few stations have moved from conservative talk to slanderous talk.

But radio talk can also be an amazing forum for average citizens. Namibia has two shows that provide an excellent model of what radio can be. Each morning from nine to ten o'clock the public radio station airs "The Chat Show." People call in with complaints. Sometimes it is a business that has bothered the callers, but often it is concerns about the police or government ministries. To an American ear the calls are decidedly calm. There are few grand complaints about "the system." Callers make specific complaints about experiences they have had, and do it fairly quietly. They relate their stories slowly and in detail. Announcers don't rush people, and seldom interject their own feelings one way or another. After a person has said all he or she has to say, the announcer tries to sum up, and then moves on to the next caller. It all seems far less shrill than American radio (but sometimes more tedious).

From ten to one o'clock there are periods of music and interview shows with experts on one thing or another. At one the action starts again. This is the time for "Feedback." Sandra Williams of NBC has spent the three-hour interval from ten to one calling government agencies or private businesses to get their reactions to comments made during the morning. Getting reactions is often quite simple—it turns out many of the ministers listen to the morning show. She records their responses and prepares to put them on the air at one. When "Feedback" begins, Williams plays a tape of the original complaint, unedited and often lengthy. Then she plays the response. On occasion she will ask a question for clarification, but usually she and her colleagues are silent, letting the caller and the minister have center stage.

In rural Namibia the radio serves a more unusual role. There are no phones, there is no mail to speak of. If you want to get hold of a person, how do you do it? You call the local radio station. For no charge you can have the station announce that Johannes should see his aunt, she needs him. Johannes may not be listening, but enough of his neighbors are that he will get the message by the end of the day. The same system is used by government bodies. When the University of Namibia branch office in Oshikati needs to talk to a student who is taking a correspondence course, it will call the local station and have it announce, "Teofilus Shicongo, your biology textbook has come in." They have never had a student not get the message. Even in the poorest, most rural places in the world, radio works.

Books

In 1990, over 650,000 different books were published worldwide (BOWKER 1993). The sheer number of titles might imply that the world is awash with books. It is certainly true that parts of the world are awash with books. For instance, U.S. publishers sold over 2 billion books in 1991 (U.S. CENSUS 1993:247). But here, as in every other form of information, production is uneven. These figures from 1990 demonstrate the huge differences in book production by country:

Country	Number of Titles Published
Bangladesh	2,795
Canada	8,126
China	73,923
India	13,837
Norway	3,712
Philippines	1,112
South Africa	4,950
South Korea	39,330
United Kingdom	63,980
United States	48,146

While North America was publishing 461 book titles per million people, Africa was producing 29. The differences are even clearer when we look at particular countries. UNESCO monitors both the number of books published per country and the kind of books being published. Some kind of books (such as "pure science") would seem to be difficult for developing countries, but one would expect that all countries would write books about geography and history. Such books would be an important part of a country's self-awareness. Yet differences here are great. Consider these figures from 1980 (CURWEN 1986:273–276):

Country	Geography/History Books Published
Nigeria	230
Tanzania	0
Canada	932
Cuba	18
Mexico	203
United States	2,673
Colombia	340
Japan	2,919
Sri Lanka	62
Germany	4,332
United Kingdom	4,024

Among developed nations there are substantial differences in publication rates, but all are publishing large numbers. For poorer nations such as Tanzania,

Cuba, and Sri Lanka, local production is minor. Tanzania, with no production of history books at all in 1980, poses a problem typical for the very poor. If citizens want to learn about their nation, they have to learn from outsiders. It is possible Tanzanian citizens are writing books on Tanzanian history and having them published in other countries, but even in this unlikely event, publication control (editing decisions, design work, printing) are all in the hands of foreigners. How would we Americans feel if every book about American history were published in foreign countries? It would seem odd indeed. Even if every foreign publisher had the best intentions, we would probably be somewhat nervous about such a situation.

Yet publishing in a developing nation can be a daunting task. Jane Katjavivi, president of New Namibia Books, illustrates the problems such publishers face. She established her company in 1990 and has been very successful in bringing out a range of trade and educational titles. But it hasn't been easy. Production costs are high. Part of the costs comes from high paper prices (it must all be imported), high printing costs (all of the local presses are small and slow), and high editorial expenses (few people in Namibia have editorial or design experience). So it costs her more to produce a book in Namibia than it did when she was working as a publisher in the United Kingdom.

While costs are higher, sales are smaller. The highest-selling trade book she has published is *Last Days to Uhuru* (1994) by David Lush. A detailed and dramatic account of the last two years of Namibia's independence struggle, the book sold just two thousand copies in its first year. Part of the sales problem is literacy (fewer than half the citizens of Namibia have finished sixth grade), part is poverty (while the book costs less than ten U.S. dollars, that is more than two days' wages for many workmen), and part is distribution. There are only a handful of bookstores in Namibia, and most of them are part of a South African chain, CNA. CNA's stores are all controlled from South Africa, so getting a local book carried in the local branch store is no easy task. The Swakopmund Scientific Society produced a book on the ecology of Namibia's Atlantic coast and wanted to sell it through CNA's Swakopmund branch. The branch manager needed permission from the regional manager in Cape Town. The regional manager went to the national manager in Johannesburg. The Johannesburg manager turned down the book because he had never heard of the Swakopmund Scientific Society. For small local publishers, large international chains can be impassable obstacles.

The only good news for Katjavivi and her peers across Africa is the African Books Collective, an organization based in the United Kingdom and funded by the Ford Foundation and various Canadian and European development agencies. The collective transmits book information to libraries in the United

States and Europe and has had a significant impact on sales. Sales may still be small, but at least African books are no longer invisible.

Despite the efforts of publishers such as Katjavivi, however, it appears that book publishing will continue to be dominated by the United States and Europe. When Africa produces less than 2 percent of the world's book titles, and Latin America just 5 percent, it is clear where the book industry is concentrated. For Jane Katjavivi, sales figures reinforce the point. Her best-selling book had "good" sales when it reached two thousand. It hit two thousand the same year the U.S. market sold two billion books. Put another way, her biggest winner sold just one-millionth of the U.S. market. She and her African colleagues understand where they stand in the book world.

Conclusion

At a time when we are talking about an explosion of information, most public information sources are constrained, one-sided, and meager. Major sources of public information have inordinate American influence. What information flow exists, flows out from the United States, with little flowing back. Often there is little available to flow in any direction. Television shows have to be produced before they can be viewed. Movies have to be made, books have to be published. A walk through the minuscule "foreign films" section of any video rental store, time spent browsing in any bookstore, all give immediate force to world information trends.

The problem would be acceptable if we were just looking at Americans' renowned disinterest in any country but our own. But when you find that so many foreign countries have little information about themselves, you begin to wonder about larger issues. What public information is available, both here and abroad? The answer is very little compared to the range of cultures, histories, ideas, and peoples that populate our planet. There *is* a world outside of Hollywood, but it is not easy to find it. Rather than an information explosion, the public media seem to be demonstrating an *im*plosion in which few voices are heard and little of the world seen.

Chapter 2 Personal Information

When are you most afraid?
—A Seattle high school student via e-mail to a
friend in Tel Aviv during the Persian Gulf War

SCHINDLER'S LIST was the most acclaimed movie of 1994. It is a monumental story of courage in the midst of horror and degradation. Yet it was a story that took half a century to get to the silver screen. Why? It's not that Schindler was totally unknown. He saved twelve hundred people—people who remembered him and told others about him. They were hardly shy—they referred to themselves as Schindler's Jews. In April 1962 his heroism was recognized in Israel before a crowd of eight hundred and a tree was planted for him in the "Street of the Just" at the Yad Vashem Holocaust memorial in Jerusalem (FIXSES 1994). In Frankfurt a small street was named after him and a plaque there reads, "Oskar Schindler, 1908–1974. Savior of many Jews from extermination in concentration camps." There was also a novel published about his exploits. He may not have been a household word, but he was hardly unknown.

Yet the movie is not the result of orderly research into World War II heroes, or the consequence of newly discovered documentation. The movie occurred because a Hollywood screenwriter happened to get into a discussion with a shop owner who had been saved by Schindler. If the shop owner had been busy, if the writer had been in a hurry, if either of them had been grouchy and uncommunicative, the conversation never would have taken place, and the sequence of events culminating in the movie never would have started. In a world of faxes and databases and two-hundred-channel TV, the necessary information came from a quiet conversation in a small Los Angeles shop.

In 1984 Stephen Jobs was the head of a highly successful computer company, but it was a company in trouble. His Apple III computers were going nowhere. IBM had just entered the personal computer market and was threatening his Apple II sales. A friend invited him to visit Xerox's Palo Alto Research Center. While touring the labs he saw a series of computer interface projects. One involved a new device called a mouse. The other created small pictures or icons on the computer screen and substituted manipulation of them for typed commands. Jobs took what he saw back to Apple and first created the Lisa, then the Macintosh. He built his computers around this new graphic user interface and breathed fresh life into his company.

Nearly a decade goes by and it is IBM's turn to be in trouble. Seen as overpriced and out-of-date, they are losing market share and not even competing in emerging markets. Finally they decide to make a concerted effort in laptop computers. Their design team walks the floors of IBM's mammoth research labs and finds an odd device that looks like a pencil eraser. It is small and easy to use and takes the place of a mouse. Just the thing to have on a laptop, where space is tight and no one wants to carry an external mouse. They use the "eraser" and IBM produces one of its first hits in the personal computing market.

All three stories remind us of what should be obvious but is often forgotten: one of our principal sources of information is other people. It is important to have television and newspapers and computer databases, but it also helps to know people. Consider these statistics from the U.S. Census Bureau (1993):

Category	Year	Number
Overseas phone calls	1970	23.4 million
	1991	1.3 billion
Travelers visiting the United States	1985	25 million
	1992	45 million
U.S. business trips	1980	97 million
	1991	152 million

These are all people activities. We are making fifty-five times the number of overseas phone calls we did twenty years ago. The explosion in telecommunications is real. But we have increased the number of face-to-face meetings at the same time. Nearly twice as many foreigners are visiting the United States as in the mid-1980s. American business trips are up over 50 percent. Whatever the method, we want to make personal contact.

What is the information value of these connections? We will look at six links that people can make. Some people seem to make all of these links; some just a few; some seem cut off from all of them. Each link has connections to a specific body of information—information often unavailable to nonmembers.

As we will see, even in an age of high technology, who you know often determines what you know.

Family

Talk about family and connections, and the first thought that often comes to
mind for Americans is either the Mafia or the superrich. Those are the family
connections that have made their way onto television or movie screens. But while
those families certainly do help each other, the influence of family extends through
all social strata. The middle class takes good care of its own children, often in
ways that are so subtle they are missed. Consider these test scores from the
National Assessment of Educational Progress comparing the knowledge of
American eleventh graders in 1990 (U.S. CENSUS 1993):

	Parental Education		
Subject	SOME HIGH SCHOOL	HIGH SCHOOL GRADUATE	COLLEGE GRADUATE
Writing	190	204	221
Math	285	294	316
Science	261	276	306

The differences associated with the education level of the students' parents are
more significant than those associated with the students' race or gender. The
differences are large for all subjects and have held relatively constant since 1980.
What you know seems greatly influenced by what your parents know.

How does this work? Walter Loban of the University of California at
Berkeley began a longitudinal study of verbal skills in 1953. For the next thirteen years he followed 211 children from all socioeconomic levels as they
moved from kindergarten through high school. Each year he had them demonstrate their speaking, reading, writing, and listening proficiency. Over the years
he identified thirty-five students who had the highest developed verbal skills,
and the thirty-five who had the lowest. Differences were dramatic. For instance,
in one measure of communication ability, it took the low group until grade six
to reach the level the high group had reached in grade one!

In describing the characteristics of the two groups, Loban states that the
high group "spoke not only freely, fluently, and easily, but also effectively, using
a rich variety of vocabulary. They adjusted the pace of their words to their listeners, and their inflection or 'imparting tone' was adapted both to the meaning
of their content and to the needs of their listeners." By contrast, the low group
"rambled without purpose, seemingly unaware of the needs of the listener.

Their vocabulary was meager, and as listeners they did not focus on relation-ships or note how main ideas control illustrations or subordinate ideas" (LOBAN 1976:70–71).

Who were these children? Loban did his research in Oakland to ensure he had a mix of students of various racial groups and social backgrounds. The kids went to a wide range of public and private schools and lived in different neigh-borhoods. What distinguished the high group from the low? Money. Race seemed not to matter, nor did the type of school attended. The big difference was the position of the parents. Professionals had no children in the low group; day laborers and the semiskilled had no kids in the high group. Loban describes the situation this way: "Minority subjects who came from securely affluent home backgrounds did *not* show up in the low proficiency group. The problem is poverty, not ethnic affiliation" (23).

What does money have to do with something as basic as learning to talk? Loban's theory was that kids from wealthier backgrounds got more chances to talk, met more people with a wider range of interests. They simply had more experience than poor kids: "Their home lives and their compatibility with the school environment exacted of them complexity of thought, functional uses of abstraction, distillations of experience into words, and imaginative foreseeing of consequences. Their need for more concepts induced language for categorizing, comparing, contrasting, and conjecturing as well as for clarifying and commu-nicating feelings and emotions" (89).

Besides general ability, Loban also was able to identify a basic style of speech that distinguished the two groups. The high group, while more able, was also more tentative—willing to condition their statements with words like "generally" and "usually," willing to recognize that there were exceptions. The low group presented ideas in a very different manner. They were "more inflex-ible, dogmatic, unwilling or unable to entertain nuances or ambiguity" (25).

So which group would you rather spend an evening with or sit next to at lunch? One group can talk in an interesting manner about a range of subjects and is concerned about your needs as a listener. The other barely makes sense, pays no attention to your confusion, and presents meager ideas as if they were the Ten Commandments. Which group is prepared for a life of meeting people and learning about the world? Which kids had the benefit of a good family?

The new problem for children of very poor families may come from a direction Loban didn't expect—their itinerant life-style. Says one expert, "They move constantly, change schools, lose friends, and lose hope" (BERNSTEIN 1994:82). Add high crime levels that keep kids too scared to go outside to play with friends, and you end up with children who grow up knowing very few people. Their only companions are their siblings and their television set. We have already seen the impact of poverty on language development. For kids who seem to be growing up in a version of solitary confinement, those problems may be getting worse. Does family matter? For some kids it's the difference between spending a childhood alone in front of a TV or traveling the world.

School

Milton Houws and his former classmates at the University of Namibia get together for a few beers about once a month. They have been out of the university for about five years now, but they still like to stay in touch. Partly they are drawn together by a shared experience—theirs was the class that rallied, demonstrated, boycotted, and marched during the last days of the colonial regime. They had been lucky. No one shot, no one even arrested. But they hadn't known at the time what would be around the next corner or waiting for them after dark. So they shared their experiences, and their bravery, and their victories over the South Africans.

Now they also share careers. All five had been computer science majors at The Academy—soon renamed the University of Namibia. Computer science majors the world over share long hours—often late hours in the computer lab, so they knew each other well even before the political events began, and now they still have computer stories in common. Whose company is doing what, what hardware works best, what large programs are being developed around town. In some ways they have become rivals as they approach the point at which some of them may move into management, but they understand they still need each other and their University of Namibia (UNAM) grapevine to stay up on developments around town. So they sip their beers, and say more than their bosses probably wish they would, and get caught up for another month.

In neighboring Botswana, Mathaelsii Leepile edits the largest weekly newspaper in the country, *Mmegi*. He works his school network regularly to get stories. Many of his old friends at the University of Botswana are now in the government and they are happy to talk with him. In fact, they complain about some of his reporters who seem shy: "Sometimes reporters act like they are afraid of us. Don't they know sometimes we want to leak information to see how people react to proposed policies?" Contacts are easy for Leepile; he is still part of their social circle and is regularly invited to the parties of government ministers. If he wants a story, he can get it.

Such school links happen. Often they are the result of shared stress. Medical students are prone to such bonding because of the long hours and high stress. Fine arts majors often forge links out of the long rehearsals and lengthy shows they share. Circumstances can create school links. But not all schools wait for links to be formed by accident. Some schools forge links as a matter of policy. The largest example, certainly the example of links formed at a tender age, is the Japanese schools.

In Japan, links are part of the system, and they begin when students enter school the first day. Students are assigned to a *kumi*, a classroom they will share with forty to forty-five other first graders. They will share that one classroom and one teacher for two years. It will be their home 230 days per year, from 8:30 A.M. to 3:30 P.M. or later. They will eat lunch in their *kumi*, they will play with their classmates during free time. They will learn together as a *kumi*, all doing the same tasks at the same time. There are no ability groupings, no "bluebird" reading group, no kids pulled out for Chapter One tutoring. They learn together.

The only break from the *kumi* is their *han*, a smaller study group which works on projects together over a long period of time. This is not an ability group, and *hans* don't go off on separate tasks. Each group works on the same projects. But these student groups do elect a leader, so children get some experience in leadership. However, it is leadership Japanese style—forming a consensus and negotiating with dissenters rather than ordering obedience. The *han-cho* learns what it takes to manage a group—the limits of power, the efforts needed to build group cohesion.

With a social system as strong as the Japanese schools building group cohesion, the results can be impressive. But there are problems. What of children who move? What of children who must travel overseas with parents running Japan's new commercial empire? Once out, how can any child become part of a *kumi* again? This problem is so severe, Benjamin Duke tells us, that half of all men transferred to a job elsewhere in Japan leave their families in the home city (1986). Those children who do transfer are called *tenkosei*, and for them to be fully accepted can take months—often not until the next biannual *kumi* is formed.

For Japanese children who have studied overseas, the transition back can be worse: "The child's absence from Japanese schools is seen as a clear handicap, for not only has he lost ground academically, but he is perceived to have lost his 'Japanese common sense' . . . the right way to do morning exercises or . . . how to bow properly" (WHITE 1987:175). In short, the child doesn't fit into the group anymore. This is an immediate problem for the child, but it is also a problem for Japanese business interests. What parent would take an overseas position knowing how much it will hurt his children? The ties that bind children to the *kumi* also bind parents to a single city.

A more subtle form of school ties was recently demonstrated by France. The French government is in the process of buying access to U.S. universities. It is an effort brought on by a decline in their place on campus. A study by the Modern Language Association in 1991 showed that while total college enrollment in foreign-language classes rose 18 percent from 1986 to 1990, enrollment in French fell 1 percent (BROWN 1994). Long term, the problem is even worse. From 1968 to 1990 French enrollments have fallen 30 percent, while Japanese enrollments are up 1,000 percent. France's response? It gave $400,000 a year for three years to be split among Harvard, Princeton, Johns Hopkins, the University of California at Berkeley, the University of Pennsylvania, and the University of Chicago. The universities can do whatever they want with the money, but presumably it will be used to improve the teaching of the French language and culture.

France isn't the only country buying access to elite U.S. universities. In many ways they are just copying the programs developed by the Germans and Japanese, both of whom have special programs of scholarships, travel, and curriculum development support. For countries too poor to write checks to American colleges, sometimes business people can fill in. When professors at Berkeley's Center for South Asia Studies wanted to endow a chair in Indian studies, they turned to South Asian business leaders and were able to bring in $450,00, more than they needed to establish the chair (CAGE 1994).

Why make such an effort to buy a piece of American colleges? According to one source, the decision to spread $400,000 around selected American campuses was "debated at the highest levels of the French government" (BROWN 1994:2). That's not much money, but the concept was important to them: "It allows us to break the stereotypes in which you associate France with wine and cheese." Shaping how people view your country is of course no small matter. Who wants to be associated with cheese? So you buy a few local champions, give away some plane tickets, and make important friends. Some might wonder if all of this is fair to Afghanistan, Uruguay, or Mozambique, none of which have $400,000 to give to Harvard, but the countries that can write such a check understand the need to do so. Making connections with college kids is a good investment in the future.

Civic Organizations

What is 1 American in 589? One Swede in 296? One South African in 6,183? A Rotarian. Goma, Zaire, may be famous for many years as the place where over a million Rwandans swarmed into exile and thousands died of dysentery. It also happens to be home to a chapter of Rotary International. It may seem incongruous that there would be Rotarians among all the filth and disease, but prior to the arrival of the Rwandans, Goma was just another small African town, a surprising number of which have chapters of international clubs.

The presence of Rotary or Lions Clubs all over the world is no accident. Both clubs have an international orientation and actively support the creation of clubs around the world. No sooner had the Iron Curtain come down than volunteers went over to Eastern Europe to help form clubs. Why rush in to form civic clubs when so many other things seem more necessary? They do it because a fair amount of evidence indicates the civic clubs can be the foundation for national success. Robert Putnam, a longtime researcher on the role of civic organizations in public life, says it quite plainly: "The quality of public life and the performance of social institutions (not only in America) are indeed powerfully influenced by norms and networks of civic engagement" (1995:66).

How do such organizations help? Putnam explains it this way: "For a variety of reasons, life is easier in a community blessed with a substantial stock of social capital. In the first place, networks of civic engagement foster sturdy norms of generalized reciprocity and encourage the emergence of social trust. Such networks facilitate coordination and communication, amplify reputations, and thus allow dilemmas of collective action to be resolved" (1995:67).

Beyond civic virtue, there is also the question of economic gain. Social connections have long been shown to be important in acquiring a job. International clubs play a role in international business—members can go to any country in the world and make contact with people who are also in business. They are a perfect place to gain insider information about local companies and to meet business leaders. At any meeting members can speak with people from other countries and gain insights into situations that are only glossed over (or ignored) in the public media.

Unfortunately, there are some limits to the links international clubs can make. One limit is the clubs' membership policies. While service clubs in the United States are usually open to women and minorities, such policies are often unenforced in the rest of the world. Women, for instance, are frequently banned (the Rotary Club in Namibia has had only one female member in its history—the U.S. ambassador). Racial or ethnic groups can also be excluded. Clubs usually bow to local prejudices. Money can also be a significant filter. Rotary Clubs often expect a member to have reached a certain station in life. Clubs in Germany are said to have informal requirements that new members make a large contribution to club charities. The few clubs in the former Soviet Union often were reserved for members of the secret police. The result is that clubs are hardly a representative sample of the local population.

In looking at U.S. civic organizations, Putnam (1995:72) provides numbers that illustrate the elite nature of civic groups and point to a second, emerging problem:

Level of Education	Average Memberships per Person	
	1967	1993
College graduate	2.8	2.0
High school graduate	1.8	1.2
High school dropout	1.4	1.1

College graduates are twice as likely to participate in and benefit from civic organizations as other Americans. It is they who meet the community leaders, they who share information, they who are most likely to develop a personal network. Yet while nations around the world are seeing the value of civic organizations and striving to build their groups, the figures above make it clear that Americans of all educational levels are cutting back on their level of civic involvement.

This creates problems. Some of the problems are obvious, like the drop (from twelve to seven million) in the number of parents who belong to PTAs or the drop in volunteers (26 percent) for Boy Scouts. We know what these changes mean for the number of opportunities our children will have in school. Other problems, like those that may result from the 40 percent decline in league bowling, are harder to specify. Yet here too we have a general sense that growing numbers of Americans are missing chances to socialize, to communicate, to share ideas over pizza, beer, and bowling balls.

Work

Au Bon Pain is a chain of French pastry restaurants along the East Coast. Like all fast food restaurants in the United States, it initially relied on a pool of young workers who came, worked briefly, and then left. Low pay, low training, and low status meant workers who cared little about their jobs or their customers. With a turnover of 200 percent a year, it was hard to even know who the workers were. Imagine working at a place where every employee was new every six months. Imagine being a customer at such an establishment.

Gary Aronson, manager of one of the stores in Boston, finally showed the industry the way out. First, he cut his work force by 70 percent and upped the hours and the wages of the employees he kept. He asked them to expect work weeks of fifty to sixty hours. He agreed to pay overtime for the extra hours, so that they now earned up to twenty-three thousand dollars in their first year, more than double the industry average. Employee turnover dropped to 10 percent a year, one-twentieth of the industry average. Employees who were around long enough to learn their jobs also learned who their customers were. According to researchers at Harvard, "Sales have soared as customers patronize the people they see everyday behind the counters" (SCHLESINGER 1991:9).

The lesson seems to be to drop casual labor—employees with little connection to their employer or the customers they serve. Identify your best employees, pay them well, and keep them on the premises long enough so they develop an awareness of their customers. When customers and employees get to know one another, service improves and sales take off. Such connections seem to be the current model for business—reach out, use electronic mail, use meals, use social events, use whatever you need, but find out where the talent is, find out what your customers want, find out what you need to succeed.

Location

With telecommunication equipment in every briefcase, what possible difference does location mean? We can work just as easily on a mountain top in Tibet as in a board room in a major business center, right? Maybe so, but there are many examples that testify to the contrary, beginning with the Internet itself.

In the twenty square miles around Washington, D.C., 1,206 technology companies have major operations. Beginning with a focus on satellite communications, such companies as Hughes, Intelsat, and GTE Spacenet set up operations. Add them to the Defense Department, NASA, MCI, and Sprint, and you begin to have a pretty big communications center. Then add the Internet. Says Anthony Rutkowski, vice president of the Internet Society, "It's uncanny how many of us in the internet business are strung up and down the accessway to Dulles Airport" (STEWART 1994b:64).

It really isn't all that uncanny. To begin with, the Internet was founded and is still partially funded by Washington. Then add the nature of Washington itself—it both produces and requires tremendous amounts of information. Take, for example, the 140 megabytes of information produced each day by the Securities and Exchange Commission. With an information factory like that, is it surprising that an information conduit is located nearby?

Then there are people. Jean Villanueva, vice president of America Online (also located in Washington), puts it simply, "We all know one another, or know who we are." Why? Carl Malamud of Internet Multicasting service points to the Net itself: "We all talk to each other—we have to, because the Net is a very complex machine." Another observer points out, "The technical and service skills required to run large data networks are scarce, and labor markets work best when people can change jobs without changing mortgages."

And then there is public policy. Says one network executive, "Technically, we could be anywhere, but the real questions aren't technical. They are public policy and social change. It's really important to be here [in Washington]." So the Net that takes you all over the world may have created cyberspace, but it is grounded in one very particular space—Washington, D.C. That's where the people networks are. That's where the human connections are made.

In his book *The Work of Nations*, Robert Reich points to other concentrations of people and talent. In fact, he invents a new description of one class of workers—"symbol analysts"—and declares it natural for these people to draw together. Because their work depends on face-to-face meetings to exchange insights and professional gossip, he looks to ever heavier concentrations of elite workers in "specialized geographic pockets" such as Cambridge, Hollywood, and the Silicon Valley. The very nature of their work as information experts, Reich states, draws them into physical proximity with one another.

But you don't have to be a leading figure in Hollywood or Cupertino to understand the need for physical proximity. For example, consider the "Singing Dustman," James Bhemgee. He wanted to be the world's greatest tenor. This is a pretty ambitious career goal for anyone, but especially ambitious for a twenty-nine-year-old "coloured" man from South Africa who is partially deaf, has a speech impairment, is barely literate, and sweeps streets for a living. The only thing he had going for him, besides an amazing voice, is he knew where to sing—the white part of Cape Town: "I knew the white people had the connections and the money. I was hoping someone would hear me and tell me what I could do" (PALMER 1994). So as he swept the streets of Cape Town, he waited until he was in the best white neighborhoods and then let loose with his best arias. One morning in 1988, his strategy worked. As he swept past the home of Angelique Fuhr, he launched into an Afrikaans song, "Without You I Cannot Live." The eighty-three-year-old Fuhr was the widow of a violinist and the mother of a concert pianist. She asked Bhemgee to come in and sing for her. He said he couldn't during working hours but could be back after lunch. He came back later that day and sang for her. Fuhr called her daughter and told her to come right over. The daughter agreed Bhemgee had a remarkable talent and started calling her friends. They quickly found a music teacher for Bhemgee and things progressed from there.

He has not become the world's best tenor. But he has come a remarkable distance. He has received coaching from some international performers, has studied music at the Royal College of Music in London, and has performed onstage in Johannesburg. Most recently he has moved to the United States, where he has enrolled in the opera program of a university in the Southwest. Maybe he will become an international star, maybe he won't achieve that level of success. But at least he has been able to get some help and to move ahead with his ambitions, all because he knew where to go—the white part of town.

Digital Friends

In 1989 Jeff Golub's Seattle, Washington, high school students joined the Learning Network. A commercial venture that links schoolrooms around the world, his students were put in a group with twelve other schools—eight in the United States and four in Europe. Assigned the task of exploring global pollution, Golub's class gathered data, and once each class period one student would go to the computer in the back of the room, print off information received from the other schools, and type in the information gathered in Seattle.

The endeavor was very organized, very scholarly, very predictable. Students enjoyed having daily contact with their peers around the world, but the quality of the contacts didn't exactly compete with MTV. Then one day a student in West Berlin broke the rules and forgot to send a message on local pollution. Instead, he wrote about what he had seen the night before. He had been to the Wall. So had lots of other people. He wasn't sure what was going on, but people were saying the Wall might come down. End of message. Each morning for the next two weeks, students rushed early to their Seattle classroom to read what was happening at the Wall. The pollution assignment was abandoned. Golub and other teachers tried to teach sixteen-year-old Seattle students about the history and geography of Berlin, starting with pictures of the Wall. Students balanced classroom lectures with personal messages and questions to their friend in Berlin. Finally, after two weeks came the longest message of them all—the Wall is down, I saw my grandmother last night, she came through the Wall—screen after screen of eyewitness description from a peer. To the students in that Seattle classroom, history was no longer dry lectures and sanitized textbooks cleared by endless state committees. History was a young boy in Berlin writing about his grandmother.

Two years later Golub's class was also hooked to the Learning Network. A new crop of sixteen year olds was linked to eleven classrooms—seven in the United States, three in Europe, one in Tel Aviv. The research subject was pollution again, and students collected local information and shared it with the other schools. The process was interesting, but routine. Then one day one of the girls in Tel Aviv started her message with "Last night the Scuds landed" and described her neighborhood. And once again day after day the students in Seattle ran into their classroom in the morning to check their e-mail. What had happened? Were they okay? The Seattle students sent questions and messages of support. The Tel Aviv students described what their lives had become.

At one point one of the Seattle students asked, "When are you most afraid?" The answer from the teenagers in Tel Aviv? They were afraid to take showers. Wet, naked, soapy, they might not hear the sirens, and if they did, they worried they might not make it to the sealed room in time to protect them from any poisoned gas. The kids in Seattle had long talks, and lots of quiet moments, over that revelation.

Microcomputers have been in schools for well over a decade now. They have been used to record attendance, to drill multiplication tables, to process words, and to simulate taking a wagon train on the Oregon Trail. But nothing compares with the impact they have had now that teachers are using them to connect students to students. Now even young students can receive very personal information instantly from across the world

At least some students can. Unfortunately, most of chapter 6 is a detailed description of how many technical barriers still remain before this kind of connection can become routine. For students on the wrong side of those technical barriers, there is no flood of electronic mail arriving to enlighten and entertain. The problems for the children on this side of the barriers are more subtle. A year or so ago I was speaking to a teacher's group and telling the story of Jeff Golub's class and their connections to the students in Tel Aviv. When I finished, there were the usual questions about the students in Seattle and Tel Aviv, and then a teacher asked a question I hadn't thought of—"How did the kids in Baghdad feel?" We don't know. No one had direct feeds to their schools while the cruise missiles roared overhead and children wondered if they would live through the night. The kids in Seattle never heard their fears, never heard which children made it through the night and which didn't.

Dangers of Personal Information

While personal information sources may be important to all of us, personal information is inherently messy. It seems a patchwork of hit-and-miss efforts. Information is available to some, but not to others. The information itself is often errant. Lies can be transmitted just as effectively as truth, as can be seen in the following examples.

MYTHS

As Rwandan refugees huddled in Goma, Zaire, and tens of thousands died of dysentery, clean water flowed on the other side of the border—back in their own country. But convinced they would be killed, refugees stayed in Zaire and died. More disturbing was the fact that many believed they were being killed not by bad water but by enemies in Rwanda: "It was the Tutsi who poisoned our food. We bought it by the side of the road, and now we are dying. God will judge this" (GIBBS 1994:35). International groups who were all over Rwanda could find no evidence to support any acts of vengeance by the new rulers in Rwanda, and had limitless evidence that the water in Zaire was deadly. It was clear to the scientists that refugees were killing themselves drinking bad water. It was equally clear to the refugees that they were being poisoned by another tribe.

Where did the refugee quoted above get the news that he was being poisoned by Tutsis? Some of the lies were circulated by a radio station, Radio Milles Collines. But much of the mythology was just handed from person to person as they hiked the roads into exile, as they sat around the campfires. Their personal "networking" continues. Information still flows. In this case it is misinformation that is flowing. But it is accepted as truth. Two plus two equals four, the earth revolves around the Sun, and the Tutsis are poisoning the Hutus. Each truth is inherently obvious to the refugee. There is no need to debate, to question, or to dig for more information. The truth has been found. And yet another murderous myth makes the rounds.

A year later it was America's turn to host a mythology explosion. In the weeks after the Oklahoma City bombing that left 167 men, women, and children dead, private communication systems burned with rumors and ravings. Using fax, phone, and e-mail, one group in Idaho ascribed the bombing to efforts by the federal government to eliminate former bodyguards of President Clinton who knew too much. Meanwhile, in Kansas City, Missouri, a woman operating an "information service" tells all she can reach electronically that the bomb is the work of the UN: "This is what the UN does when they go in and overthrow a country. They produce unrest in the country first" (BAYLES AND FOSTER 1995:9). With the power of electronics, talk that formerly crossed a barroom now crosses continents. Mythology goes digital.

TRIBALISM

The South Africans showed the world just how destructive tribalism can be. When they ruled Namibia (1915–1990) they practiced what they called "cultural diversity." What this amounted to was reserving the central part of the country (better land, higher altitude for cooler temperatures, easier access to railroads) for white farmers—a policy initiated by the Germans when they had ruled. The corners of the country were broken out for individual tribes and named accordingly. There was Bushmanland, Ovamboland, and so forth. Each had its own administration, its own educational system, and its own language. It was a textbook example of divide and conquer, with a bit of the Tower of Babel thrown in for good measure. The South Africans created diverse cultures—exactly what they needed to maintain their rule.

Eventually the Namibians were able to achieve their independence, and they worked hard at undoing the damage left behind. They went to a single official language—English, created a single national school system, and tried to reduce the importance of local chiefs. So far they have been remarkable in their ability to create a unified country. But examples from all over the world make it clear that building true and lasting unity will be difficult. For one thing, some leader sensing opportunity seems ever ready to play one group against another. In Central Africa, Rwandans are being urged to exterminate one another and Kenya looks to be fairly close behind as President Moi seems to want the Masais to drive the Kikuyus out of the country or out of existence. To quote Moi, "We have said in the past that when a multi-party system is introduced, it will create tribalism, divisions, and hatred and so on. This has now taken place" (HUBAND 1994:18). As long as his party had absolute power, the world according to Moi was perfect. The minute there was opposition, he found a tribe to blame it on and made the tribe pay the price.

Tribalism, of course, is not limited to Africa. In the United States many of the sparks flying in the "culture wars" can be traced to groups that function in total isolation. In her excellent description of textbook censorship, Joan Delfattore traces an encounter between American tribes. The Hawkins County School Board in rural Tennessee changed to a new reading series. The new series was fairly standard fare in that it promoted multicultural awareness along with reading skills. A conservative group of parents was opposed to the new series and brought their complaints to the school board. At that point there was a clash, brought on in part by the total lack of awareness by both sides that there *was* another side:

> Like many fundamentalists who become involved in textbook controversies, Frost associates mainly with people who think much the way she does. She and her family are not separated from the secular world as the Amish are, but they read primarily religious newspapers and magazines, avoid movies and television programs, and socialize with others of the same religion. It came as a great surprise when churchgoing local school officials, including some of her former school mates, did not agree with what seemed perfectly obvious to her. On the other side, the school officials took it for granted that everyone supports multiculturalism, environmentalism, and the other contemporary "isms" presented in the Holt books.
>
> (DELFATTORE 1992:17)

An ugly fight ensued, fueled greatly by the surprise each side had that another view *even existed*. Everyone they talked to, everything they read, convinced them that everyone thought exactly as they did. So who could object? Each tribe went to the school board meeting assuming they would easily prevail. Neither side understood there was another side. How could they? They had no contact outside of their own tribe.

A common hope among those watching the burgeoning of e-mail communication systems is that these new communication links will help people meet more people and encounter fresh views of the world. Jeff Golub's class is an exciting example of how good such communication can be. He proves e-mail will let us reach beyond our local tribe. But there is no guarantee it will happen. While surfing the Net, will we look into areas that are totally foreign to us or will we steer directly to the familiar? Will we try to link up with our political opposites? Or use our limited time to support our allies? There is nothing in the medium that would automatically lead to new kinds of behavior. So why shouldn't we expect people to form tribes in cyberspace?

INEPTITUDE

Walter Loban's research on language development poses a problem for those born to the poor—what do you do if you recognize your language skills are weak? You don't talk comfortably, you find reading a chore, mixing with others is painful. Should your parents' income sentence you to a lifetime of limited conversation? What if you were lucky enough to be born into the middle class but are shy? You sit in meetings but never talk. At lunch you can never move the conversation to topics that interest you. You tend not to join groups because making small talk before or after meetings is agony. When you travel you tend not to meet many people and can go days without talking.

There are responses both an individual and an individual's culture can make. The Japanese *kumi*, in which students stay together for two years at a time, may look impressive by current standards, but two years is tiny compared to what American students used to have when they shared one-room schools. We used to have the same children and the same teacher for six or eight years. We got to know each other very well. Now that we have newer schools, the first thing we do is break students up by grade and then by ability. Now many elementary schools are moving to different teachers for different subjects. Children as young as first grade may have three or even four different teachers during the course of the day.

Oddly enough, while American grade schools atomize classes, some American universities are going in the opposite direction with cohort scheduling. One group of students is scheduled for the same set of classes—English, chemistry, history, and so on. The idea is to let professors take advantage of common classes, to give them a chance to relate assignments from one class to another. Socially, cohort scheduling gives students on huge campuses a chance to meet and get to know one group of students very well. It gives average students some of the special opportunities usually reserved for students in special honors programs or enrolled in smaller elite institutions. Does it help? One study showed colleges using this approach reduced their dropout rate 4 percent (*Realizing* 1995).

In the workplace, one effort underway to encourage more involvement involves new "groupware" communications software. Each person on a team sits at a computer terminal (located anywhere in the world), typing into a word processor. One portion of the computer screen shows all the comments made by others in the group, one portion of the screen allows for your responses. Now there is no waiting for your turn to speak, or trying to shout over a more aggressive team member. As you have comments, you make them, and they are displayed along with everyone else's. Groupware may not be a sure cure for the shy, but it lowers the threshold for inclusion, making it easier for all to be involved and for all ideas to get out on the table.

POVERTY

The truly poor are restricted from networking on two accounts. One is money, the other is time. Too poor to join fancy clubs, travel the world, or attend expensive colleges, they know very few people. They also don't have time. For many women of Africa it is routine to spend three hours a day gathering wood for a fire, or two hours walking to the nearest source of water. When do they have the time to sit and talk with people? Middle-class people who lose their jobs find themselves facing the same situation, plus an additional wrinkle. With no income they suddenly can't afford travel or membership dues. With no job, all their time goes into finding work. In addition, the minute they lose their job, they lose their computer link to their peers around the world.

In truth, the problem of poverty is insurmountable. The poor are excluded from much of the world's information and no one has even begun to outline a solution to that problem.

Summary

Most of the world's knowledge isn't sitting in books or in computers. It is sitting in heads around the world. Individuals gain access to that knowledge through their families, their school, their club memberships, their co-workers, and through travel. For some the process of acquiring this information is easy—they are born to the right family, attend the right school, have the money for club memberships and travel. Others seem to have everything going against them. They have few connections handed to them, and they have few of the skills needed to build links on their own. The consequences of a lack of personal information may seem minor to those who have it, after all they already have so many other sources of information they may not even need or appreciate this one. But the consequences are clear to those who don't have it and can be summed up in two words—Who's hiring?

Chapter 3

Organizational Information

*[The Internet] is run by people who believe information
wants to be free. That may be incompatible with what
commercial entities want to do with it.* —CHARLES FRYE

1993 MAY BE REMEMBERED as the year public universities went public. Pushed,
prodded, and cajoled by various governors and state legislatures, universities across
the United States agreed to be more forthcoming about what they did and how
they did it. It wasn't an easy battle, but so many states took on the battle
simultaneously—in what one university administrator called "legislation by fax"
—that universities withered under the pressure and agreed to tell the public what
was happening on their campuses.

What did they agree to tell? Typically, universities would now publish
annual reports in which they detailed the number of students who graduated
within six years of entering, the number of programs that were accredited, the
pass rates for students on state and national licensing exams, the job placement
rates of graduates, the average high school rank and entrance exam scores for
incoming students, the scores of juniors on new national "midcollege" assessment tests, the amount of crime on campus, and the racial, ethnic, and sexual
composition of the student body.

Some of this information, such as graduation rates, placement rates, and
crime statistics, had been required by federal law for years but had been buried
in reports quietly mailed to Washington and never seen in the local papers. Some
of the information was new. The number of programs receiving formal accreditation from external bodies is a good indicator of a campus's strength. When
South Carolina started collecting and publishing that data on its universities,

other states followed suit. Test scores for juniors, usually a general test on verbal and quantitative skills, was also new, but was growing in popularity as a way of seeing if required general education courses do what college professors claim—boost students' general knowledge and skills.

For obvious reasons some universities and some faculties have been reluctant to release this information even at the direct request of their legislatures. When the Wisconsin legislature demanded that the twenty-six campuses of the University of Wisconsin system release data on the student evaluation of faculty, the faculty union immediately threatened to sue. Various campuses chose more devious responses. One department had previously asked students to respond to twenty-two questions on its faculty evaluation forms, including such questions as "The instructor is readily available for consultation," and "The instructor seems well prepared for class," but once it became clear that the student responses to these questions would become public knowledge, the department stopped asking the questions. Their theory seems to be that the best way to hide information is never to collect it in the first place.

Meanwhile, across campus, the Office of Information Technology is writing home pages for the World Wide Web. Pretty pictures of the campus logo accompany a list of majors offered, the exploits of leading faculty, descriptions of the campus and community. Electronic sales literature, the campus home page goes out to anyone with an Internet connection and a desire to surf the Net. By one count five thousand such home pages are being created each day. But what is on these pages? More important, what is *not* on them?

The technology is available to carry information to the corners of the earth. Organizational structures are there to ensure that only pretty information makes the trip. In viewing how organizations—whether universities, medical centers, or appliance stores—handle information, there are three useful ways of looking at their information flow: internal information, exchanges between organizations, and information released to the public. Each information flow is going through changes, but there are still strict limits on what can be known by whom.

Information within the Organization

There is a general sense that organizations are changing—becoming more open with their employees, knocking down barriers to communication. We certainly have some well-publicized examples of companies that have done just that, but each organization is different. Each has different leadership and a different culture. To help think about those differences and their effect upon information flow, let's look at two different approaches to internal information flow. Examples of each approach can be seen all over the world. But whatever the geography and whatever the local circumstances, organizations either share information with their employees or hide it.

OPEN INFORMATION SYSTEMS

Some organizations make a conscious effort to share information. Employees of these organizations are allowed and encouraged to know what is being done and why. A review of two strategies used shows the kind of effort open information flow requires.

JAPANESE FACTORIES. The corporate culture of Japan has been described many times, especially in recent years as American business writers try to decide if we should be in love with Japan or deathly afraid of it. For me, a more useful resource on Japanese corporate culture comes from Robert Cole (1971), who wrote about Japanese factories from the factory floor and did it more than twenty years before it was fashionable. Cole describes the Japanese factories of the 1960s, a period of great transition, a period in which the warts were still visible.

The Japanese firm of the day was already forming the unique melding of worker and management that is so frequently noted today. But as Cole observed, that melding was less the result of some nebulous homogeneity of Japanese culture than it was of specific actions on the part of Japanese employers.

CONSULTATION AMONG WORKERS. Long before quality circles and team-work became buzzwords for the factory floor, Cole found substantial efforts among workers to control their work. As one electrician told him, "In the Tokyo plant, when you have a job to do, you sit down with two or three guys, each expresses his ideas about the best way to do the job; then gradually you sort out the best proposals and a decision is made" (1971:139).

LEISURE NETWORKING. For factory workers under thirty (they typically married at thirty), co-workers were the people they went out with after work, the people they spent holidays with, the people they joined on outings. Management often helped, setting up company recreational facilities and promoting company friendship organizations. On the other hand, Cole found one worker who was skeptical of too much company involvement in such groups. As he saw it, true friends would not need "organized friendship" (1971:139).

INFORMALITY. While Japanese workers are supposed to always be polite, Cole found his fellow workers "gregarious, spontaneous, quick to anger, and quick to express joy" (1917:141). This range of emotions and freedom of expression was partly the result of an exceptional informality on the factory floor. Although typical Japanese language has a range of verb forms to reflect social positions, age, and skill differences, these verb forms were dropped on the factory floor. They all used more intimate, more informal forms of address, ignoring social distinctions that would be important in other places.

BREAKING BLUE-COLLAR, WHITE-COLLAR DISTINCTIONS. Prior to the Second World War, there were huge differences between blue-collar and white-collar workers. After the war, efforts at democratization softened those distinctions substantially, although some differences remain. Salary differences narrowed, as did differences in job security. Significantly, so did the difference in worker appearance. Blue-collar workers commonly arrived and left the factory in a suit, white shirt, and tie. And although their social groups were still primarily class-bound, Cole found many instances of blue- and white-collar workers who went out together after work.

REGIONAL COALITIONS. A major influence in bridging the gap between levels of employees was geography. Those who came from a particular place often knew each other before coming to work at a company or were drawn to each other by similarities in dialect and social custom. Cole found these vertical groupings often connected people from top management down to blue-collar workers.

AGE COALITIONS. Workers who came to work for the company the same year tended to maintain their connections throughout their careers. This resulted in continued relationships even after some of them had become supervisors. For those who were of lower status, their age mates were an informal channel of information about upcoming management developments, while managers were able to solicit reactions to possible policy changes through a group that would respect their privacy.

NO PERMANENT ENEMIES. One of the surprises Cole observed on the factory floor around him was the apparently inconsistent relationships between people: "It was not uncommon, in the Tokyo die-cast plant, to see a Communist leader idly chatting with a foreman who tried to split the union or see a worker who had angrily given the foreman hell at a section meeting offer him a cigarette on a break the next day" (1971:137). Part of this is a cultural bias against permanent enemies. The larger your circle of contacts, the better your chances of getting aid when you need it. But part of this is a conscious effort on the part of management. They know even the most militant worker will change with age. So they forget past sins. They also keep talking so they can keep in touch with workers. A worker who screams at them is a worker who will at least communicate with them.

Some of these communication channels, such as age or geographic cliques, are an accident of the local culture, some are the result of management efforts, but in either case, it is clear the culture of the Japanese factory floor supports multiple contacts between employees. They talk to each other across levels and through a variety of circumstances.

DISNEY WORLD. Red Pope's pair of articles entitled "Mickey Mouse Marketing" (1979) do a marvelous job of defining team-oriented organizations in America. He describes the experience his two children had as temporary Disney World employees, comparing their experience to that of typical bank employees and pointing out that Disney builds a very unique culture. The culture begins with names. Employees are "Cast Members" and "Hosts." Each of them, from temporary ticket taker to corporate vice president, wears a name tag that contains only one word—his or her first name—no job titles, no Mr., Mrs., Dr. The point is to break out of the hierarchy chart and give everyone a common purpose—to serve as hosts for all of Disney's "Guests" (they don't have "customers").

Team membership begins at Disney University, where each new employee takes "Traditions 1." This is an explanation of Disney philosophy and organization, down to a description of each division of the company and how it all relates to "the show." This orientation takes four eight-hour days and is required before any person can start any job—even something so simple as street sweeping or ticket taking. Employees are paid for this training period, are given lunch, and are treated like royalty, including having their picture placed on the front page of the Disney newspaper.

Team spirit is also built by the provision of a host of employee services, from restaurants to car pools, and by the annual reassignment of senior personnel to low-level jobs. For one week directors and vice presidents sweep streets, flip burgers, and join the cast on Main Street U.S.A. The regular employees know they are coming and are invited to share ideas with these senior people.

From an information-flow perspective, Disney's approach does two things remarkably well. First, by training even its lowest-level employees in a serious manner, it creates employees who understand the organization that employs them. This pays off directly when these employees have customer contact. Even though they are street sweepers, they can help a lost customer find the parking lot or catch a bus or locate a first-aid station. In short, it improves customer service. Indirectly, this training gives these employees a better chance to participate in the improvement of the company. Simply installing suggestion boxes may not produce many good ideas, if they are submitted by people who don't really know much about where they work. With no understanding of what their employer does or why the employer does it, people are in no position to suggest useful improvements. When Disney employees talk to the vice president flipping burgers next to them, there is a very good chance the suggestions they make will have enough sophistication to have some real value to the company.

This gets to the second benefit of the Disney approach. Between the titleless name tags, the range of social activities, and the week-long work stint of senior managers, every effort is made to mingle employees at every level. There are the usual corporate newsletters, but serious efforts are made to make personal bridges, informal contacts, that help information flow through the organization. While it is one thing for a manager to say "my door is always open," it is another for a low-level employee to actually walk through that door. Presumably an employee who would be unwilling to enter the hallowed halls of the corporate offices might be willing to talk to a man just as hot and sweaty as he is after a long day in the sun. There will always be differences between senior managers and entry-level employees, but Disney has shown a culture can be created that reminds both they are working on the same team toward the same ends.

PROBLEM CASES. Although many organizations around the world have used strategies to improve communications, there are considerable barriers to overcome. One of those barriers can be the employees themselves. Consider one example. My university has been stably and ably led since its inception over a century ago. Our last major change took place half a dozen years ago, when our former chancellor reached retirement age. Since change occurs so seldom here, the new chancellor was brought in with much pomp and circumstance. There was a formal inauguration attended by over one thousand. There were meetings and receptions and banquets and faculty teas. An extrovert, the new chancellor went everywhere and saw everybody. Finally, a year after arriving on campus, he started making the rounds of department coffee lounges. He had an especially pleasant visit with the English faculty, talking about recent literature for over an hour. As he was about to leave, one of the senior English professors stuck out his hand and introduced himself. When the chancellor responded with his name, the professor looked a little confused and asked, "What do you do here?" A now equally confused chancellor replied, "I'm the campus chancellor." "Oh" was all the professor could manage. He hadn't heard that the campus had a new chancellor. He thought he had been talking to a new professor.

That a professor on a relatively small campus would not even know the name of the campus head says a great deal about this particular professor, but it also says something about our culture. Many individuals may have some connection to an organization, but their connection is purposely tenuous. They want no more to do with that organization than their job, or their paycheck, requires. They won't show up at the company picnic, read the company newsletter, or tune in to the company grapevine.

These iconoclasts, or isolates, have been studied extensively. One study (RICHARDS 1976) found isolates ranging from 27 to 50 percent of organizations studied. But this apparently varies widely with organization type. In his research at a midwestern university, Goldhaber found only 7 percent of the professors were isolates. Whatever the percentage, a study by the Office of Naval Research (ROBERTS 1975) found isolates were less experienced, more insecure, and less motivated than their peers who were involved more actively in organizational communications. As people move up the ranks or spend more time with the organization, apparently they become more integrated.

In one sense, though, all these studies miss the point. Whether iconoclasts are 7 or 50 percent of an organization, or young or old, a good question would be why we have them at all. One is hard pressed to imagine any Japanese organization reporting 7 percent alienated employees, much less 50 percent. U.S. organizations not only have huge numbers of isolated employees but still manage to survive. Part of this is cultural mythology. In one of the most ironic examples of careful corporate communications efforts, Lucasfilms discovered through some internal research that there was almost no horizontal communication between editors, cinematographers, and artists. It responded by carefully restructuring its softball teams so that no team could have more than one person from the same department. This, of course, is a very insightful and clever way to encourage communication between departments (GOLDHABER 1990). Yet this is the same organization that brought us three Han Solo adventures (*Star Wars* one, two, and three), all showing the struggles of the isolate buccaneer of the future (carefully named Solo just in case any viewers were too slow to understand what he was supposed to represent). This kind of conflicted attitude is normal for our culture. Part of us knows that group activity is rewarding, even satisfying. But part of us wants our own space too. We, and the organizations that employ us, manage to juggle these mutually conflicting views of the world, but it isn't always easy, and communication often suffers in the process.

CLOSED INFORMATION SYSTEMS

Not every organization is willing to share information even with its own employees. There are multiple reasons for their approach, and multiple techniques at their disposal, but the effect on information flow is drastic—there is none.

AFRICAN BUREAUCRACIES. African nations are young, as are their corporations. One consequence of this is a shortage of experienced managers. There simply hasn't been enough time for a class of managers to develop. Add to this the corruption of a number of governments, where appointment as a manager has more to do with political loyalty than management skills, and you end up with fewer good managers.

But quality of managers isn't the only issue. Good, bad, or indifferent, managers work in a culture. In Africa that culture includes strong ties to one's family and tribe (BLUNT 1992). Those ties involve obligations, obligations that may conflict with obligations to an organization. The culture also centralizes power. This is sometimes called a "hierarchical" structure, but "paternal" may be a better label. Hierarchies may concentrate power at the top, but there is also power at other levels. Middle managers normally have power over their units. African middle managers have much less power.

The quickest way to understand the nature of an African organization is to stand outside any CEO's office. The waiting room is always full. In addition to the usual traffic that leaders draw, people who would normally be shunted to a subordinate wait to see the top man personally, feeling that some family or community connection gives them the right to be seen. And the manager will usually see them. His kinship responsibilities require that he receive these people. If he does not, his next family get-together will be very unpleasant for him.

The consequence of this culture for top managers is very long days, extreme stress, conflicting values and obligations, and little support from subordinates. The workload can't be shared. The multiple demands can't all be met. The job simply cannot be done. Add to this a climate of scarcity and you have an impossible situation. There aren't enough jobs to give to all the relatives. There aren't enough resources to help all in need. Every year brings less income and more poor relatives who need help. The only thing worse than being a top manager is being an unemployed cousin.

The consequence of this culture for information flow is even worse. First, everything flows through the CEO. All correspondence, all personal contacts, all phone calls, focus at the head. This means that only the head gets this information, and it means that since even the hardest-working CEO only has twenty-four hours in his day, the amount of information that comes in is restricted to the number of people the head can see and the number of letters the head can read. Furthermore, because much of the information coming in is private, even if the CEO wanted to shared it, there would be problems. And, of course, the CEO is not likely to share information that may involve decisions that, while good for his kin, are not good for the organization. How do you announce you have hired one more unqualified relative? You don't. So organizational information comes to the head and stays there.

The pervasiveness of this culture was clearly illustrated by an incident at the University of Namibia during the spring of 1994. Stories began circulating that funds were gone and student tuition would need to be raised again. Students went on strike demanding that the head of the university stop hiring people until costs were brought under control. They wanted the university head to stop using his power. But ironically, their method of protest was to march to the home of the president of Namibia and demand that he resolve the problem. Faced with a problem, they went straight to the top. Faced with a request, the president saw the students and took action. Each were acting out typical African roles. It never occurred to the students that there might have been other ways of solving the problem. It never occurred to students to speak with subordinates on campus or subordinates in the national government. One only talks to the top man. They responded to the excesses of one top man by going to another top man. No student saw the irony in this. The culture won.

As long as this culture remains unchanged, organizational information will be limited in Africa. Little will be known and little will be shared. Organizations are set up to focus information inward to the head, and to use that information in ways that often cannot be made public.

TAYLORISM. Another approach that closes information flow comes from Frederick W. Taylor's *Principles of Scientific Management* (1947). The basis for Taylorism is the attempt to stop the waste of human effort. To quote Taylor, "We can see our forests vanishing, our water-powers going to waste, our soil being carried by floods into the sea; and the end of our coal and our iron is in sight. But our larger wastes of human effort . . . are but vaguely appreciated" (5). Having worked for many years as a laborer and then as a foreman in a steel mill, he knew firsthand how confused and wasteful a shop floor could be. His "scientific management" was largely an effort to bring some organization to the factory floor.

Read more than eighty years after its first publication, there are two aspects of Taylor's work that stand out, one positive, one negative. Taylor's strength is his definition of management's role. He saw the management of his day as having two major weaknesses. First, it didn't really understand much of the work it was supervising. As Taylor put it, "These foremen and superintendents know . . . that their own knowledge and personal skill falls far short of the combined knowledge and dexterity of all the workmen under them. The most experienced managers therefore frankly place before their workmen the problem of doing the work in the best and most economical way" (32).

Since they couldn't really lead, the response of the foremen was to push. Hence, their second weakness, a reliance on incentive programs to get more work out of employees. What's wrong with incentive programs? First, they didn't work. Employees resisted all efforts to be pitted against their peers, as Taylor found out from personal experience (in one of his more unpopular periods a friend took to warning him about which routes to use when he walked home). But even when employees could be induced into increasing their effort, if the efforts were mis-guided (or unguided by an ignorant manager), the only result might be more waste or personal injury.

Taylor's response was to envision a new role for management that at first sight seems obvious: "The managers assume . . . the burden of gathering together all the traditional knowledge which in the past has been possessed by the workmen and then of classifying, tabulating, and reducing this knowledge to rules, laws and formulae which are immensely helpful to workmen in doing their daily work" (36). In short, management had to learn the best way to do a job and then take responsibility for training employees in this method. For the first time, they had to fully understand the nature of the work they were supervising.

Now for the problem of Taylor. While Taylor is not kind to managers, com-plaining about how little they understand the work they supervise and how much they rely on unworkable incentives to control workers, he is downright brutal when describing workers. One laborer is described as "a man of the type of the ox . . . so stupid he was unfitted to do most other kinds of laboring work, even" (62). In describing the needs of managers to train workers, he justifies the need by saying, "The man suited to handling pig iron is too stupid properly to train himself" (63). These are pretty rough descriptions of his fellow citizens. It was such descriptions that made labor extremely anxious about Taylor's methods. It is such descriptions that make it difficult for contemporary readers to embrace Taylorism.

What does the Taylor model do for information flow? To begin with, it assumes two classes of human beings. One class needs lots of information as it makes its decisions. The other class needs to show up at work on time, keep its mouth shut, and wait for orders. One group has all the information; the other group has none.

SILENT CO-WORKERS: PAPER MACHINE NUMBER 16. Lately there has been a great deal of talk about how new information technologies will change the rel-ative role of workers and "empower" all employees. Maybe so, but there is no shortage of examples in which technology is being used to supply even more information to management while sending little information in the direction of workers. Consider the situation of one group of paper-mill employees. The Wisconsin River Valley in central Wisconsin has long been home to paper mills. Of late, computers and robots have moved onto the mill floor and taken their place alongside the union papermakers.

As part of the Just-in-Time manufacturing processes that are being employed by publishers and other manufacturers, paper coming out of the dryers of the paper machine usually already has an owner. There is a printing plant somewhere that wants the paper in a certain width, in a certain size roll, on a loading dock on a particular day. All those orders are in a computer two blocks from the paper machine. A scheduling program determines what orders have to be processed in what sequence. That schedule takes control of the paper as it is pulled onto massive rolls weighing thousands of pounds. The computer-controlled machines trim the roll to the right width and stop the roll when it has gotten to the right size. Next a UPC label is printed by the computer and glued to the roll so it can be distinguished from all the others. The roll has been created to specifications known to the computer.

At this point the roll starts moving. Rollers and elevators take the roll two blocks to the warehouse. Because of the huge weight of these rolls and because of the ease with which paper can be damaged, no humans are involved while the roll moves from paper machine to warehouse. It travels silently down the belt for fifteen minutes before a piston raises one side of the belt and rolls the paper into another series of elevators and rollers until the paper is deposited on floor level in the warehouse.

Now the paper roll has to be routed. The roll is pushed onto a platform that makes up the foot of a Y. A scanner reads the UPC label on the paper and sends the identification to the main computer for interpretation. If a truck is waiting for the roll, the computer has the platform push the roll down one side of the Y, where it rides belts for one hundred yards to the loading dock. While the roll makes the trip, the computer prints out the shipping label at the dockside printer. Finally, the paper arrives and is placed by machine on a wooden pallet. Here is where humans finally come in. The computer has calculated the best routes for the trucks and determined which rolls go on which trucks. People have to drive up in a forklift, put the roll on the right truck, and give the shipping forms to the driver.

If the roll will not be shipped for a few days, it needs to be stored. This is done by robot. Of course, these robots do not even vaguely resemble the robots of television or movies. They much more closely resemble the bumper cars in carnivals, but bumper cars reinforced to carry two tons and fitted out with a flat metal top about three feet wide and four feet long. They sit like a row of taxis waiting for a fare until their radio receivers pick up a signal giving them a location to go to. Then emitting an intermittent "beep" and flashing a yellow light to warn people of their approach (there are rarely people in this part of the warehouse), they follow a set of wires hidden in the concrete floor to where the paper roll waits. In two quick motions the roll is tipped on end and then slid onto the robot's back. Beeping, the robot platform follows the wire "road" up aisles and around corners until it gets to the shelving area of the warehouse.

In systems like these, information flow is from machine to machine. There are people to oversee the computer software and repair the electronics, but they are few in number. Most employees do other tasks while machines around them work in total isolation. Imagine working next to machines that follow orders you never hear, machines reading bar codes you don't understand, machines filling orders you never knew came in. For the workers of Machine Number 16, this is the age of invisible information.

THE COMPUTER AS SPY. For many workers, the computer can be the perfect surveillance device. Shoshana Zuboff's massive investigation of computers in the workplace, *In the Age of the Smart Machine* (1988), refers to this role as the computer equivalent of the eighteenth century's panopticon. Originally invented by Jeremy Bentham, the panopticon was an optical instrument that allowed an observer in the middle of a prison to see into all the cells yet remain unseen. Since prisoners had no way of hiding, and no way of knowing if they were being observed, they would behave. The panopticon was a device for control.

For many workers, the computer serves the same function. It sees every move they make while on the job, yet they cannot see the computer's "eyes" buried deep in the back of their computer, recording every piece of information that floats by, sending it off to a report only the office manager sees. Does this kind of information gathering effect employee behavior? Absolutely. Says one mill employee, "With this information on the computer, there has been a psychological effect. We know there is something that will tell on us exactly. We can't fudge it now, so we hustle more" (ZUBOFF 1988:346).

At the same time the computer is watching employees more, supervisors are talking to their workers less. They are often relying totally on the computer for their information. Says one foreman, "In the old environment, the supervisors would arrive at the same building as the craft and greet you in the morning. He would be able to walk around and talk to you, and he would see how you were doing. You had the camaraderie of communication through the visual. Now you are basically just dealing with computers and checking on people. I can't see my men in the field now, because I look through the computer" (ZUBOFF 1988:332–333).

A great deal more information can be seen through a computer. Semis now arrive from the factory with places for satellite dishes. The Global Positioning System (GPS) lets the home office see exactly where each truck is located. Other satellite systems allow the communication systems to bring back information on engine conditions. Is the engine overheating? Is it being driven too fast? Is it overdue for maintenance? Computer operators sitting in the home office can "watch" semis as they go down the highway and may often know more about the driver's situation than the driver.

Newer systems are adding similar features to excavating equipment but bring in a new twist. Using a series of satellite links plus a local beacon, a system can tell not just a bulldozer's location but also its depth. Now, as a dozer works its way across an open pit mine, both the operator and a manager in the home office can see how well the bulldozer is staying on the desired elevation, whether it is grading too deep, too shallow, off line, or matching the ideal dig.

Such tools do exactly what Taylor would have wanted. They let management understand and control the processes of the company. Without question they produce better, more accurate processes. They also place workers in a fishbowl unlike anything seen in the past. When someone sitting in an office a continent away can see how fast you are driving, how deep you are digging, what speed you were going when you changed gears, you now have a job without any semblance of privacy. This may be an unforeseen effect unanticipated by management drives for improved quality, but it is an effect that is very real to employees. This loss of autonomy is well understood by every truck driver in America.

Organizations that have closed information systems can change, but it will not be easy. African CEOs aren't going to change overnight just because e-mail is suddenly available, nor is there much reason to expect isolates to read e-mail any more than they do company newsletters, nor can we expect workers who have spent their lives being treated like "a man of the type of the ox" to decide today is their day to write a letter to the CEO.

The switch to a more open culture can be made. Levi Strauss may be the best example, because it was able to make changes with a largely blue-collar work force—the kind of people that normally are asked to check their brains at the door. It also had to make some decisions about trust: "We share as much information as we possibly can throughout the company. Business literacy is a big issue in developing leadership. You cannot ask people to exercise broader judgment if their world is bounded by very narrow vision" (HUEY 1994:21). The result has been improved information flow and five straight years of record profits.

But some of the recent failures of reengineering efforts demonstrate just how hard it is to move from one structure to another. Those who wish to move in with digital communication systems and high expectations of instant results would do well to understand the organizational structure they are building upon. Each structure already has ways to promote—and block—information flow.

Information Flow between Organizations

While there has been a great deal written about the quality of workplace communication, much less has been said about the nature and amount of communication *between* workplaces. What do organizations tell each other? Quite a bit. Furthermore, there are now international conventions on how organizations will exchange information electronically. But as always, progress is uneven and barriers exist at every turn. Here is where we stand.

BUSINESS PARTNERS

Business organizations have a long history of working together. While we normally think of Japan's Keiretsu as the primary example of linked businesses, Peter Drucker (1995) traces such linkages to the classically American enterprise General Motors and William Durant's efforts to link GM's assembly plants with parts producers. By being able to manage the total cost of the car, from parts through finished product, Durant was able to give his company an unbeatable advantage. As a practical matter, this meant companies involved in the assembly stream had to share design, engineering, inventory, and cost information.

Business partners don't have to be as tightly linked as the companies within General Motors. Retailing provides us with examples of very different companies that are finding new ways of working together. Wal-Mart is the best example, allowing suppliers to stock products directly on its shelves. Wal-Mart saves inventory costs but has to give over sales information—suppliers know far more now about which stores sell what when. Such information sharing doesn't come easily. To quote Drucker, "Economic-chain costing requires information sharing across companies, and even within the same company, people tend to resist information sharing" (1995:58). The reasons for resistance are obvious—the more a supplier knows about Wal-Mart, the more it is in a position to tell Sears. Nevertheless, the cost advantages of closer working arrangements are so significant, companies are willing to take the chance.

BUSINESS ACQUAINTANCES

Businesses with loose relationships to one another obviously share far less information than businesses that are essentially part of the same enterprise. But they do share information. The syringe supplier needs to know how many syringes are needed, where they should be sent, and what payment terms will be used. The hospital needs to know that syringes are really on the way, when they will arrive, what charges will be, and how the company will acknowledge receipt of payment. Currently this, and billions of transactions like it, are being done by phone, fax, mail, and sales rep. This process is about to change.

Electronic Data Interchange (EDI) is as much concept as reality, but the concept is important. In essence, it is simple. All the information I need for ordering is on my computer, all the information you need for shipping is on yours. Why don't I just have my computer call yours and we can both spend our time more profitably? This is EDI. No phone calls, no faxes, no order forms to be keyed in or invoices to be typed. Get rid of paper, the people used to process the paper, and the time delays and typing errors that paper permits. Hook the computers to each other and keep the data flow entirely electronic.

There are only three problems with turning this concept into reality, and it may yet turn out that all three are insurmountable. The first problem is technical. It is all very good to say that computers should talk to one another, but of course, not only do computers not talk, but if they did, they would each speak a different language. They all have different operating systems and different approaches to telecommunications. So a data stream coming in from the PC at the syringe company might seem pretty odd to the VAX at the hospital. There are standards. In general the United States has settled upon the ANSI X.12 standard for information transmittal. Unfortunately, the rest of the world has a different standard, EDI for Advanced Commerce and Transportation (EDIFACT). There was some talk about having all the United States move to the international standard by 1997. Now the standards committee has backed off the requirement to 1999.

In the meantime, even if we could agree on a telecommunications standard so companies put all their data in the same form and in the same order and sent it at the same speeds with the same error checking, that just gets the data in the door. Now we have to connect that data with the data already in the computer. But the order information you send me may be different from the order information I have been typing into my computer for decades. I enter it in a different order and use different size fields for product names, or different representations for dates. The result according to one study: "Out of the 50,000 companies using EDI today in the broadest definition, probably half get EDI transactions from a handful of customers and treat it like it came in on a fax machine" (FRYE 1994:87). In other words, they rekey all the EDI orders they get so the data fits their usual record-keeping process. The same study estimated that just 10–15 percent of the companies using EDI can process a large portion of their orders without human intervention.

Cost and security are the second barrier. Right now, EDI traffic is carried on Value Added Networks (VAN), proprietary services used to carry traffic between businesses. Such networks provide links between companies and guarantee security—for a price. Companies would like to move to cheaper carriers, such as the Internet, but are concerned about security. For the time being, companies have to bear the higher costs of a VAN.

The last barrier, inertia, may or may not be going down, depending upon who you talk to. In 1993 President Clinton signed a memorandum that all federal procurement for items valued at less than twenty-five thousand dollars must be done via EDI by 1997. Says a manager in the Defense Department, "If you're a vendor doing business you'd have one way of dealing with the government." Given that kind of spur, estimates are that the fifty thousand companies now using EDI in some form will increase five- to tenfold by 1997.

The only problem is that the federal government itself has a poor track record for using EDI. Says one EDI software vendor, "The president's memorandum was issued in 1993. Wouldn't you think the 40 to 50 [federal] sites connected would be ardent users of the system? They're not. The DOD has been unable to make it work" (FRYE 1994:87). Why not? Inertia: "The majority of sites [military bases] are hesitant to change. Many vendors have gotten very discouraged at not finding enough RFQs [requests for quotation] to bid on, so they cancel. For every 500 vendors we sign up, we lose 300. It's frustrating."

Such reluctance to change shouldn't be too surprising. EDI saves paperwork and time only if computer systems and corporate processes can be changed to allow information transfer of a kind we haven't seen before. Inherent in the process is a national and even international standardization of business practices down to the details of one's corporate databases. Information flow at that level won't be easy, quick, or cheap.

Organizational Information and the Public

How much will organizations tell us about themselves? Not much. Some limits are inherent. No one expects Coca-Cola to suddenly publish the formula for Coke, for instance. Other limits seem based more on hostility to the general public. Two examples of information hiding demonstrate this hostility clearly.

TOBACCO COMPANIES TALK TO THE WORLD

Tobacco companies have been under pressure for many years now. For a while it appeared cigarettes would gradually fade out of the American scene and tobacco companies would adjust quietly. A number of factors turned the peaceful fade into open warfare. One, of course, is money. No one walks away from a profitable product without second thoughts. On the other side, legal pressure on tobacco companies has been growing. Florida attempted to charge tobacco companies for all the extra health expenses cigarette consumption added to Florida's health care system. The Justice Department is investigating the industry for fraud and perjury before congressional panels. The Environmental Protection Agency (EPA) is pressing for a law to ban smoking in the workplace.

Faced with both this opportunity and these threats, tobacco companies have fought back. One of their more novel responses came in July 1994. Philip Morris placed three-page ads in forty major newspapers debating the validity of statistics used by the EPA. The cost for the ads? $64,000 a page. (If you haven't got a calculator handy, $64,000 times three pages times forty papers comes out to over $7 million!) Since $7 million would pay the salary of every statistics professor in the United States for quite some time, this sudden interest in statistics is truly a novel event.

These July 1994 ads are titled "Decide for Yourself" and are reprints of an article entitled "Passive Reporting on Passive Smoke" printed in *Forbes Media-critic* magazine. In dense, eight-point type, the reprinted article criticizes the statistical methodology used by the EPA. It claims that some studies showing no effects from secondhand smoke were ignored by the EPA, that the EPA twisted the figures it had to prove a point it was determined to prove, and that epidemiology itself is a weak science ("So it is with epidemiology. It is a blunt tool.") (SULLUM 1994:7).

What can the tobacco companies be thinking? A public debate over "epidemiology"? Do they expect guys on the loading dock to discuss the validity of a 90 percent confidence interval? Smokers tend to be less educated than non-smokers, with high school dropouts far more likely to smoke than college graduates. Are these the people who will spend their free time debating correlation versus causation?

But for R. J. Reynolds, numbers may be the whole point. As long as the debate remains on epidemiology and confidence intervals, no one asks about the 150,000 American children the Food and Drug Administration claims are made sick each year by secondhand smoke. What illnesses do they get? What do they look like? How badly are they hurt? By supplying $7 million worth of numbers, R. J. Reynolds kept people looking at numbers and away from pictures of kids. We will never know what R. J. Reynolds was really trying to accomplish with its ads (that would be proprietary information), but its $7 million is a reminder that organizations can use information to shape a debate. Information is not neutral, and its presence may not be a sign of strength or truth or honor. It can be a weapon to hypnotize or deafen.

AT&T AND EVENTUAL TRUTH

On 17 September 1991 American Telephone and Telegraph had a day it would rather forget. Its New York–area long-distance lines went out, blocking five million calls. Worse yet, the outage blocked necessary air traffic signals, leaving tens of thousands of air travelers grounded. The American air traffic control system is so interconnected that while the blockage occurred in New York, flights were disrupted as far away as Boston and Chicago and flights in the air were endangered. The only good news for AT&T that day is that no flights crashed or collided.

The cause for the problem was quickly identified. AT&T provides its own power for its switching stations. When its power plant malfunctioned, the system automatically went to batteries that were designed to provide six hours of service—plenty of time for an error to be fixed. Unfortunately, when the batteries came on line, the alarms that were to notify workmen of a problem went unnoticed for six hours. The batteries went dead and so did the phone lines.

By 18 September 1991 AT&T had two problems. One was to get long-distance service up and running again. This was done within seven hours. The second problem was to rebuild its reputation and to hold off competitors MCI and Sprint, which were now going after AT&T's customers with charges that AT&T was unreliable as a service provider. William Benoit and Susan Brinson (1994) have spent years investigating AT&T's response to this second problem. What they found is not a pretty picture.

Benoit and Brinson begin with the assumption that companies in AT&T's position have five possible responses: deny responsibility, evade responsibility, reduce the offensiveness of the event, apologize profusely, correct the problem. One would think a major corporation would just get to response four and five—apologize profusely and get about fixing the problem—but that's not the route AT&T took. AT&T's first response was to evade responsibility. Their press releases of 19 September blamed their workers. One group of officials said technicians at the station had failed to notice alarms. A vice president went further, saying workers "violated company procedures by failing to inspect equipment when the company converted to its own power" (ANDREWS 1991).

Blaming its own employees was not only an ugly strategy, but also turned out to be ineffective. The workers were represented by the Communications Workers of America. The union did its own investigation and was able to rebut management the very next day. Among their findings was the fact that audio alarms didn't sound and visual alarms were hidden behind new equipment. Most embarrassing was the revelation that workers were not even present at the time of the alarm because they were at a class to learn about a new alarm system!

AT&T spent the next two days in apparent confusion. They now stated that technicians were not at fault. Now it was management personnel who had not followed procedures. Finally Robert Allen, chairman of AT&T, wrote a letter to AT&T employees trying to clarify what had happened. "We were inconsistent in explaining what had happened," he told his employees, but this "was not because we sought to excuse ourselves but because events were moving so fast," leading to "misinterpretations of exactly what had happened" (RAMIREZ 1991:27).

Finally, on 23 September, six days after the service break, Chairman Allen prepared an ad to be printed in the *New York Times,* the *Wall Street Journal,* and the *Washington Post.* In it he finally took the blame, admitted that the cutoff had been a major problem, explained how it had happened, and described steps the company would take to prevent a similar problem in the future. Allen stated the service disruptions "not only affected our customers but also stranded and inconvenienced thousands of airline passengers." Furthermore, "the recent disruption underscored a fundamental truth: our services have a crucial impact across the economy, across society. They affect people's work and personal lives in the most crucial ways." He ended the first paragraph of the ad thus: "I apologize to all of you who were affected, directly or indirectly." He then went on to describe steps the company will take.

To the cynical, Allen's response could be seen as a strategy of last resort—blaming employees hadn't worked, so he had to admit the company itself was at fault. On the other hand, it is true that in the early days there was confusion and local managers might not have understood the whole reason for the problem. The fact that they immediately blamed their employees is not a good sign, but at least they admitted the truth when pushed by the union. Six days after the disaster the company chairman himself was out in public taking the blame, describing the circumstances of the problem and describing the strategy the company had adopted to solve it. Ultimately the lesson of AT&T's response may be that blame shifting doesn't work but complete honesty does. Organizations can present the truth to the public and benefit from their honesty. Unfortunately, not all organizations accept that premise.

Summary

If we accept the proposition that much of the information in our lives comes from the organizations for which we work and the organizations upon which we depend for goods and services, where do we stand? The answer seems to depend upon who "we" are. For American employees, organizations appear to be more forthcoming. The nature of employment has changed so that at least some employees have more information about their jobs. For some employees, there is already more information floating around the workplace than they want. Over time the number of isolates may decline, but as long as Han Solo is a cultural icon, we can expect some number of our peers to model their behavior on him and keep their distance from the organizations around them.

On the consumer level, political and economic forces seem to support more openness and accountability. But results have been tentative at best. There may be less outright fraud, but there are still consistent efforts to hide and mislead. Private organizations seek to maintain their reputations and their market share. Public organizations seek to maintain their privileges. Caveat emptor still applies. We may have microwave towers, optical fiber, and worldwide satellite links, but that doesn't mean the information coming to us from organizations is more plentiful or more honest.

Chapter 4 Professional Information

Participation in the making and administration of the law
shall be kept accessible to Lincoln's plain people.
— ALFRED REED

ANDREW M. ODLYZKO is a mathematician at Bell Laboratories. He recently made one of his more remarkable calculations. According to his figures, nearly half of the one million papers that have ever been published in the field of mathematics have been published in the last ten years. It is that kind of calculation that has led to much of the excitement over the future. With so much more science being done, surely tremendous benefits for all are just around the corner. And of course many benefits have already been seen.

Yet for all the explosion of information coming from scientific and professional fields, it is worth taking a look at the nature of that information, its quantity and its quality. For quality is an issue. This is not to say that bad science is being practiced and we are all being duped by doctors relying on false data. But it is clear that professional information has it own rules—its own forms. And like anything else, it has its own strengths and weaknesses. The best way to start looking for these characteristics is with a definition of professional information.

The Nature of Professional Information

One of the best descriptions of professional information comes from the science historian Thomas Kuhn. His well-known book, *The Structure of Scientific Revolutions* (1962), is principally an explanation of paradigms—accepted approaches to problems. Kuhn describes the development of scientific disciplines. In each case, he says, some new synthesis of ideas is created, a synthesis sufficiently useful and attractive to gain the support of the majority of the next generation's practitioners.

That synthesis, or paradigm, not only changes the way people look at their field, but the way they write about it as well. Prior to the creation of an accepted synthesis, individual scientists have to build their field anew in each piece of writing, justifying their actions from first principles. The explanation of these first principles can now be left to textbooks in the field; scientists can begin their discussions at a later point. But this shift also changes who can read their work: "No longer will his researches usually be embodied in books addressed, like Franklin's *Experiments on Electricity* or Darwin's *Origin of the Species*, to anyone who might be interested in the subject matter of the field. Instead they will usually appear as brief articles addressed only to professional colleagues, the men whose knowledge of a shared paradigm can be assumed and who prove to be the only ones able to read the papers addressed to them" (KUHN 1962:20).

For professionals in the field, these accepted principles mean they can describe their work more quickly and efficiently. But notice what has happened to their audience. They go from writings which can be understood by anyone with general interest to only those who have shared a specific kind of training. The information of their field is locked up in articles only peers can understand. Of course there are still translators, science writers or legal authors, whose principal business is to present professional information to the laity. But those participating in the profession write for each other—not for outsiders.

This encapsulation of information within a professional context may define professional information, but it also describes the first problem with professional information—little of it is directly accessible to outsiders. Unfortunately, this is not the only limit on professional information flow. There are at least four barriers, each of which severely restricts even what the professional elite can know, and certainly restricts what the average person can learn. We will review each of the four barriers in turn.

CULTURES OF EXCLUSION

Professions are made up of people. Almost from the origination of professional societies, the question has been *which* people. Who will be allowed to participate in the profession, and who will be excluded. American legal education provides a good example here.

In the early 1800s law schools got off to a rocky start. Many universities, led by the University of Maryland, made the decision that lawyers should have a thorough knowledge of history, political science, and philosophy as well as law.

This meant the law course took four years. This was far too long and expensive, so many would-be lawyers simply read the available publications and took an apprenticeship. Finally, in 1829 Harvard dropped the standards of its law school and taught only common law. "Students were permitted to come and go as they pleased (provided they paid their fees), and examinations were abolished" (BLOOMFIELD 1988:38). Law school was now palatable and students began attending. Other colleges followed Harvard's lead and set up law schools divorced from other training. Now just a two- or three-year course (and not particularly rigorous at that), college law began to attract students.

Once law schools were firmly established, they changed the rules. Christopher Columbus Langell became dean of Harvard Law School in 1870. Besides raising Harvard's standards and changing teaching techniques (he introduced the case method), Langell upped the years required to get a degree. Other major law schools followed suit. Studying law became more expensive and more prestigious.

While Harvard was raising its standards, a terrible thing was happening out on the Plains. In 1865 the University of Iowa opened a night law school. It enrolled women, working men, blacks, and ethnic minorities. Worse yet, the idea caught on. By 1916 there were almost as many students in part-time and night law schools as there were in the more expensive day schools.

The old guard was not going to stand by and watch all these new and inferior competitors enter the field, so it struck back. In 1913 the American Bar Association (ABA) asked the Carnegie Foundation to study legal education in the United States. Three years earlier a Carnegie study had reviewed U.S. medical schools and recommended closing many of them. The ABA expected a similar result. They were wrong. Alfred Reed did the review for the Carnegie Foundation and came back supporting the night schools. "The night school authorities," he concluded, "see most clearly that the interests not only of the individual but of the community demand participation in the making and administration of the law shall be kept accessible to Lincoln's plain people" (BLOOMFIELD 1988:44).

This wasn't what the ABA had wanted at all. But it also wasn't enough to stop them. The ABA's next step was to ask its Council on Legal Education to begin accrediting law schools. The accreditation ploy worked much better. The Depression cut down jobs for lawyers, and so local bar associations and state legislatures were more interested in cutting down entrants into the field. They were ready to listen to the ABA, and by the end of the Second World War, it was fairly common for states to admit to the bar only graduates of ABA-accredited law schools, all of which made law a graduate program. If the training period could be pushed to seven years, then poor people trying to get law degrees through night school were put in an intolerable position. Attending school only part time, it would be a decade or two before they finished both a bachelor's degree and a law degree. Few people have that kind of dedication, or the resources for such endless study.

So much for night schools. Now only those who had already received a bachelor's degree could attend law schools. Universities did a nice job of filtering out the competition—women, working men, blacks, ethnic minorities—"Lincoln's plain people."

American lawyers weren't the only profession to fight to keep people out. French engineers very carefully kept their ranks free of the poor and middle classes by using a traditional filter—education. The École Polytechnique was established after the French Revolution as a democratic institution to ensure the technical competence of French bureaucrats. By 1816 the monarchy had been restored, and with it admission requirements were changed to ensure only the elect passed through its doors. Abstract mathematics and literary study were the first filters. By 1860 knowledge of Greek and Latin were also favored. The value of Greek to engineers was never demonstrated, but the real function was clear: "This preference made it still more difficult for students to gain entrance unless their parents could afford an expensive secondary education as well as two or three years of special preparation for the entrance examination" (PORTER 1995:140). These barriers were maintained until the First World War. The elite classes held the profession for a century.

The fight for exclusion continues. In her description of the Computer Society of Tanzania, Suzanne Grant Lewis (1992) describes how this group was shaped by the desire to improve the professional status of members. One method they used was to limit membership to those who had specific educational credentials. It didn't matter what experience people might have had; unless they had the right college degree, they could never be members. They also required that members be trained in large computer systems as well as in microcomputers. Because few universities had the resources to pay for mainframe computers, this further limited the number of people qualified to be members. Their third approach to exclusivity was to eliminate those with hardware or technical training. This was to be a group for software people only.

Having removed as much competition as possible, this group of elites then started seeking perks for themselves. First, they set up a special committee that was to advise the government. As the few "qualified" computer people in the country, their elevation to national advisors seemed natural to them. To further boost their status, they began offering courses to managers. This not only gave them visibility but also confirmed their mastery over technology. They became the fountains of computer knowledge.

In these three examples, and in countless others, it is clear one of the functions of professions is to keep people out. The device may be duration of education, it may be a special kind of education only available to the select few. Whatever the device, the consequence has been too often to filter out people who might not only benefit from their memberships but also bring special abilities to the very professions that don't want them. One wonders what American legal systems might be like if they were, in the words of Alfred Reed, "accessible to Lincoln's plain people." A wealth of personal knowledge is inaccessible to that profession, inaccessible by the choice of that profession.

BOUNDARIES OF INFORMATION

While professions may fight to limit access to the club, they can be exceptionally open among themselves. But even that openness can have limits. First, two quick examples of how intraprofessional communication can work in the ideal. In Canada a group of chartered accountants decided to move into accounting for the information technology field. Deciding that there were new opportunities here for their profession, the Canadian Institute of Chartered Accountants set up a special interest group in information technology, and within a year had 220 members who had joined a special e-mail facility that let them exchange information, files, and news about the field (DAGENAIS 1993:44). They wanted to talk to each other, so the means were found and a system developed practically over night.

In Africa a medical group called SatelLife has put together a medical network called HealthNet. With ground stations in Zambia, Uganda, Tanzania, Kenya, Mozambique, Malawi, and a dozen other countries, the system links medical professionals via satellite with their colleagues in the United States, Canada, England, and Russia. A physician with a question in Kenya can use the system to get information from her peers around the area, or from experts in any of the industrialized nations. The system is also used to "publish" an electronic version of *HealthNet News*, the *African Medical Librarian's Bulletin*, *World Health Organization Digest*, and the *AIDS Bulletin*.

In both examples, professionals needed to speak with each other, found a means, and got systems up and running. The Canadian example is remarkable for its speed; the African example is remarkable for its level of international cooperation.

But for all the examples of professionals reaching out, there seem to be unfortunate examples of boundaries on where professionals will look for information and who they will listen to. Recent research conducted by *Scientific American* illustrates how severe these limits can be. The table below provides the percentage of all published mainstream scientific journal articles that are published by scientists, highlighting the problem immediately (GIBBS 1995:92):

Country	Percentage
United States	30.817
Japan	8.244
United Kingdom	7.924
Germany	7.184
India	1.643
Israel	1.074
South Korea	.546
South Africa	.415
Chile	.176
Zimbabwe	.024
Bolivia	.010
Gambia	.005

Scientific American's analysis covers the year 1994 and includes articles published in journals listed in the *Science Citation Index*. The message is clear—slip below such emerging industrial nations as South Korea and South Africa, and science disappears. This message was articulated directly by Jerome Kassirer, editor of the *New England Journal of Medicine:* "Very poor countries have much more to worry about than doing high-quality research. There is no science there" (GIBBS 1995). With those words, the scientific output of 80 percent of the world is dismissed.

Is there no science there? The scientists working in developing nations think there is. They think they do good science, work that is ignored by the editors of major journals. The story of Dr. Luis Benitez-Bribesca illustrates their case: "When I was a resident in Boston, I was able to publish papers in the *American Journal of Pathology* with a couple of well-known American patholo-gists. They flew through to publication with no problems. After that, I went to the University of Bonn in Germany and published two papers in *Nature*. Then I came back to Mexico with more experience and maturity. But now when I have sent papers to the same journals, they have been rejected immediately" (GIBBS 1995:98).

Ignored by the major journals, where can they publish? In local journals. The problem is that such journals are unknown and unread by scientists in lead-ing countries. Seventy percent of Latin American journals are not included in any index. With no index, there is no way to locate them. Any articles published in them are largely invisible—unknown, unused.

What information is lost? Much that is medically important. Says one researcher, "Take cholera, for example. Right now cases are increasing in Mex-ico. Our researchers have interesting findings about some new strains. . . . Scientists searching the literature will not find the papers published in Mexican journals, because they are not indexed" (GIBBS 1995:94). So information that could save lives is unknown outside the country of origin. In the world of jumbo jets, the impact of that ignorance is just one flight away. Richard Horton, editor of *Lancet*, points out, "One of the reasons why infectious diseases such as the Ebola virus are emerging is that economic changes in developing countries are bringing humans into contact with previously isolated ecosystems." The ecosystems are no longer isolated, but our information systems still are.

Will advances in telecommunications solve this problem? No. First, the problem isn't technical, it is personal—exclusion of information arriving from sources outside the "club." Whether the research results arrive from Mexico via snail mail or e-mail won't matter until research results from Mexico (and the rest of the developing world) are treated with respect. Advanced communication systems may speed the delivery of information from industrial nations to poorer nations (assuming adequate phone systems and local computers), but the reverse flow requires changes in attitude, not in technology. Until those attitudes change, professionals have created blind spots—areas of information they refuse to see because the information exists beyond boundaries established by the professions themselves.

WALLS OF NUMBERS

One of our expectations for professionals is that they will combine expertise with impartiality. One way we expect to observe those traits is in professionals' use of numbers. Their formulae require expertise to create and understand, and produce results that appear far more impartial than any words. And such formulae do exist. One international example is available in the medical field. Physicians working in intensive care units (ICUs) are faced with constant dilemmas. Patients are in critical condition, and the very fact that they need the attention of an ICU implies that a substantial number will not recover. For the hospital it is often difficult to be sure the ICU is staffed and equipped in such a way as to give patients the best possible chance of survival. You know some patients will die. How do you know if too many are dying?

One attempt is the APACHE (Acute Physiology and Chronic Health Evaluation) score, developed by Doctor William Knaus throughout much of the 1980s. Cooperating ICUs from throughout the United States collected thirty-four physiologic measures on hundreds of patients. They collected information on temperature, blood pressure, heart rate, respiration rate, and white blood cell count, among others. Over the years they were able to reduce the measures from thirty-four to twelve, which were most predictive. They were also able to associate a number with each degree a patient's measures varied from normal. For instance, a patient would be given four points if his heart rate was above 180, three points if above 130, two points if above 110. He would also get points if his heart rate were abnormally low (two points if below 70, four points if below 49).

The points in the twelve categories were added up. The higher the score, the sicker the patient. Knaus found that only 1.9 percent of patients with scores under four died, while 3.9 percent with scores between five and nine died. With scores near the top of the range (over thirty-five), 84 percent of patients died.

APACHE scores have been important to Dr. Rodney Glickman, director of the intensive care unit of Windhoek Central Hospital in Windhoek, Namibia. He computes his scores once a year and posts them prominently so new staff can see them. Most years his hospital significantly outperforms the American benchmarks. Glickman also uses the APACHE scores in research. His hospital changed homeodialysis treatment for severe malaria in 1993. After the new treatment 40 percent of patients died; before, 60 percent died. Because he was using two different groups of patients, he needed to calculate APACHE scores to be sure the drop in the mortality rate wasn't due to other circumstances. The APACHE scores confirmed that both groups of patients were equally sick—the new treatment was solely responsible for the improvement in patient survival.

This is the way we expect to see numbers used by professionals—objectively, and in the public interest. At least one historian says this is only part of the story. Theodore Porter has written a two-hundred-year history of numbers in government and has come up with an interesting thesis: professionals use numbers in much of their communication with the public because it gives them power. In truth they have far less faith in numbers than it would appear. Among themselves, they understand the limits of quantification. But if you want to convince a skeptical public, numbers do just fine. For illustration, he cites three groups of professionals who have used, and refused to use, numbers in public decisions. The first two groups didn't need numbers to get their way. The third group, Americans, did.

In the early years of the English life insurance system, English actuaries were asked by the government to produce standard risk tables. They refused. The idea was silly to them. How could there be standard risk? In making decisions over who to insure and how much to charge, they used tables for part of the decision, but much of what they decided was based on learning about individuals— who drank too much, who was sedentary. They made individual decisions and refused to accept the government proposition that there was such a thing as a standard life. They were strong enough professionally to hold to that position —to limit the power of numbers.

So were French engineers. Graduates of elite schools, state engineers controlled the design and placement of bridges, canals, and railroads across France. Well trained in mathematics, they could understand the forces on suspension bridges well before their American counterparts. Yet these elite engineers knew the limits of numbers. In plotting the path of the state railroad system, they calculated carefully the costs of each main line. Yet they also knew no formula could tell them absolutely which town to put on the line and which town to bypass. So they didn't try. They made their decisions behind closed doors and had enough authority to make their decisions stick.

Where did numbers become the key to power? In the United States. In a sea of conflicting regional and class interests, with no identified group of elites with the authority to impose their will, numbers became the weapon with which to rule. In 1936 Congress passed a law that all government projects must have a positive *cost/benefit* analysis (the first use of the term). With every congressman anxious to build dams and roads and airports all over his district, there had to be some way to choose among projects before the country was bankrupted. Now there was a way. Project sponsors had to total up all financial benefits, list all costs, and only projects that showed more benefit than cost could be built.

Sound fair? In many respects it was. Now there was some way to select between projects other than to simply choose those favored by the most powerful political groups. But the fact that numbers were involved doesn't automatically make decisions politically neutral. Porter details one project by the Army Corps of Engineers to illustrate how numbers can look far more neutral than they really are. The Savage River Dam in western Maryland was begun in the late 1930s and stopped when it was clear it was not economically justified. By the corps' own formula, it would return just thirty-seven cents for every dollar of costs. But in 1945 local political pressure to finish the dam was building. Hearings were held, and again it was shown that the project made no sense financially. But the pressure didn't go away. So General Crawford of the Army Corps went back to his formula and came back to the hearing three days later with a surprise. He had "found" benefits of $180,000, enough to make the project financially viable. The fact that the benefits were just guesses largely pulled out of the air didn't matter as much as the fact the numbers now said what the politicians wanted them to say. The corps could now build the dam.

Porter's point is that professionals know the limits of their numbers. Nothing is as precise as it sounds. Most formulas contain educated guesses and professional judgment. No two life insurance policies, train routes, or dams are exactly the same. But faced with a need to appear scientific and objective, especially in this country, the numbers are cited and given far more weight than they warrant. In times of need, professions will use numbers to hold off the public.

At the same time, knowing the power (and arbitrary nature) of numbers, professions will also fight to ensure numbers are not used against them. One way to do this is to eliminate measurability where it might reflect on *them*. Abbott describes the importance of reducing measurability:

> As results become less and less measurable, there is less and less need to prefer one treatment to another, and thus a weaker professional hold on the problem area. Since the results of psychotherapy are famously difficult to measure, psychotherapeutic schools have become interchangeable and the problems they treat have become an inter-professional battleground. On the other hand, results that are too easily measurable lead to easy evaluation from outside the profession and consequent loss of control. They may also make it easier for competitors to demonstrate treatment superiority if they have it.
>
> (1988:46)

The problem measurable results poses for professions is amply demonstrated by the education and legal professions. The perennial drop in the very public Scholastic Aptitude Test scores gives critics annual ammunition to use in calls for changes in the education system. Similarly, annual crime statistics give the general populace materials to use in complaints about the legal system. Both professions may try to deflect criticism by questioning the statistical validity of the measures, but the damage is done. A public yardstick is available, and both professions have been found wanting.

Not every profession is so unlucky. Accountants aren't held to measures like number of tax defaults or misfilings per thousand. Dentists aren't subjected to annual counts of cavities. Chiropractors don't face an annual backache index. It is relatively certain that none of these professions will develop such a measure either. They want autonomy. Measurability reduces that autonomy.

The result is that professions tend to have a curious relationship with numbers. Internally, there are in fact formulas and calculations of value, but not of absolute value. Professionals understand the limits of their numbers. Yet pressed from the outside, professions may present numbers as a ploy to gain authority. At the same time they may reject numbers that reflect on them and make their work more transparent and accountable. Numbers are a two-edged sword, wielded with great care. The consequence for consumers of professional information may be an unnoticed but very real loading of numbers in the public realm. The precision we see may be smoke; the numbers unseen may be mirrors.

BOUNDARY WARS

While professions need to hold their own again a skeptical public, they also need to fight other professions for the right to take on public problems. Abbott cites the rise of psychiatry as an example: "The direct referrals reflected the psychiatrists' rapid, entrepreneurial expansion into areas of social control long dominated by other professions. With the help of a popular front organization, the National Committee on Mental Hygiene, psychiatrists in the twenties tried to seize control over juvenile delinquency, alcoholism, industrial unrest, marital strife, and numerous other areas. This brought them into violent competition with the clergy and the law among older professions, and psychology and social work among the newer ones" (1988:23).

This is probably not the historical view of psychiatry presented in commencement addresses. But to a nurse practitioner who feels in a constant war with physicians, physician assistants, and every other classification of health-care provider, it may present a view of the health-care field truer than the fantasies we see nightly on television. Professionals, no matter what their field, fight for their piece of the pie.

The fact that professions compete with each other is not automatically a bad thing. Competition may drive them to excellence. But it does create two problems for information flow—one for those inside the professions and one for those outside the professions.

For those inside, a lack of respect for competing professions can lead to ignorance about those professions. A common example can be seen in professional conferences. Let's take one of the more entertaining conferences as an illustration. The Modern Language Association (MLA) is a group for literature and foreign language professors. Each December thousands of their members descend on a major city for seminars and presentations. And each December the local paper does an article laughing at some of the titles of the presentations.

On 27 December 1993, the MLA arrived in Toronto. I don't know what the local media thought of this group, but if they wanted to follow the tradition of poking fun at all these quaint professors, they might have looked through the conference program and gotten a chuckle from titles such as "Queer Theory Inside and Outside the Academy" or "The Poverty of Theatricality: The Problems with Histrionic History." How about "The Cultural Politics of Modern American Poetry in Ephemeral Media?"

Lost in the chuckles is another interpretation of the MLA program. Of the more than six hundred talks available to members during that chilly week one might ask if there were any that looked beyond the profession to the larger world. Could members hear ideas about developments in other professions? Could they hear about developments that might shape their own profession? Was there any presentation that might have helped these literature professors break their isolation? Actually there were six out of six hundred. Listed under the heading of "Science, Technology, and Humanities," conference attendees could have heard these presentations: "Culture in Science," "Reconfiguring the Discipline in an Electronic Age," "Literature and Human Nature," "Teaching in the Electronic Age," "Textual Research in the Electronic Age," and "Scientific Metaphor and Epistemology."

These six talks might be referred to as the 1 percent reality check. For 1 percent of its allotted time, the profession tried to see what was over the next hill. The program tells us nothing about the quality of these talks, or about how well they were attended, but at least a small attempt was made. For professional groups, 1 percent is not an altogether bad ratio. But it is an awfully small window on the world. These professors will return to their campuses having learned nothing about the issues that dominate the discussion in the next building over from theirs. Parochialism and professional competition leave them ignorant of the most intellectually stimulating and socially demanding issues of their time. Meanwhile, off they go for yet another seminar on histrionic history.

The fact that professions can become so totally entrenched in their cubicles of insight may be damaging to them, but it is also problematic for the rest of us. Long before chaos theory and complexity theory, there was Bertalanffy's general system theory (1968). At its base is a very simple concept—forces interact, creating results far more complicated than any single effort can account for. So isolating any one force tells us little about larger systems. We need "a general science of wholeness." With luck, there might even be common elements of systems, letting us apply knowledge learned about one system to other systems. But in any case, there would be a "tendency toward integration in the various sciences, natural and social" (BERTALANFFY 1968:38).

Ideally there would be integration of the sciences and professions because there is a need to match the integration that occurs in the great real world. Take a current social problem. Is the current struggle with gangs in America a consequence of education? parenting? poverty? television? racism? drugs? religion? Pick one and you have people who need to respond: teachers, parents, businessmen and -women, television producers, politicians, cops, clergy. Periodically each profession or group is singled out in public discourse, each is blamed and shamed. But what if the causative agent isn't one group but several or all? Now what? Do the principal actors have a common ground? Do teachers talk to cops? Does anyone talk to television producers? When do parents and business owners sit together? Systems theory is very clear on the impact of multiple sources of conflict. It is less clear on how to create a solution from discrete groups, especially when groups may be competing with each other for social prestige and employment security.

From the public's perspective, the ideal solution would be the equivalent of a 911 number for each problem. One of your children has been injured?

Dial 911 and let them decide if the proper response is an EMT from the fire department or an ambulance from the hospital or a poison control expert or a combination of all three. Which office covers which problem is of no interest to you. Turf battles can be sorted out after your child is safe.

But who do you call if the kid down the street starts wearing gang clothing? Is there a number that sorts out which provider handles which problem? Would the professional bodies allow such a clearinghouse? Would they even know about the other professionals? Is there any avenue by which they could work together? Do they understand each other? Why should you have to care? If there is a single fallacy built into the current competitive system of professional information, it is the belief by professionals that knowledge comes in nicely packaged bundles called professional degrees and that there is a direct map between certain degrees and certain problems. We are surrounded by tragedies that illustrate the error of that logic.

Summary

The discussion above is not meant to demean the efforts of professions. In the many thousands of articles they generate each year are research results that are literally lifesavers. We seem to be at a particularly productive time in the history of science, and all of us benefit from the results they achieve. But professions respond to institutional forces too, and those forces shape where professionals look for information, where they don't look, who they have helping them in their search, and who they exclude. Those forces practically guarantee that even if the information produced by professions continues to expand, some areas will continue to remain in the shadows.

Chapter 5 — Commercial Information

If you can't come to us, we'll come to you.
—*Advertising brochure for the American Management Association's courses*

E<small>LZEBE</small> E<small>RASMUS</small> is one of the most powerful women in Africa, yet it is unlikely even one hundred people know who she is or what she does for a living. Her surroundings hardly speak of power. Her company occupies under a thousand square feet on the ground floor of Kenya House—a very ordinary office building on a side street in Windhoek, Namibia. The company offices are clean, but hardly lush. Temporary partition walls separate a dozen or so desks, each supporting a computer. Young women sit at each computer, sometimes making small talk as they respond to their computer screens or answer phones. The atmosphere is so relaxed you would never know that each computer query or phone call means a business transaction that will or will not occur, a home that will or will not be built, a fugitive that may or may not be apprehended.

Erasmus runs the ITC Credit Bureau. In her computer files are records of all eighty thousand Namibians who have a credit account anywhere in the country. But just as people and merchandise move across borders, so does credit information. The microwave relay towers that connect Namibia to South Africa connect ITC to Johannesburg, and satellites connect Johannesburg to the main office in Chicago. So with the click of a mouse and a selection from a menu, she can check on any of South Africa's two million creditors as well.

What can she know about creditors? Their names, their spouses' names, their previous names, current and previous addresses, current and previous employers, current banks, current loans, current payment activities, current purchases, current and past legal actions. As creditors stop at a store and try to make credit purchases, stores make inquiries about their credit worthiness. As a result, she can tell where they are shopping, what they are buying, and how much they are spending. Some days she can sit in her Windhoek office and practically "watch" a creditor walk from store to store in a Capetown mall a thousand miles away.

Her information has value—great value. Retailers want to know if they should give merchandise out on credit. They not only pay for a credit evaluation on a potential customer but also help build the information base by supplying details on what is being purchased. Banks need the same information and supply the same updates. Police also want the information, but they pay in kind—not in cash: "Tell me where Mr. X is currently shopping, and I will tell you when Mr. Y will be released from jail so you can have a bill collector waiting for him at the gate." It's a handy relationship.

Namibia is a new country and so has almost no laws on privacy or on commercial information. So Elzebe Erasmus makes her own laws. She has a sense of fair play, so she allows any creditor to see his or her own credit report (at least those who know that such a report exists and where it is housed). But she doesn't like trouble. So spouses can't see each other's report. After all, a wife might want to know what happened to the jewelry purchased on credit two years ago, or a husband might want to know why his wife opened a separate bank account last month. Questions like those could get ITC brought into divorce court and who needs that kind of unpleasantness? So the "law" of Namibia consists of the personal preferences of Erasmus. And she says hands off spousal records.

Laws on privacy may vary from country to country, but the laws of economics do not. The laws of economics in the information age say that information has value—it is a product that can be sold, just like socks, cars, and toothpaste. Who's doing the selling? A recent Information Industry Directory lists forty-seven hundred organizations worldwide in the information business. They range from the International Potato Center in Lima, Peru ("a computer-readable database covering literature on potato and sweet potato research") (MORGAN 1992:725) to the Metals Economics Group, Ltd., of Halifax, Nova Scotia ("online access to the MineSearch database, which contains project profiles and detailed economic and geologic data"). The directory provides staffing information about each organization ("4 information professionals, 4 management professionals, 2 technicians, 2 sales and marketing, 1 clerical, 2 other"), address, phone, and year founded. In two thick volumes the directory details the industry.

But even two volumes don't really cover the industry, because the information industry goes beyond database companies. It comes in many forms, including continuing education, proprietary training, consulting, research services, and "cybrarian" services. We will review all these fields.

Commercial Databases

We've had a hundred years of databases. They started right here in the United States. Our Constitution, which requires that a census be conducted every ten years, created the first one. Among other things, the census is needed to determine how many congressional seats will be awarded to each state. But, of course, once people start collecting information, it is hard to stop. Even in 1880 the U.S. Census Bureau was collecting masses of data. In that year it had two hundred different census forms that contained a total of over thirteen thousand questions (U.S. CENSUS 1990). Included in this mass of data were questions on agriculture, manufacturing, mining, electricity, and, yes, some questions on the original subject—the population of the United States. No wonder it took seven years for the results of the 1880 census to be published.

With the 1880 census data released in 1887, it was not until 1887 that states could begin the redistricting process. It was 1887 when the Commerce Department began analyzing the status of the nation's agriculture and manufacturing (or at least analyzing the status of the agriculture and manufacturing that existed in 1880). Worse yet, the country kept growing. If it took seven years to do the 1880 census, how many would it take to do the 1890 or 1900 census? Would it be 1905 before anyone knew how many people were living in the United States in 1890?

One solution might have been to ask somewhat fewer than thirteen thousand questions (a solution that is being debated again a century later), but there was another way of solving the problem. In 1879, nineteen-year-old Herman Hollerith, recent graduate of Columbia University's School of Mines, got a job at the Census Bureau with the help of a former professor. Able to witness the census procedures and problems firsthand, he worked for the government until 1884 and then got out. He took what he knew of the problem, took his engineering training, and began making machines that could count.

Hollerith's solution was to take information from handwritten ledger books and put it on small cards. Information was represented as holes at various positions on the cards. For instance, if the person represented on the card could read, there was a hole in column seven, row nine. Then he built a machine that would "read" the cards. This first card reader was not a thing of beauty. Cards had to be inserted one at a time. A top plate was lowered onto the card. Where there were holes in the card, pins were able to pass through the card and into a series of small cups, each containing mercury. The pin-mercury connection completed an electrical circuit that advanced a counter for each hole in the card. Every hole in the card was a piece of information that could be counted, and added, as fast as a person could take out one card and insert another. It may not have been pretty, but it worked. Hollerith's machines won a competition held by the Census Bureau and were chosen for use in the 1890 census.

In one sense, the rest is history. Flushed with his success with the 1890 census, Hollerith formed the Tabulating Machine Company in 1896, merged the company in 1911 with several others that made time clocks, scales, and coffee grinders, and was enjoying a very happy retirement when his company was renamed International Business Machines (IBM). Other companies got the idea for machine tabulation, entered the business, and an industry was born.

It may not be directly relevant to our discussions, but a couple of historical details should be mentioned. The year 1890 was a turning point for Hollerith and the industry he founded, but it didn't make him instantly rich. His first sale, by the way, was not to the census, but to the army surgeon general, who wanted to add up days lost to illness. After selling that one machine in 1889, the Census Bureau ordered just six in 1890, and Hollerith had to promise to provide electrical power to the machines, maintain them, and resolder panels on the machines when a type of calculation was changed. He was held responsible for all down time (ten dollars per day) and had to do all the work personally, since he was still six years away from forming his company. In 1890 the company was him.

His machines worked well. The 1890 census was completed in under three years (versus seven for the 1880 census), and at a savings of $5 million in processing costs (despite the fact that there were thirteen million more people in the country now and the Census Bureau asked twice as many population questions). Hollerith's reward for this feat? In 1894 the Census Bureau sent all the machines back to him. After all, the census was over. They left it up to him to warehouse the machines. They also left him wondering how to feed his family until the next census. He sold his horse, canceled his family's vacation, closed his shop, moved his family in with his mother-in-law, and wandered Europe in search of orders for his machines. By 1895 he had contracts with the French and Russian governments, and with the New York Central Railroad. These kept him going until the 1900 census, by which time there was a new census director who was less enamored with his machines. The Census Bureau waited until Hollerith's patents expired and began building its own tabulators. It wasn't until 1911, when Hollerith refocused his machines on commercial applications, that his new company was able to have good growth and stable income. So for Hollerith, the real reward for his efforts came not in 1890, but twenty years later, when he was in his fifties.

So perseverance and sacrifice are also part of the story. But let's get back to the issue at hand—information storage. So far we have moved from ledger books to punched cards. The common punched card is still around in a few billing systems, but generally we have moved on to magnetic tape and disks. The storage device of the moment is the CD-ROM, with storage space for 640 million bytes. That's the equivalent to 640 million characters. Considering the punched card held just 80 characters, the jump in capacity is substantial (it would require eight million punched cards, a pile five thousand feet high weighing twenty-three tons, to match the storage capacity of one CD).

With storage devices so cheap and easy to use, it becomes increasingly possible to store more and more information. We could add new fields to a credit record, for instance, keeping track of more payment information or adding more personal information—there's plenty of room. Or we could start including pictures. In fact some places have. State Farm Insurance has begun storing pictures of cars they insure, and pictures of damage done to cars in accidents. Both help in cases of theft or fraud. How much storage room does a picture require? Inexpensive scanning equipment will produce an electronic image that only requires 80,000 bytes of storage, far more than the 200–300 bytes we might need for a credit record, but still a reasonable number. These days a gigabyte (1 billion bytes) disk drive costs under five hundred dollars. For less than five hundred dollars State Farm can store and retrieve the pictures of twelve thousand cars—four cents per car. That seems pretty cheap insurance against theft or fraud.

For the moment it is enough to consider what a century has produced. We began with one man who believed that a machine could be used to store information. This is a conceptual breakthrough far exceeding any of the technological miracles that followed. By putting information in a machine rather than in a book or on a sheet of paper, he did something every bit as revolutionary as the soul who first pressed characters in clay tablets. We can enhance or change the concept, but the concept is central to our age—a machine can hold information.

The next step is elementary to any business. We now have a product—information. Now what we have to do is sell that product. Whether it is Elzebe Erasmus with her credit records, or the potato board with its research database, or the metals group selling geologic data, there are large numbers of people whose business consists of selling peeks into their database. That may not seem like much of a business, but it is enough. In her history of the commercial database industry, Martha Williams of the University of Illinois provides a clear sense of just how fast this industry is growing: "Over the 16-year time period from 1975 through 1991, database records have grown by a factor of 77—the number of records increased from 52 million to 4,060 billion, while the number of databases has grown from 301 to 7,637—a factor of 24" (1992). This kind of growth in databases has led to a similar growth in database companies—from 105 in 1975 to 933 in 1991.

What's in these databases? Records can be citations, abstracts, news stories, biographical records, chemical data, recipes, software, descriptions, or virtually anything else. And the records aren't just text anymore. Within the last few years both sound and image databases have been started. By 1991 there were 145 image databases and 27 audio databases commercially available. The other big area of growth has been in full-text article databases. As recently as 1985 it was normal to put bibliographic information in a database but to make readers go to the original magazines to read the articles they wanted. With the huge drop in the cost of storage, it is now possible to put the entire article in the database, and that is exactly what database companies are doing. The table below shows exactly how fast this change has occurred (WILLIAMS 1992:xvi):

Database Type	1985	1991
Bibliographic	1,094	1,425
Full-text	535	2,040

In just a six-year time span, the number of databases featuring the entire text of an article increased fourfold.

The other aspect of data collections that has changed over the years is U.S. dominance. In 1975 the United States had more databases than the rest of the world combined, but not much more (177 to 124). Sixteen years later the rest of the world has vastly increased its collection of databases (to 1,893) but still hasn't been able to keep up with the explosion of growth in the United States (to 4,368). Here is the breakdown by region (WILLIAMS 1992:vxiii):

Region	Number of Databases
Africa	8
Asia	34
Australia	146
Far East	189
East Europe	13
West Europe	1,797
North America	5,396
South America	54

By any measure, databases are an American phenomenon. Africa, Asia, Eastern Europe, South America—each have less than 1 percent of the world's databases. North America (mainly the United States) has 71 percent.

What kind of money can such databases generate? The large number of companies getting into the business gives some indication of the health of the industry. But there are specific indicators as well. Database companies can charge for information in two ways: they can charge for online time or they can put the data on a disk and sell the disk. Each can pay quite well. Here are a few examples:

CIRCUITWRITER NETWORK

This is an online service that "provides access to news and information of interest to the ministry and members of the United Methodist Church." The database includes such things as "Methodists Make News," "Catch the Spirit Monthly Program Guide," and "Bottom Drawer—short stories, anecdotes, poems, quotes, and comments that may be used to illustrate the theme of a sermon." All this and more available for eighteen dollars per hour prime time, nine dollars per hour during off hours (MARCACCIO 1992:242).

CLAIMS/U.S. PATENT ABSTRACTS

This online service covers U.S. patents in chemistry, aerospace, engineering, electronics, nuclear science, and technology. Fees are $140 per connect hour, plus 75 cents for each record printed. Want the whole database on a CD-ROM at your site? You can have that too, for just $1,895 per year (MARCACCIO 1992:247).

POLITICAL RISK COUNTRY REPORT

This database "contains the complete text of 85 country reports assessing the political and economic conditions in the 85 countries most important to international business, forecasting the 18-month and 5-year outlooks for finance, investment, operations, and trade." Charges are $107.00 for each connect hour and $5.13 per paragraph printed (MARCACCIO 1992:959).

BUSINESS PERIODICALS ONDISC

This is a full text database with all the articles from three hundred journals and comes with a proprietary ProQuest computer to run the fifty to sixty disks that arrive yearly. Subject coverage includes accounting, data processing, and a dozen other business subjects. The price is $19,900 per year (NICHOLLS 1991:227).

WITH MANY THOUSANDS of databases to choose from, obviously both the subjects and the charges vary widely. But the four examples above at least give some flavor of the opportunities available. From fillers for Methodist sermons, to personal credit histories, to analyses of national stability, there is plenty of information for sale, and plenty of money to be made in the process.

What information is *not* available through such databases? In our discussions of organizations, we already reflected upon the information organizations (and governments) feel uncomfortable sharing. But the subject of commercial information sources raises another issue—the need for information to have a market for it to be collected and stored.

For instance, in the thousands of commercial databases, there is no database on government services for the poor. Nor is there a database on recipes for people on food stamps. Nor is there a database on strategies for helping the illiterate. Where there is money, there are databases. Where there is no money, there is no information. The many thousands of databases available all have one quality in common—they meet the needs of customers—people who have money to pay for information.

Continuing Education

Linda Kuhl is a CPA. Much of her year is as the public expects—nearly endless hours from 1 January to 15 April, with a more reasonable workload the rest of the year. What the public doesn't think much about is the sixty-plus hours she spends every year as a student. The first forty hours are required. Her professional society, the American Institute of Certified Public Accountants, requires that she take the courses to maintain her membership. Last year she sat through four workshops on taxes and one on estate planning, all taught by or approved by her profession.

Her cost for all these courses was substantial, usually $225–$350 per day in tuition, plus transportation, meals, and a hotel room. This is all in addition to her association membership and publications. The cost to her partnership was also substantial, since her studies required her to be out of the office and miss all those billable hours. Yet she had no real choice. Her professional association demands members attend courses no matter how many years they have been licensed or practicing. The association sets the standards, they teach or approve the courses, they test and certify members.

Such courses can be big business. The American Management Association aggressively pushes its courses, and people must be enrolling one way or the other since the AMA offers over twenty-five hundred courses each year (MARCHAND 1986:261). They aren't the only ones. In America alone, one estimate says that $60 billion dollars is being spent on corporate-sponsored continuing education.

Besides professional bodies, other sources for continuing education may be larger companies that manage their own training. Extreme examples would be the Rand Corporation, Wang Laboratories, and Northrop Corporation, which offer their own graduate degrees. Many other corporations have training sites that would be the envy of most junior colleges.

Then there are the professional trainers. The American Society for Training and Development (ASTD) is their home organization, listing a membership of twenty-three thousand. These may be everything from public school teachers who do a little moonlighting evenings and weekends to full-time professional trainers who travel the circuit doing workshops on everything from word processing to public speaking to business writing.

And don't forget universities. Most have an office assigned to continuing education, some an entire education center dedicated to the continuing education and training of business people. Part of their interest goes back to initial mission statements that recognized a public service and community outreach responsibility. Part of their interest is cash. Tuition and fees from evening courses can be hefty and can not only supplement the income of professors but also let the institution test the waters for new programs. Furthermore, such outreach efforts let them build bridges to important business leaders.

Not that the United States is alone in its continuing education efforts. Part of the huge rush to modernization in China has been a major effort to upgrade the technical skills of its workers. Of course with a different culture the effort has taken a slightly different direction. One method that has proven especially effective is television teaching. In China 1 million people per year participate in broadcast and TV universities; 610,000 have already been awarded university diplomas through television study. This isn't too bad, considering that continuing education was brought to a complete halt during the cultural revolution and only allowed to begin small-scale operations again in 1979 (KEMING 1988).

In areas such as Shanghai, television has been an especially important source of training for managers, with Shanghai Television University producing six times as many graduates in the areas of finance and economics as all other higher education institutions combined. Nevertheless, not just anybody can get a diploma via television: "[Students must] Uphold the Chinese Communist Party; love the motherland, people, and socialism; observe discipline and law; study hard; have high school graduation level or equivalent schooling; have good health enabling one to both work and study; be below the age of forty. People with infectious diseases, pregnant women, and disabled persons who are not able to take care of their own daily life are not qualified to apply" (KEMING 1988:95).

Affirmative action policies don't appear to have gained much ground in

China, but that isn't the only problem the Chinese television universities face. Because of significant problems with the technical quality of both television and radio signals, much of the information broadcast has to be repeated in face-to-face tutoring sessions. The resulting run-up in costs is large, with the program needing three hundred full-time faculty and staff members at the broadcast station and over one thousand full-time faculty at the various tutoring stations, all to serve sixteen thousand students. Nevertheless, the program works. A study of Shanghai Television University graduates found a very high percentage performed well in tests of management ability, verbal skills, and scientific research.

So it goes around the world. Universities, professional organizations, and companies themselves have recognized that training needs continue for a lifetime. Such needs provide a steady market for education services. Such needs also create a new problem for the unemployed. Returning to Linda Kuhl, what if she were laid off by her accounting firm and could no longer afford to pick up fifteen hundred to two thousand dollars a year in continuing education costs? Not only would she lose her membership, but she would be publicly reprimanded in the association newsletter. The professional group that builds her skills, also holds an iron fist over her head—hers and every other professional's. In some real senses, this is a captive market.

Proprietary Training

Continuing education is normally the purview of universities, professional bodies, and major corporations. Proprietary training, on the other hand, can be done by anyone from local piano teachers to international tutoring services. And while conservative forces in the United States call for increased privatization of education, it is clear that training is already a huge private business both in the United States and worldwide. By one estimate there were over 1.4 million students enrolled in resident proprietary school programs in the United States in 1987, with another 1.5 million taking home-study courses. Those numbers equal a full quarter of all American students taking postsecondary education (LEE 1990).

Nor is this interest in trade schools anything new. Historians can point to a want ad printed on 20 March 1728 in the *Boston Gazette* in which Caleb Phillips offers a home-study course in shorthand (LEE 4). In the Civil War era H. B. Bryant and H. D. Stratton formed a chain of fifty trade schools in fifty cities. By 1890 businesses were beginning to hire women. In response, proprietary schools began enrolling, for the first time, more women than men, a trend that has continued for the last century. After the Second World War the GI

Bill offered support for veterans who wished to attend approved institutions, and "nearly twice as many veterans chose enrollment in a vocational school than in a college or university" (LEE 1990:10). By the mid-1960s over a million and a half students were attending proprietary school to study trades, business, cosmetology, and barbering. When the 1972 Higher Education Act put financial aids for proprietary schools on an even footing with colleges and universities, enrollments again surged.

Despite the success of proprietary schools, there has long been concern about the industry. During a series of investigations conducted during the early 1950s by the Veterans Administration, the General Accounting Office, and others, it was found that some private career schools had billed the government for students who had never enrolled, falsified cost and attendance data, and trained students for careers with few available jobs.

These complaints were revisited in the early 1970s during debates over the Higher Education Act. As one critic has put it, "Students attracted by sophisticated advertising and unfillable promises may enroll in schools [that] do not offer the quality of education . . . the schools claim is available. This is the case particularly in regard to certain technical occupations, where . . . the students are offered courses of study for which jobs are unavailable" (LEE 1990:14).

Although this complaint was made in 1972, it can be heard today. The industry is largely unregulated, and studies of graduates show the quality of programs to be uneven at best. Two studies done in the 1970s asked for graduates' opinions and found them fairly unhappy with their educational choice. Only 65 percent of proprietary school graduates said they would repeat their choice of school, versus 90 percent of public school graduates (LEE 1990). A second study conducted in the 1970s found only 33 percent satisfaction from proprietary graduates versus 60 percent satisfaction from public school graduates.

Unemployment numbers also look unimpressive. One New York study conducted in the mid-1980s found that only 35 percent of proprietary students actually completed their studies, and only 64 percent of them found jobs in a field relating to their training. Another study during this time found that while 12.7 percent of public technical school graduates were unemployed, 26.3 percent of proprietary school graduates had no jobs. A third study found little difference in employment rates.

Despite these problems, this industry enrolls nearly three million students and takes in billions of dollars in revenue. One reason may be the students they serve. Studies consistently show proprietary schools enroll students who are more likely to be older, poorer, female, and black. This is to say, proprietary schools seem to reach a group of students who are underserved by other avenues of education.

Consulting

There's an old joke that says a consultant is someone who borrows your watch to tell you the time. Apparently a lot of companies are happy to loan their watches to consultants because in 1993 alone the top ten consulting firms brought in revenues of over $8 billion and employed over forty-five thousand consultants (BYRNE 1994). The table below shows just the top five consulting firms, their three-year growth rates (1991–1993), and the number of consultants they employ (BYRNE 1994:65):

Firm	1993 Revenue (in millions of dollars)	Three-Year Growth (%)	Number of Consultants
Anderson Consulting	2,876	53	22,500
Coopers and Lybrand	1,351	50	7,650
McKinsey	1,300	31	3,100
Booz, Allen & Hamilton	800	54	4,600
Gemini	516	125	1,700

Beyond these large firms are thousands of one- and two-person operations selling advice. All together 1993 saw eighty thousand individuals calling themselves consultants collecting $17 billion for advice. What kind of advice do consultants sell? Much of the work involves change. In a business environment in which companies look to new markets around the world, in which customers demand new and better products at lower costs, in which organizations seek to streamline both to cut costs and speed product development, change is the order of the day. Outside experts can help direct that change—for a price. During 1993 AT&T paid out $347 million for consulting services alone.

Beside change, the other big motivation to hire consultants is globalization. Determining which markets to enter, locating plants overseas, finding and training local executives, all require information companies may not have. Increasingly consulting firms are positioning themselves to supply just that kind of international help. Consider the international aspects of these major consulting firms (BYRNE 1994:94):

Anderson Consulting	150 offices in 46 countries
Arthur D. Little	36 offices in 23 countries
Booz, Allen & Hamilton	Staff from 73 countries working in 75 countries
Boston Consulting Group	Half the staff is based in Europe
Ernst & Young	Head of consulting services directed projects in 20 countries
McKinsey	63 offices in 32 countries
Price Waterhouse	400 offices in 118 countries

With this kind of international expertise, much of what these consulting firms sell is access to foreign markets. For instance, Coopers and Lybrand helped Burger King identify business partners, suppliers, and site locations in China. Arthur D. Little revamped the information systems of a Dutch telecommunications company and then used the knowledge they gained to do a similar revamping for companies in Switzerland and Portugal. Price Waterhouse helped merge two snack food companies that extended across six countries in Europe.

Gaining this kind of international expertise is not easy or cheap. Anderson Consulting spends $40 million annually just on international travel costs. All the consulting firms heavily recruit international students graduating from U.S. MBA programs. With international graduates on their staffs, the firms have an instant insight into local customs, a grasp of the language, and often contacts with local leadership. The high-priced salaries of these MBAs can be recouped by selling their services to companies looking for just this kind of knowledge.

What's the future of the consulting industry? No firm can maintain growth rates of 50, 80, or 100 percent. Besides, in a world with more and more information available online, and international networks linking individuals around the planet, it would appear that so much information is available from other sources that consultants would eventually become redundant. But there are two problems with predicting the demise of the industry. First, much of the information consultants sell is not publicly available. Companies that know who to contact in Hong Kong for quick service on a building permit (and how much to pay) are unlikely to give that information away free. Second, packaging counts. The number of books available on reengineering may be approaching infinity, but no book has the same impact as a team of bright-eyed young people in five-hundred-dollar suits who can talk about the job they just did for leading company X in exciting locale Y, saving millions for all involved at absolutely no effort. Information in ten-point type just can't compete. If it could, companies would spend twenty dollars for a copy of Tom Peters's latest book instead of paying him tens of thousands for personal appearances. Sizzle still sells.

Selling Research

Two billion dollars is pretty good revenue. It's not up there with IBM or AT&T, but it is still enough to get you into the Fortune 500. Except in this case, the recipient of these billions isn't a company at all, but ten research universities in the United States. They brought in $2.79 billion in 1988. The top one hundred research universities in the United States collected over $11 billion that year (MATKIN 1990).

That major American universities engage in significant research efforts is probably not news to people (people might be more surprised by how frequently American universities were criticized in the last century for their lack of science teaching). With the Morrill Act of 1862 giving land to public universities (land-grant colleges) on the condition they teach agriculture and mechanical engineering, the move to science at this country's universities was underway. We now expect it to be a major feature of any college. Still, some colleges or universities do more research than others. By one estimate, while there are over three thousand colleges in the United States, only two hundred can be called research universities, and this number quickly falls to two dozen when we look for the most active research centers.

It is those two dozen leading research universities that have collected the lion's share of research revenues. And it is at those two dozen research universities that the 1980s saw a significant shift in focus. Gary Matkin's study of four major research universities, *Technology Transfer and the University*, follows the Massachusetts Institute of Technology, Harvard University, Pennsylvania State University, and Stanford University through those years. His descriptions do an excellent job of explaining how universities become billion-dollar players in commercial research.

To begin with, American universities were originally assigned the job of performing basic research. It didn't have to be that way. The government could have set up special research centers. But it didn't. With few exceptions, basic research in this country was done at universities. Applied research was to be left to companies to do on their own. But through the 1970s and 1980s universities moved into commercial research. Matkin enumerates several forces that encouraged the move.

First, the basic research of universities began to pay off commercially. In both electronics and biotechnology, university research seemed to have an almost immediate payoff. This is probably most evident in the case of MIT. One recent study there showed that 404 companies in Massachusetts had been founded by MIT graduates, and that these companies employed 160,000 people and had gross revenues of $27 billion. MIT's influence was even more pronounced in the area of high technology, where 156 of the 216 high-tech companies in the Boston area were founded at MIT facilities. Clearly, basic research was already paying off in a big way.

At the same time, concerns over international competitiveness made leaders wonder if more research could be turned to commercial advantage. And then there was the federal government, which changed the patent law in 1980 so that universities could now take patents on discoveries made under federal contracts. The feds also pushed universities toward commercial ventures by both cutting support for basic research, leaving it up to the universities to determine how to fund their research efforts, and encouraging "leverage" of federal grants, in which commercial ventures would supply part of research funding and the government the rest.

With universities now looking for ways to commercialize their research, they quickly came up with two approaches: selling general information, and licensing research results.

SELLING INFORMATION

For twenty-five thousand dollars, you can join thirty other members of the Diamond Consortium at Penn State. Formed by Rustum Roy in the university's Materials Research Center, the consortium performs research on industrial applications of diamonds and shares the results with corporate sponsors. Corporate members of the consortium attend two research workshops per year, receive a quarterly newsletter, and have informal information transfer sessions with any of the seventeen faculty members in the department.

MIT has a number of similar programs, plus a broader Industrial Liaison Program (ILP), which has 325 members contributing over $8 million per year to the campus. The money funds research in a number of fields. In return, the professors at MIT give research briefings, prepare special seminars, conduct visits through their facilities, travel to corporate offices, prepare reports for a special ILP newsletter, and field phone calls from ILP members. Faculty are supported by a special ILP staff of administrators and clerks, including a group of four administrators in Japan.

Part of the attractiveness of such programs is the access to the best research labs in the world. Part is the chance to join other corporations in sponsored research. With each company paying part of the cost, a company can get far more research done than it could normally afford. The phrase "$25,000 will buy you $250,000 worth of research" is used frequently. In some fields the benefits may be far greater.

LICENSING RESULTS

While research labs are producing general research, they also can produce specific products, such as gene splicing techniques or new technology patents. Because federal law now allows universities to patent discoveries even if the research was done with federal money, universities now have patents to sell. Here universities have choices. They can sell the license outright or they can take an equity stake in the company licensing their discovery.

Licensing can be very lucrative. When a Harvard researcher, Mark Ptashne, discovered a lambda repressor important in bioengineering, General Electric offered the university half a million dollars for the patent rights. Start-up companies, who might be the first to use such patents, seldom have huge sums to buy the rights. For them, universities will sometimes take a stake in the company. In one of the most profitable examples, the University of Pennsylvania was able to receive $7 million for its stake in a start-up company, Wharton Economic Forecasting Association.

Universities have done well from both shared research and product licensing. They have support for their research projects and new help for construction efforts. When then-governor Jerry Brown vetoed funds for a new electrical engineering building at UC–Berkeley, the campus had little choice but to turn to industry. And they did so very effectively. Within four years they were able to build the $5 million building they wanted and generate $18 million in cash and equipment for their projects, all by tapping their Computer-aided Design/Computer-aided Manufacturing (CAD/CAM) Consortium.

But two problems remain. The first is ethical conflicts. An example of such a conflict occurred when MIT became caught between two corporations: Magnetic Engineering Associates (later known as Sala Magnetics) and Magnetics International. MIT produced some technology that both companies wanted to license. The license was awarded to Sala Magnetics. The executives as Magnetics International questioned the decision. They became especially bothered when it was revealed that MIT owned a piece of Sala Magnetics. Now the losing company charged that MIT was trying to get rich by licensing technology to itself. Because the original discovery was funded with National Science Foundation money, Magnetics International called on Congress to investigate the possible abuse of federal tax dollars. The NSF did in fact investigate, much to the embarrassment of MIT.

The second problem is structural conflict. UC–Berkeley can find corporate sponsors to build and staff a new electrical engineering building. Could they do as well building a poetry building? A women's studies building? A poverty studies institute? Selling research may provide an important income stream for troubled universities. But it is a stream only available in some areas. It is a stream that waters part of the campus and leaves the rest high and dry.

Cybrarians

The seventeenth of November 1995 is a day Jim Clark will probably remember for some time. It is the day he became a billionaire. As founder and CEO of Netscape, he watched his company's stock hit more than $110 per share just months after its initial public offering. For that matter, it was only eighteen months since the company had been founded, just four years since the chief product of the company had first been published, and just five years since the idea of a "Net browser" had first been conceived.

What could possibly drive numbers like that? What product could possibly have that much value? The computer industry has had its share of instant millionaires, but usually it takes more than a year and a half to make your first *billion*. The answer lies in access to information. The jury may still be out on whether the Internet will be the chief information highway of our future and whether the World Wide Web will be the chief organizing principle for that highway, but if they are, then putting the front end on that information machine may in fact be worth all the money. For what is casually called a "Web browser" would in fact become the chief means of access to the Internet's information store. Think of it as the front desk of the cyberlibrary. If you control the front desk, the card catalog, and the check-out counter, you have more than a little power at your disposal. Maybe you charge to check out books. Maybe you charge local retailers to put up advertising signs on your desk. Maybe you aren't sure where the money will come from, but assume locating in a rich neighborhood will probably lead to income somewhere, somehow.

What Clark and his competitors have their fingers on is a new approach to information. Before, people made money by creating information. Now, people may be able to make money by finding information and delivering it to your door. Your public librarian had a piece of this action before, and may keep some of the business in the future, but the old library approach is highly labor-intensive, meaning total costs are high but individual income for workers in the industry is low. Few people would trade paychecks with a librarian.

But if we can automate and improve information access, then income is divided by fewer laborers. If a single company with just a few hundred workers can supply the information that used to be handled by tens of thousands of old librarians, then there should be a dollar or two to be made. Maybe even a billion or two. This is what Clark's shareholders are looking for. Whether or not they find it, the very fact they would gamble so much tells us we are at a major moment in the commercial development of information.

Summary

It is no great news that information is an industry worth billions. This chapter looked at only a few corners of that industry. We can assume that, like any other young industry, it will continue to grow. We will see more databases for sale, more data on a disk available to anyone with the money, more people and companies repackaging information in the form of short courses and evening degrees and consultant reports. There is money to be made in this industry—just look at any of the boy billionaires that have already made their fortune in these new gold fields.

What we haven't seen yet is how the interplay of money and information will work out. It may be that the profit motive will drive the generation of fabulous new sources of information, leading to better lives for everyone. It may be that the profit motive will lead to the hiding of information, with corporations and even universities grabbing onto their information and holding out for the highest bidder.

We also haven't heard much yet about how people will pay for this information. The phrase "$25,000 buys you $250,000 of research" may be a cornerstone of much of university commercial research efforts, but it begs the issue of the small businesses that don't have $25,000. And it totally ignores individuals who may have nothing at all. Will public libraries continue to be the access points for those who want information without cost? How much can libraries afford to buy? How much can they continue to give away? In short, we really don't know how much of a barrier money will be to information.

But we can make some estimates. One British survey (MURDOCK AND GOLDING 1989) on incomes and their relationship to expenditures for traditional information sources showed these results:

	Weekly Expenditures (in £)		
Weekly Income (in £)	TV/AUDIO EQUIPMENT	NEWSPAPERS, BOOKS, MAGAZINES	CINEMA
60–80	.57	1.51	.03
100–125	.91	2.00	.02
150–175	2.73	2.48	.09
225–250	4.51	2.98	.11
325–375	5.33	3.50	.15
550+	10.19	5.54	.28

Income directly affected the amount spent on every major source of information. To quote one observer, "Just as once only the wealthy could afford manuscripts, now electronic information is being supplied to elite buyers on a first-use basis" (LARSON 1992:46). The next three chapters underline just how difficult that struggle for information access will be, especially for some.

Part II

Transmission Problems

Chapter 6   Information Exiles

Those who have recently achieved their independence, must take care this time not to miss the last train of the twentieth century.   —MATHIEA EKRA,
minister of state, the Ivory Coast

THE GODS MUST BE CRAZY is a very funny movie. It portrays a group of Bushmen in the Kalahari Desert living a simple life in harmony with nature. One day a pilot flying overhead throws a Coke bottle out his window. It lands near the Bushmen, who have no idea what the object is, what to do with it, or why the gods have sent it to them. After initially appearing to be a useful object, the bottle causes jealousy and hurt. They decide to throw the bottle back up to the gods, but it keeps falling back, so finally one elder is selected to walk to the end of the earth and throw the bottle off. Along the way he meets white people whom he aids, especially a white woman who knows nothing about nature and is quite helpless.

The movie, and its sequel, present a world that might have been written about nearly two centuries earlier by Rousseau or any of his English peers. It is classic romanticism—the natural man living a life of harmony and health until he encounters the scourge of civilization with all its weaknesses and follies. Two centuries later, romanticism still has its appeal. In a world of faxes and e-mail and traffic jams, the idea of moving off into the hinterlands sounds good. On occasion, many of us do just that. For most, it is just a short fishing trip into the countryside or a few days at the beach. Others are most ambitious, flying thousands of miles to escape the daily grind. Of late even the Kalahari is getting visitors as ecotourism gains popularity with those able to cover the plane fare.

Groups fly into Maun, Botswana, ride through the desert in jeeps, and even stay a few days with Bushmen families, sleeping on the ground and gathering gourds.

The simple life. If we could just cut our electronic shackles and get back to nature, we could have the quality of life the Bushmen enjoy. Then again, maybe we'd better not. Maybe there is a side to poverty and isolation that isn't put in movies. Maybe if we looked beyond movies to the true state of the Bushmen and other of the world's poor, we might see that a life of ignorance is a life of powerlessness. No one knows that better than the Bushman. For the tale of the Bushmen, and of the village of Tsumkwe, Namibia, where the film was made, show how little possibility exists for "natural men" to walk the earth in harmony with nature. For the truth is, when we are aren't lying about them in movies, we are stealing their land and shooting them down.

Two books about the Bushmen that are far less funny but far more honest are *The Harmless People*, by Elizabeth Marshall Thomas, and *The Bushman Myth*, by Robert J. Gordon. They and numerous other accounts describe in detail the large-scale slaughter of the Bushmen during this century. Nor has the destruction of the Bushmen stopped. Thomas describes how into the 1960s Afrikaner farmers in need of laborers would simply drive into the Kalahari, tempt Bushmen into their trucks with sweets or small gifts, and then drive off to their farms, where the Bushmen would work for meager food and a few trinkets. The effect of their abduction on the families left behind was described by Claude McIntyre in 1955:

> At Rama and Gautsika Dam I was immediately recognized and assailed by wailing women demanding the return of sons and husbands who had been similarly removed. . . . Food supplies in the vicinity were exhausted [and] the whole band should . . . have trekked . . . but they were waiting . . . in the hope that the men who had been taken away would be returned. . . . I was . . . shown girl wives with children and aged women whose supports . . . had been removed by force by farmers from the Police Zone. Within the last fortnight since the Marshall expedition had left, another four Bushmen had been removed from the band by farmers.
>
> (GORDON 1992:170–171)

In the 1980s the South African military needed trackers for its war against Namibian guerrillas. They went out into the Kalahari and hired all the men they could find. Those who survived the fighting in Angola came back to the Kalahari with pockets full of rand and no place in a subsistence culture to spend it. So the state opened a bottle store in Tsumkwe, where the money went quickly on beer and liquor. In her horrifying 1988 appendix to *The Harmless People*, Thomas describes how every person she knew in the 1950s is either murdered or becomes a killer under the influence of liquor. Coke bottles a mystery from the sky? Hardly. The South Africans sold them Coke—and rum to mix it with.

The story of the Bushmen reminds us that there are no islands of primitive peoples living peaceful lives away from the rat race of civilization. There are only victims whose land and labor can be taken at will—cultures overwhelmed by highways, diseases, and drugs—individuals who are totally consumed by alien forces that sometimes destroy out of calculated maleficence but often destroy without even being aware of the damage they do.

The Bushmen are fighting for survival. And they are quickly learning the rules of the new warfare. Forming alliances with Australian aborigines, Himbas, and other indigenous people, they are pressing their legal claims and making sure they get their share of air time on the six o'clock news. Forming the Nyae Nyae Farmers Cooperative, they are developing ways to market local products and handicrafts, as they train themselves in the methods of modern business. If courage and energy were sufficient for victory, one could be much more sanguine about their future. But the Bushmen face overwhelming odds. Virtually every development in the information age leaves them more vulnerable and demonstrates the problems faced by people like them around the world.

To understand these problems, a good place to start is Tsumkwe, Namibia. Established in 1959, the village started out as little more than a farm where experts hoped to teach Bushmen cattle-raising skills. Tsumkwe is not an easy place to reach. You begin by driving four hours north of Windhoek on two lanes of asphalt. Then you turn right—east—into the Kalahari. For the next four hours you bump along over gravel and sand, leaving a long cloud of dust in your wake. You pass a few hills and a few trees, but no people or structures, as you drive hour after hour through a grassy plain. Occasionally you see another car or truck, but only occasionally. After the first couple of hours you feel a sense for just how isolated this community is.

The Germans wanted it that way. When they ruled the country from 1885 to 1915 they put their settlers on land that had water, good pasturage for cattle, and easy access to markets. During the South African occupation from 1915 to 1990, the policy remained the same. Nonwhites, especially the Bushmen, were pushed to corners of the country, while white farmers and merchants controlled the middle. And so the Bushmen, who once controlled much of the center of Namibia, were pushed out to the edge, out to the desert. They had once been miners and traders, but that part of their land was taken from them. Reduced to hunting and gathering, they struggled to pull a living from the Kalahari.

The extent of their isolation becomes increasingly clear as you bump along the gravel road hour after hour. For the first hundred kilometers there are phone lines strung along the right side of the road. They stop at a government agricultural station. Fifty kilometers farther your car radio fades into static. For the next hundred kilometers there is just the sound of gravel popping up against the underside of the car. There are no people here. At one point I passed two Bushmen cattle herders waiting for a lift into Grootfontein. They were still there eight hours later as the sun set. I picked them up on my return.

After such a long, silent drive, Tsumkwe just seems to pop up out of the low brush. It would be easy to miss. There isn't much there, and what there is, is spread out. There is an intersection—another thin gravel road crossing yours. To your left is the school, set back fifty yards from the road. A set of block rooms, it enrolls three hundred in grades one to ten. Across the intersection is the only store. It looks like an old gas station. Also made of blocks, it is about thirty feet square and painted white. The inside is dark and largely empty. Shelving bolted to the walls contains a scattering of food and household goods. There are two low coolers, each about four feet long. One has soft drinks, the other meat. The center of the store stands empty.

Back out at the intersection, the road to the right is Main Street. On one side is the police station, then the gas station. Some days there is gas, some days not. Next is the home of the rural development official, followed by the home of "the Bushman movie star," as he is known locally. No one in town has seen *The Gods Must Be Crazy*, but they remember the filming. Across the street is the clinic. All these buildings are set well back from the road and separated from each other—space is not a problem here.

There is one residential street with eight houses for government workers. The first one is the town leader's. He also gets the generators in his back yard. Down the street are seven more houses, all about twenty years old, ranch-style brick with single-car attached garages and grassy front yards. It looks like it could be a suburban block from western Texas.

Driving the short distance up the gravel streets, there are few Bushmen to be seen. The storekeeper is white, the government officials black. The rural development officer, Charles Chipango, is on leave to study computer science at the University of Namibia. A student of mine, he drove me back down the residential street but kept going past the end, past the gravel, past the electricity out onto a dirt track. In a few hundred yards we came to the Bushmen. One group was living in a collection of square block structures about eight feet on a side. There were eight or ten such buildings. Across a small field were smaller stick-and-mud homes. We bounced over the dirt track through fields of mahango and corn.

As we came around one bend we had to stop. A Bushman was passed out drunk in the middle of the track. We edged around him and found the "shebeen" that had supplied him. In a clearing was a small structure—four poles about five feet high, with a lattice of branches across the top to provide shade. Sitting in the shade was the wife of one of the government officials. She had a two-liter box of wine, a boom box, and a small half-pint whiskey bottle. For ten rand she would fill the old whiskey bottle with wine. The twenty or so Bushmen at the shebeen would pass the bottle around, dancing barefoot in the dirt as they drank. It was just 1:00 P.M. and she was doing a good business. Profit margins were among the best in the world. She bought the wine for twenty-two rand a box. She could fill the ten-rand bottle thirteen or fourteen times from one box. Twenty-two rand becomes one hundred and thirty with no taxes and no overhead. Not a bad profit margin.

The shebeens farther down the track didn't have any business yet. But it was early. Each had a forty-gallon plastic garbage pail sitting in the shade. Homemade beer was brewing in each pail. By night each would be empty, to be refilled the next day. That was the second Tsumkwe. The dirt paths and stick houses and home-brewed beer back off the road, out of sight, back past where the gravel and electricity stop. For these people there are no happy natives living the simple life of *The Gods Must Be Crazy*. The gods out here seem hostile, or cruel.

Obstacles

The world is full of small towns, and Tsumkwe bears some similarities to the faded logging towns of northern Wisconsin or the Indian reservations of North Dakota. And, like those other small, rural towns, Tsumkwe illustrates every single obstacle to full inclusion in the new age of information.

GEOGRAPHIC ISOLATION

Tsumkwe isn't four hours from markets, it is four hours from a *road* to markets. Besides which, most Kalahari Bushmen don't live in Tsumkwe, they live in small bands farther into the desert. If they wish to sell handicrafts or skins or visit relatives (or see a doctor), they have to travel a full day or more just to get to Tsumkwe. The distances hurt economically—products in the local store are far more expensive than in Windhoek because of shipping costs, yet Bushmen get less profit from their own goods because of shipping expenses. The distances also hurt personally. Relatives who move to a larger city are essentially gone forever.

LACK OF COMMUNICATION

It makes no economic sense to run phone wires across the Kalahari. So there are no phones. The only connection to the rest of the world is a radio phone. It is difficult and expensive to use just for voice communication. Nobody will be hooking up to electronic mail anytime soon, and four-hundred-channel TV doesn't seem to be in their future. There is mail. Once every week or two someone volunteers to drive the four and a half hours to Grootfontein to get it.

LACK OF INFORMATION

The general store in Tsumkwe sells no newspapers. Radio reception is only possible with a really good antenna and then only at sunup and sundown. At those times the faint signal is as likely to come from Botswana as Namibia. Television sets don't exist.

LACK OF EDUCATION

The school in town is less than twenty years old and appears solid. The problem is the teachers. They have broken into two factions—the qualified and the unqualified. The qualified teachers either have university degrees (one is a Peace Corps volunteer) or have attended a teacher training college. There are four of these teachers. They are outnumbered by the eight unqualified teachers who have completed eighth grade and little else. These teachers tend to be both unqualified and uninterested. One regularly comes to class drunk. Another sleeps at his desk most of the day. His fellow teachers can tell when he is asleep—his students climb up into the ceiling area under the roof and look down on adjoining classes. A third teacher was finally run off when he was confronted with numerous students who said he paid them ten Namibian dollars for sex. The battle between the two groups continues, with the unqualified teachers generally winning a maintenance of the status quo.

INABILITY TO SPEAK OR UNDERSTAND
THE DOMINANT LANGUAGE

Namibia has had several national languages. During the German occupation it was German (it is still the principal language of commerce), under the South African, Afrikaans. With independence in 1990 the official language became English. The problem for the people of Tsumkwe is that the official language has never been Bushman. The language problem affects their children (and the problems they have in trying to learn), it affects their ability to keep up with the world around them, it affects their ability to defend themselves in a court of law. Anthropologist Dorothea Bleek recognized over half a century ago the problems Bushmen had in courts:

> [Bushmen] are dreadfully afraid of the white man, particularly the policeman, who appears to them merely an arbitrary tyrant as they don't understand the laws . . . half the convictions of Bushman under the game laws would not take place, if the accused did not let

themselves be frightened into owning to the police. . . . [The Police]
take care not to warn the natives that anything they say will be used
against them. When Bushmen appear in court they have no idea of
what would be accepted as defense or in mitigation of sentence, and
the interpreting is mostly done by native constables who are anxious
to please the white policemen they serve under and to "make a case."
(BLEEK 1922:48–49)

To the Bushmen, every encounter with the legal system must seem like something out of Kafka.

POVERTY

One of the cruder ironies of the information age is that rich people get their information practically for free, while poor people pay dearly for every morsel. Be it
a telephone call, a newspaper, a drive to the store—all cost more in Tsumkwe
than they do in Beverly Hills. They cost more in absolute terms; they cost astro-
nomically more in relative terms—as a percentage of a day's wage. How many
Americans would work an hour for a newspaper, two hours for a phone call, a
day to see a movie, a lifetime for a home computer? Yet for those on the edge
of survival, information is more important. If every evening for a month goes
into making a basket, what kind of baskets are selling in Windhoek? What size?
Will the new crafts store in Tsumeb pay more? Are tourists coming to Tsumkwe
who might buy it? The poor can't afford wasted effort—unsold production. Yet
they know almost nothing about the world. Where a phone call costs more than
a basket, you don't call around to check markets.

The Bushmen of the Kalahari are an extreme example of people who are
disconnected from the new age, but they are, unfortunately, not alone. All over
the world are people and groups who, for various reasons, are off the information highway. The consequences for them are the consequences always faced
by the powerless. The reasons for their predicament are worth further elabora-
tion. Some of the reasons, such as poor education, we will describe in later chapters. For now, we will concentrate on four of the information problems most
frequently faced by the poor: geographic isolation, lack of communication
channels, language problems, and lack of computer systems. Each problem
deepens the isolation and weakness of the poor.

Geographic Isolation

The importance of location was already described in chapter 3. Whether it is
the concentration of Network experts in Washington or Reich's information
capitals of Silicon Valley, Hollywood, and Washington, the new age seems

to be drawing leaders together, not dispersing them across the planet. Electronic links are used to supplement face-to-face contact, not replace it. To fully make contact with people and their supply of information, you still have to be able to get there from here.

Unfortunately, there are a number of circumstances that limit travel. It is easier to get to some places and increasingly difficult to get to others. The explanation comes from three current phenomena: airplanes, roads, and fear.

AIRPLANES

Airplanes, of course, make travel very fast, with a New Yorker being able to get to London in about six hours, Los Angeles in five, Chicago in two. But what if a New Yorker wants to fly to Des Moines? Or Fargo? Or Green Bay? Our traveler suddenly discovers the hub-and-spoke approach to air routes. Getting from hub to hub is quick, there are many flights, and there are often good airfares. The spokes are the problem. If the city at the end of the spoke is a big one, you at least get a big plane and stewardesses with drinks and peanuts. If the city at the end of the line is a small one, you may not even get a rest room. You also lose time. Besides the layover to catch one of the infrequent flights to the boonies, when you do board you discover your little plane takes as long to fly from Chicago to Stevens Point as the big plane took to get from New York to Chicago. Then add cost. The cost of a flight is only marginally determined by distance. Much of the cost is in airport fees, so it matters little whether the flight travels two hundred miles or two thousand. Add the lack of competition on remote flights and you often have two-hundred-mile flights costing *more* than two-thousand-mile flights. For all these reasons, major airports are filled every evening with commuters asking themselves, "Why do I live in Green Bay, Duluth, Oshkosh . . . ? If I lived here I'd be home by now."

The hub-and-spoke system exists in Africa, but with a very interesting twist. Johannesburg is a major hub, but because of its southern location and because of past trade sanctions, Nairobi, Kenya, also developed as a hub, but so did Frankfurt and Paris and London. The fact that Frankfurt, Germany, would be a hub for flights between African countries at first seems silly, but it has a fairly sound basis. First, begin with the fact that African nations don't really trade much among themselves. Namibia and Botswana are neighbors and share a huge border, but the border happens to be the Kalahari Desert—no roads, no commerce. Namibia and Angola also share a large border. Angola has been at war with itself for twenty years—no safe travel, no commerce. This litany could be repeated for country after country. Then add colonialism. African countries may be politically free now, but their major industries are owned by Europeans. Money goes to Europe, exports go to Europe, managers come from Europe. Then there are donor programs. Consultants come from Europe, aid checks come from Europe, students go to Europe. The result is that air travel from any African country to Europe is often far more significant than to any other African country. It can also be faster to Europe. Windhoek, Namibia, to Frankfurt, Germany, is nearly five thousand miles. The flight is direct and takes just under ten hours. Windhoek, Namibia, to Mozambique is nearly one thousand miles. The flight requires a change of planes and an overnight stay in Johannesburg. Your friend flying to Frankfurt will have had breakfast and be reporting to his manager at Siemens while you are still trying to clear customs in Mozambique. So since there are already so many flights filling the air to and from Europe, why not make it a hub? As an acquaintance discovered, the shortest route from Namibia to Gambia was through Frankfurt. The effect of all this on African unity is subtle, but important. It is often easier for a European to get to parts of Africa than it is for an African. It is also often cheaper.

ROADS

Every year some small town in Nebraska lobbies the state to have its name placed on Interstate 80. No matter that it may be fifty, sixty, eighty miles or more off the highway, it wants a sign saying that this is the exit to North Farmington or East Libertyville. It's hard to blame them. As a small town struggling to stay alive, a freeway that goes by with no mention of your distant existence is a slap in the face and a nail in your coffin.

This concentration of people and businesses along interstates in the United States, and the skyrocketing land values around each exit, demonstrate both that we still move people by road and that technology affects behavior. Part of the advantage of interstates is that they are wider and safer and graded to reduce inclines and declines, and supported with an infrastructure like truck stops and highway patrol. But they also match the technology of the car. There is constant talk of "smart roads," with wires that send signals to cars to direct them with no need for human steering, or talk of other interesting high-tech devices. Maybe we will see them, maybe we won't. In the meantime we already have one device that goes well with interstates—cruise control. Set it, take your foot off the gas, and cruise for hour after hour. The difference in the way drivers feel at the end of the day is noticeable. The change in their behavior is also noticeable. Would you rather drive 100 miles on two lanes of asphalt, or 120 on an interstate? 130? 140? No trucks to pass, no sharp bends or sudden hills that might hide a hay wagon or school bus, no Sunday drivers making sure they stay safely below fifty-five while you look desperately for a place to pass. Equally important, no small towns with stop signs, no twenty-five-mile-per-hour zones, and no local cops looking for tourist income.

While the United States moves its highways from two to four lanes and leaves behind the two-lane towns and villages, much of the world follows suit. Korea, which as recently as 1970 was excited about having a single highway connecting Seoul to Pusan, now has enough highways and cars that it can afford semiannual gridlock traffic jams. Europe has dug under the English Channel and through the Alps. In the First World, getting there becomes less and less a problem.

In the developing world, it is becoming more true that you can't get there from here. In Bangladesh roads get in the way of annual floods. Sometimes the roads win, creating far worse floods in other parts of the country; usually the floods win—leaving people cut off from food and medical help. In Africa the long-dreamed-of Cape-to-Cairo route seems more and more remote as even existing routes slowly disappear. A recent World Bank review of transportation systems in Africa summed up the problem:

> Roads and railways are poorly maintained, while complicated customs and administrative procedures add to delays and costs. Inefficiencies when goods are handled at terminals, and transferred from one transport mode to another, are compounded by delays in the interactions between the agencies involved in transit. For Mali's imports from Europe, for example, delays in African ports and terminals take longer than the sea section of the journey. For Uganda, Malawi, and Eastern Zaire, Tanzania potentially offers the cheapest access to the sea, but the poor state of Tanzanian roads and railways rules this option out.
>
> Worsening security has added to costs and risks. Many traditional —relatively efficient—routes have been closed by civil unrest or political differences between countries. The closure of major corridors from Beira, Nacala, and Maputo, on the Indian Ocean, and Lobito, on the Atlantic, has severely affected the economies of LLCs [land-locked countries]. For Malawi by the late 1980s, for example, additional transport charges since the closure had caused cumulative losses of more than $75 million.   (WORLD BANK 1995)

Around the world, many places are becoming more isolated, not less. Whether it is the crossroads in Nebraska desperately hoping for a sign saying it is only fifty-eight miles from the interstate or the small city in Zimbabwe hoping the rains stop long enough for trucks to get through, we are leaving much of the world behind.

FEAR

Sometimes the world we leave behind isn't very far away. The great interstates we travel pass over or around neighborhoods we seldom visit. Recent American literature increasingly builds plots around chance detours off the highway. Whether *Grand Canyon* or *Bonfire of the Vanities* or lesser known works, there is increasing discussion of the dangers of entering into "that" part of town. A recent spate of killings targeting European and Japanese tourists has much of the world wondering whether "that part of town" is really the entire United States. Meanwhile, our State Department keeps up a list of countries unsafe for Americans.

It would be nice to say that all this was just hysteria to be solved by a session with a counselor, but the dangers are unfortunately real. In Algeria and Egypt and Florida they really do target and kill tourists. In every inner city in America children are killed daily because they were standing on the wrong corner or sleeping in a bed within Uzi range of a crack house. In much of the world being the wrong religion or color or nationality or tribe can get you killed. Jews still aren't safe in Germany, neither Jews nor Arabs are safe in Israel, and in central Africa on any day one tribe can rise up and kill tens of thousands of their countrymen. It happens over and over again. In South Africa, Amy Biehl, an American Fulbright scholar, drove several friends to their homes in the black township of Gugaletu. A gang of teenage boys saw her white face, stopped the car, dragged her out, and beat and stabbed her to death. As her friends tried to stop them, they screamed, "Why are you doing this?" The boys answered, "She's a settler." The campaign slogan of South Africa's Pan-Africanist Congress (PAC) is "one settler, one bullet"—genocide reduced to a bumper sticker. The whites in South Africa aren't as good with slogans, but they know how to kill. Just before Christmas 1993 a group of young white men in military fatigues set up a roadblock outside Johannesburg. They stopped all the motorists coming down the highway. If the people in the car were black, they killed them—men, women, and children. In one case they cut the ears off a victim as a trophy.

The effect of fear on information flow is obvious. In January 1994 a large member of journalists came to South Africa to explore life prior to the elections. Within a week of each other two film crews, one Polish, one German, tried to tape what life was like for children in the black townships. One crew was robbed of all its equipment, one crew was beaten and then robbed. The story of childhood in the townships will go untold. Tourists are neither ambassadors nor scholars, but they do carry some information about their country when they travel and bring back some awareness of the world when they return. Fifty thousand fewer tourists ventured into Egypt in 1993. The number not daring to enter the United States may be as high. Student-exchange programs have grown rapidly as parents and children understand the benefits of learning a foreign language and culture. But before Japanese students come to the United States they are shown a videotape of America that prepares them to live in a country where crazy people walk down the street legally armed and dangerous.

Rotary International funds one of the larger student-exchange programs. When PAC demonstrators outside the trial of Amy Biehl's killers spotted Biehl's mother and changed the chant of "one settler, one bullet" to "one American, one bullet," Rotary Clubs in South Africa immediately put three exchange students on a plane back to the United States and arranged to have a further thirty-four put on a long tour of Namibia. (Oddly enough, PAC president Clarence Makwetu later complained about how few campaign contributions his party was getting from overseas. Apparently, "one American, one bullet" fell flat as a fund raising slogan in the United States.)

The biggest losers from fear are the poor who live in the nations and neighborhoods where travel is unsafe. Not only are they the preponderant victims of crime, but their own access to information, already severely limited, is further restricted. One American example may best illustrate. In 1992 the *Chronicle of Higher Education* reported a new phenomenon. College students from inner cities weren't going home for the summer. A growing number of black students found jobs on their rural campuses, or in the adjoining college towns, and stayed year round. When approached for interviews they were very candid about why they had made their choices—they were afraid to go home. The consequences for these students were clear—loneliness as they were cut off from family and friends. The consequences for the inner city are equally real, if less obvious. These are the young men and women who could be role models in the old neighborhood. For high school students confused about the procedures of college applications, they could be guides. For students needing academic help, they could be tutors. For adolescents struggling to confront the world, they would be a voice of reason. But instead they are mowing lawns and planting pansies two hundred miles away in the safety of small-town America. The loss for the children left behind mounts yearly.

Lack of Communication

Getting information from point A to point B requires some kind of communication medium. I need a way to get it there. In the United States I may have a wide range of options—I can telephone, fax, send a note via Internet, or drop a letter in the mail. I have a range of communication channels. Would that it were so in the rest of the world. The physical bounds of information flow are still with us whether we are looking at phones, mail, or e-mail.

PHONES

Phones are crucial not just because they are so important in maintaining personal and professional connections but also because they are the medium used for data transmission. As the world becomes one large Wide Area Network, the phone lines and switches become our information highways. Where the phone lines go, information follows. Unfortunately, there are many places where the phone lines do not go.

Let's start with America. The U.S. Census Bureau (1993) says we have fifty-one lines per one hundred population. That's not the best in the world (Sweden leads with sixty-eight, followed by Switzerland at fifty-eight, Canada at fifty-seven, Denmark at fifty-seven, and Finland at fifty-three), but it is well above average. Assuming some phone sharing, just about everyone can get to a phone at home. But there are exceptions. About one in four American Indian, Eskimo, and Aleut households don't have a phone, and 53 percent of American Indian households on reservations have no phone (VANDEWATER 1994). And the rural South is still a problem, with 12 percent of households in Mississippi and New Mexico having no phones, followed by Arkansas at 11 percent.

Bad as the numbers are for parts of America, the following countries have just one line per one hundred people: China, India, Kenya, Nicaragua, Pakistan, Philippines, Sri Lanka, and Zimbabwe (U.S. CENSUS 1993:856). Between China and India we have essentially half the world's people working off one line per one hundred people. Dozens of other countries have just two, three, or four lines per hundred people. For most of the world, the phone is not an accessible technology. It is literally true that half the world's population is waiting to make its first phone call.

Brazil represents one form of the problem. With only seven lines per one hundred people, ten million Brazilians want phones but can't get them. Even after paying two thousand dollars for a line, customers have to be lucky to use their new phones—only 57 percent of calls placed actually get through (MARGOLIS 1994). Under conditions like these, new businesses are at a huge disadvantage. Imagine being a business start-up and having to wait a year until customers could call in an order. Brazil's problem derives from an unwillingness to challenge the state monopoly. Foreign businesses may not compete and local companies can't meet demand. Meanwhile you wait years for a dial tone.

Propping up a state telephone industry is the cause for much of the problems with Eastern European phone systems. Germany is essentially having to rebuild systems from the ground up in the former German Democratic Republic. In one former East German university it was easier to call the United States than to call across campus. It will take years to create modern phone capacity in that part of the world.

In Africa the problem is a bizarre combination of poverty and foreign aid. Zimbabwe's phones aren't the worst on the continent, but they are currently drawing the most unfavorable press. Part of the problem stems from foreign aid. Five European countries have been very happy to pay for state-of-the-art digital exchanges, but they will only pay for exchanges purchased from their own corporations. As a result, Zimbabwe has five different exchange switches with five times the maintenance difficulties it might otherwise have. But even so it can keep the exchanges up and running. The real problem is the "last mile." No foreign donor is waiting to pay for the lines out to homes. Putting them in is expensive and time-consuming, so customers wait. The new digital exchanges are only being used at 40 percent capacity—there is plenty of room for more traffic, but there isn't either local money or foreign interest in building the "on ramps" to this particular information highway.

The costs of installing phones may be an insurmountable obstacle in much of the developing world. Residents and businesses there are hit by three special problems, each pushing phones out of reach. First, labor costs are high. Throughout Africa there is a shortage of people with technical skills. The reasons for this are reviewed in a later chapter. For the moment it is enough to consider the effect of the shortage—phone technicians are in short supply and so draw good salaries. Second, much of the Third World is still rural. That means it takes longer lines (and higher costs) to get to customers. Telecom Namibia estimates it costs almost five thousand U.S. dollars to hook up one rural phone. That high cost helps explain why a relatively well-off country like Namibia only has sixty-five thousand phones serving a population of 1.5 million. Because of high labor costs and high installation costs it is often more expensive to get a phone in Africa than in the United States. We know the Third World has less money than the United States (dramatically less as we shall shortly see), yet their phone costs are higher. As a consequence the vast majority simply don't have phones.

Where phones *do* exist, it is fascinating to see how they are linked to the rest of the world. Driving through southern Namibia the Kalahari stretches on mile after empty mile. You can drive a long way without seeing a building or a person, or another car on the highway. But there's no shortage of microwave towers. The banks in Windhoek need to connect to the main computer of their headquarters in Johannesburg. For thirty-five cents per kilometer the channels are kept open for them and everyone else with business connections to South Africa. The links to the South are state-of-the-art.

Calls to the North are another matter. Half of Namibia's population, but none of its corporate owners, live along the Angolan border. Four years after independence from South Africa, optical fiber is finally being laid to the north. Gradually digital switches are going in. In the meantime, a person looking at a map of trunk lines would be forgiven for not noticing that Namibia is no longer a South African colony. Most of the rest of the Third World has similar vestiges. Can't remember if a country used to be a colony of England or France or Portugal or Germany? Follow the fiber or the satellite uplinks—it's not too hard to trace history.

Third, telephones are vulnerable to violence. A particularly ugly example exists in South Africa. For much of the last decade, there has been a constant battle between supporters of the African National Congress and the Inkatha Freedom Party. Thousands of people have been killed, with thirty to forty dying on an average weekend. Social services cannot handle this kind of strain, and one of the first pieces of infrastructure to go is the telephone. Lines are cut and can't be repaired because of the violence; repair crews are robbed of their trucks and equipment. As a consequence, at one point in 1994, in East Rand townships ten thousand people were waiting for phones to be installed and five thousand phones were out of order. In Soweto Township twenty-seven hundred families were waiting for phone installations while fifteen hundred phones were out of order. According to Telecom's communication manager for that region, "The East Rand townships are inaccessible. We have cables there and all we need to do is just connect. If it were not for the violence, all those people would have had phones" (MOROKE 1994:5).

MAIL

Anatoly Vorovov, director of a Russian network linked to the Internet, sums up mail delivery in much of the world: "Here you can send e-mail to Vladivostok or Boston in five seconds. Or you can wait three months to get a magazine by mail." Unfortunately for the world, Vorovov is wrong about the Internet (it is fast but unavailable to more than a tiny fraction of the world's people) and right about mail.

Part of the problem with mail is that as a physical entity it moves no faster than people. It may fly part of the way at 500 miles per hour, or ride the back of a mail truck at 55 miles per hour, but often it is just moving as fast as a person can walk. None of this compares very well with electronic mail traveling at 186,000 miles per second. But not all mail is equally slow. Take the United States. Recent audits have shown mail in some major cities being hidden, held, or trashed. In Washington, D.C., eight hundred thousand first-class letters were found after being stashed in parked trailers for three days. In Chicago firefighters found over a ton of mail hidden in a letter carrier's home (FARLEY 1994). In general, the U.S. Postal Service agrees there are problems with traffic congestion in metropolitan areas. It appears people in U.S. cities simply have to wait longer for their mail.

In the developing world mail traffic is even more odd. David Lush heads the Media Institute of Southern Africa (MISA) headquartered in Windhoek, Namibia. His organization creates a monthly newsletter preaching press freedom issues in Africa. He describes his mail experience this way: "When I mail my newsletters to Europe, they are there in 5 days. Zambia [one of the countries adjoining Namibia] takes 4 weeks. Zimbabwe takes 4 weeks. Mozambique takes 5 weeks. Angola . . . well, if it arrives at all, it takes 5 weeks. Half the time it just disappears" (1994).

There seems to be an ironic connection to costs as well—the worse the service, the higher the cost. Here are MISA's mailing costs for the same three-kilogram package of newsletters:

South Africa	$4.40
Malawi	$57.75
Angola	$63.00
Zambia	$63.00
Tanzania	$68.25

The same forces that make it easier to get from Namibia to Gambia by flying through Germany make it faster to send mail six thousand miles than six hundred. The infrastructure to get to the corporate home office in Europe is maintained. The infrastructure to get to the country next door may never have existed. This has economic consequences. Sub-Saharan Africa has created the Southern Africa Development Community (SADC) to try to build economic ties within the region. But if it takes five weeks for a bid to be mailed to a neighboring country and another four for a contract to come back, what kind of "community" is there? As Lush puts it, "As far as communications are concerned, we might as well be part of the European Economic Community, SADC doesn't exist" (1994). The mail reflects and reinforces old dependencies.

ELECTRONIC MAIL

In theory, electronic mail—e-mail—could be a communications life line to the development world. As the network leader in Moscow pointed out, when mail takes three months to arrive, e-mail looks especially good. Not only does it provide speedy access, but it provides crucial access to expertise. But two examples illustrate the difficulties involved in making electronic mail a reality for all.

SADC REGIONAL EARLY WARNING SYSTEM

A major effort is underway to get weather information to governments in Southern Africa. NASA overflights are able to identify weather patterns that might produce rain (Cold Cloud Duration figures). In the past, those were collected in Florida and transferred by diplomatic pouch to various African governments. The process took three weeks, which meant the data was largely useless. The purpose of the new system was to downlink the information directly to Harare, Zimbabwe, where it could be communicated to ten SADC centers.

The project has been underway for three years and has succeeded in getting information to five countries on a regular basis. The other five are still offline after three years of trying. Why? One problem is local expertise. Workers at the local meteorology department could not install the internal modems purchased by the project. The second problem was phone companies. Some could handle digital data, some could not. Often the data moved quite well over international lines and then got lost as it passed over antiquated local lines. Work continues on the last five countries (FREELAND 1994).

AFRICAN UNIVERSITIES

E-mail systems could also be a great benefit to African universities. The unending decline in the average standard of living coupled with political turmoil and political oppression has left the average university in dire straits. Faculty salaries are so bad, professors either leave the profession outright or leave by taking second jobs while their university teaching commitment is reduced to the fewest possible hours. University libraries are hit by a double problem: lower budgets and increasing book prices. The result is weaker and weaker collections. By one estimation, 80 percent of what is known about Africa is located not in Africa, but in the libraries and government offices of Europe and the United States. As a result, someone wishing to study Africa might be well advised to do most of his or her studying outside of Africa.

For a university student in Africa, access to those foreign libraries could be crucial. One guideline says libraries should have one hundred books per student to ensure a range and depth of coverage. The library of the University of Namibia contains eight books per student. (Students are only allowed to check out five books. If they took out more, the library could disappear overnight.) The university is actively seeking to build its library collection, but since it perennially operates at a deficit, major allocations for books are unlikely.

The United Nations has a project underway to link African universities and their libraries. It is providing computer equipment, modems, and expertise. What it can't provide is phone lines, and that is where problems begin. Computers communicate at various speeds. The slowest communication speed—300 baud—would transmit thirty characters per second. This page contains slightly less than three thousand characters, but let's keep the math simple and round up to an even three thousand. At thirty characters per second, it would take one hundred seconds, or almost two minutes, just to send this one page.

Of course there are much faster links possible. A 14,400-baud modem is easily found. Since it transmits 1,440 characters a second, this page would be gone in just over two seconds—almost fifty times faster. Surely, this would be the way to go, especially since African telephone charges are often three or four times what a similar call would cost in the United States. Except for one problem. Africa's phone lines can rarely handle high speeds. Despite repeated attempts, the UN can't even reach Madagascar at 300 baud—the slowest possible rate. Lines elsewhere often lose messages at speeds above 1,200 baud (120 characters per second). As a consequence, not only do African phones cost more per minute, but messages take more minutes to send than they would in the United States. This combination means some of the world's poorest people have to pay the world's highest charges for electronic mail. As a result, people who might be helped most by e-mail are limited in its use.

Language Problems

When it became independent in 1990, Namibia did a very strange thing—it adopted English as its national language. It was a strange move because almost no one in the country spoke English. The largest black tribe, the group that had carried on most of the guerrilla war against South Africa, the group that led the revolutionary movement, spoke Oshivambo. The group that lost, but was able to stay on under a policy of national reconciliation, spoke Afrikaans. The merchant class spoke German. The other rural tribes spoke Damara or Herero. No identifiable group spoke English. It was like the Canadians foregoing French and English and deciding to make Portuguese the national language.

But there was a great deal of sense to the decision. Since Afrikaans and German were identified with colonial oppression, neither could be accepted. Oshivambo was spoken by the majority of the population, but picking one tribe's language over any other would stand in the face of national unity. Another choice was needed. Why not go with a language spoken in other parts of Africa, a language spoken around the world?

Actually, on a day-to-day basis, there are plenty of strikes against English—nightly TV news that few people can understand, schools being taught in English by teachers who can't speak English, a merchant class still loyal to Afrikaans and German. It will probably take a generation before the average Namibian can order a meal in English, or count change, or read an auto repair manual.

For a poor country in a remote corner of Africa, they have set themselves a significant task.

Does it make any sense to put themselves in the predicament when they have so many other problems as well? It does to the leaders of the country, most of whom spent long years in exile, living throughout Europe and North America, experiencing firsthand the powerlessness of people who can't speak the dominant language. They returned home in 1990 determined not to repeat that problem.

This question of language in the information age is a crucial one, and Namibians aren't the only ones wrestling with it. In India senior politicians have recently demonstrated against the compulsory English-language portion of the civil service exam. They point out that English is only spoken by a thin layer of rich Indians, while 43 percent speak Hindi and the rest speak one of fourteen other major languages. Supporters of English point out, "English, like air conditioners and cars, is a sign of economic inequality. But it is often the only means of communication in our multilingual society" ("Talk" 1994:12).

There are also a number of technical forces that heavily favor English as the language of the new age. First, English dominates the world of computing. Both the British and the Americans like to claim their nation as the birth-place of computing, but in one way it doesn't matter which did what—both are English-speaking nations and English is all over computer technology. English-speaking nations produce the hardware and the software for the world. Two of the three biggest computer companies in Japan are IBM and Apple (with NEC fading fast). Microsoft is the world's operating system.

This dominance of English, by the way, doesn't necessarily mean perma-nent dominance by Americans. Yourdon's *Decline and Fall of the American Programmer* describes the upsurge of foreign software houses, notably those located in India, and points out that programmers there also speak English and can produce excellent programs for a tiny fraction of what American pro-grammers charge. English-speaking software can flow back into the United States as fast as it flows out. But in either direction, it is English that matters.

Communication technology is another field in which the English lan-guage dominates. We have already discussed the growing use of computer net-works and the phone links between buildings and between nations. The signal that travels down that wire is essentially a long series of binary shifts—high or low voltage, high or low frequency—the communication equivalent to 1s and 0s, the binary code of computers. We take the letter A, agree that it is 01000001 in binary code, and send it down the wire as low frequency, high, low, low, low, low, low, high (or any other recognizable series of shifts from one state to another), and as long as the computer at the other end of the line is using the same code book, it recognizes that it was just sent an A.

There are a number of these codes. One of the major codes is ASCII (American Standard Code for Information Interchange). Notice the first word. Americans wrote it and use it extensively, and have exported it widely. It is a very efficient code, especially if you are transmitting the letters Americans know best—English. Extended ASCII even contains codes for special letters in Spanish, French, or German. But there it stops. Neither it, nor any of the other major international codes, can encode Kanji of Japan, Hangul of Korea, or the characters of China, the Bushman of the Kalahari, or the hieroglyphics of Egypt, or . . . There is a very extensive list of languages and alphabets unknown to international codes. So if you are sitting at a computer in Kyoto and want to sent a message to a branch in Indiana, the language you use is . . .

While English is the native language of the Internet and so appears naturally, sometimes it is enforced. Discussion groups all have a moderator who answers questions about signing on and off the list. Sometimes moderators also screen messages; usually they stay out of the way. Before coming to Africa I joined a group discussing international development. It was a good group and I learned a lot from the posted messages. But one day a member from Argentina posted a message in Spanish. For the first time, the moderator jumped in and wrote a message condemning the Argentinean and reminding the rest of us that the official language of the group was English. For academics and government officials around the world, the message is you can get amazing resources over the Internet, but you have to ask for them in English.

Lack of Information Systems

The developing world has far more advanced computer systems than people normally think. The fact that some of these countries, notably India, are now *exporting* computer software shows the level of expertise that has developed. Basic business systems and normal government systems are routinely available. Partly this is because businesses and governments have the same needs around the world. Partly this is because developing countries may actually have *greater* information needs in some circumstances. As one systems developer put it in describing a government system in Sudan, "The Sudan is host to a bewildering array of international aid agencies, multilateral and unilateral donors, lenders and operative agencies. In the early to mid-1980s, over 200 foreign or international organizations were involved in refugee relief and famine assistance efforts alone. Without major [computer] reforms, the Sudanese government lacked the capacity to monitor the activities of these various actors" (CALHOUN AND DELARGY 1992:26–27).

He goes on to say, "It does not exaggerate . . . to say that the cost [of poor computer systems] may include an element of national sovereignty." Keeping track of all the foreigners in one's country performing quasi-governmental activities is certainly an unusual use for an information system, but surely an important one. More recently, human rights organizations were in Ethiopia to help build new computer systems. They entered over one hundred thousand computer files in an attempt both to help identify the estimated fifty thousand killed during the seventeen years of Colonel Mengista Haile Mariavis's communist rule and to help provide evidence to identify their executioners. Six miles away, forensic teams began exhuming bodies from mass graves.

While information systems are both present and necessary in the developing world, there are a number of barriers preventing them from being as useful or as common as they are in the developed world. One problem is weather. The equator is hot. At temperatures of 130°F computers overheat and shut down. Newer microcomputers are better in hot climates than older mainframe computers, but they are still vulnerable to overheating. The response, air conditioning, solves the problem, but it restricts computers to air-conditioned areas, often centralizing their use—the very opposite of the international trend toward distributed systems.

Electricity may be a bigger problem, with wide voltage spikes and brownouts that raise havoc with equipment. Surge suppressors and uninterruptable power supplies (UPS) are a standard requirement but, of course, push up the cost of computer systems.

Lack of local service may be the biggest problem. The whole system may be useless for want of an RS-232 adapter. Networks can be unused because no one can find an extension cord. The rural areas of Russia were so notorious for being short of the kind of things we could find in any U.S. hardware store that when IBM won a contract to begin installing computer systems in rural Russian schools, it set up a packaging system in Scotland that put the school's entire computer network on one pallet and then shrink-wrapped the whole thing. On the pallet would not only go the usual computers but also printer paper, computer disks, and lengthy extension cords that could link the computers to the school's one electrical outlet that might actually work.

In Africa the lack of local repair facilities is actually made worse by donors who bring whatever computers consultants are comfortable with (usually a brand from the donor nation), even though they may be totally incompatible with already-existing equipment and totally foreign to any local computer store. They don't have parts for them, they don't have service manuals for them, they are just more computers that have to be boxed up and shipped halfway around the world for expensive repairs. One survey in Tanzania found only 55 percent of computers brought in by donor groups could be serviced locally (GRANT LEWIS 1992).

Shortage of qualified personnel is another serious problem. Information technology is a new and rapidly developing field, so information-system managers worldwide are struggling to staff their operations, but problems in the developing world seem especially acute. Partly this is a consequence of the general weakness of educational systems, partly this is a result of the odd orientation of African universities toward liberal arts and away from technical subjects (a situation that has drawn increased attention from the World Bank). But the results can be startling. In 1993 the University of Namibia graduated one computer science major! In 1994 it graduated three. The University of Uganda only began a computer science program in 1992. For much of Africa, a cadre of well-trained computer professionals simply isn't being created.

The lack of educational programs in computing unfortunately results in part from government attitudes toward computers. Rather than seeing computers as a growth industry or as a means of catching up with the rest of the world, African governments tend to see computers as a drain on their treasuries and as a threat of employment. Fear of the computer is not universal. One of the more passionate statements ever made in favor of computer information systems came from Mathiea Ekra, minister of state and president of the National Commission on Informatics of the Ivory Coast. He said in 1983, "Those who have recently achieved their independence, must take care this time not to miss the last train of the twentieth century. . . . Ivory Coast now has the possibility to enter fully into the information era and to recover from its economic crisis (JULES-ROSETTE 1992:122). Unfortunately, the economic crisis of the Ivory Coast seems to be getting worse, and the current government seems interested in derailing the last train of the twentieth century.

How Poor Are They?

Money isn't everything. The next two chapters make it clear that even rich people can assert their right to be ignorant. But for people of good will with normal human curiosity, money matters. For virtually every problem discussed in this chapter, part of the solution is money. Need to see the world? Buy a car or a plane ticket. Trouble getting communications? Launch a satellite or lay a phone line. Problems with language? Hire a translator. Need a computer system? Buy one. It's a little too flip to say money would solve everything, but people driving around with a cellular phone in their hand and a gold card in their wallet may not even know there is a problem.

For much of the world's population, the problem is not only serious, it is getting worse. A few short pages on world poverty is hardly fair to the subject, but may at least indicate why most of the world's people won't be part of anything we would recognize as an information age.

Let's begin with specifics. South Africa has the most healthy economy on the continent. Yet a short drive from Johannesburg, two-thirds of adult blacks in Northern Transvaal receive no cash income (DAVIE 1994). In nearby Lebowa, 74 percent of blacks receive no cash income. Those who are lucky enough to find work aren't much better off. Most jobs are in agriculture, where a month's pay averages R 175 (about fifty dollars). But few will find work. One study concluded there are jobs for less than one-third of the available workers in that region.

How do people with no or little money live? Obviously not very well. Disease is common; about one-third of the children are malnourished, and the average housing density is twenty-one people per dwelling. (No, that's not a misprint; the tiny shacks outside of Johannesburg house an average of twenty-one people each.) All this would be tragic if we were describing the poorest people in the world. But we aren't. These are citizens of the wealthiest country in Africa. Elsewhere in the continent it gets worse—much worse.

How much worse? We can't really tell. In a 1992 survey completed by the World Bank, Mozambique appeared to be the poorest country in the world, with a per capita gross domestic product of sixty dollars. But at least Mozambique could report. Angola's government couldn't fill out the World Bank survey because the government controls only a small portion of the country. Much of Angola has been locked in civil war for twenty years. In places under extended siege, 1993 saw the first reports of people eating neighbors killed in the shelling. Elsewhere in Africa intertribal wars left genocide as a bigger problem than poverty. We do know that in the African countries that still have a functioning national government, and can provide statistics, things are so bad that eight out of ten of the world's poorest countries are African.

In sum, we have one large section of the world where every new year means a declining standard of living—more desert, more AIDS, more babies, fewer jobs. There is no reason to expect African economies to improve and every reason to predict further decline.

Conclusion

It is no enduring criticism of the new age to say that not everyone will share in the benefits. The move to agriculture hurt—and continues to hurt—traditional hunters and gatherers. The industrial age had its own set of horrors. It only takes a little Dickens to see the costs of that revolution. It would be naïve to assume information and its benefits would be equally available to everyone.

On the other hand, it seems particularly callous to ignore those being left behind. The poor, cut off by geography or language, are powerless and they know it. They understand that living away from information does not free them from the stresses of the modern age—it leaves them to be victimized. The "noble savages" of this century are in reality poor, drunk, and isolated. Others will determine their fate. Others may or may not even bother to tell them what future has been selected for them. The poor won't even know the discussion is occurring, much less have a chance to join in.

If information is the last train of the twentieth century, we are leaving many people and whole regions of the world behind. Those left behind know there is nothing in their condition to celebrate. Ecotourists may join them in the desert for a few days, but the tourists know enough to get back on the plane when the rains come.

Chapter 7   Tyranny

*Everyone has the right to freedom of opinion and
expression; this right includes freedom to hold opinions
without interference and to seek, receive and impart
information and ideas through any media and regardless
of frontiers.* —UNIVERSAL DECLARATION
OF HUMAN RIGHTS, *Article 19*

IN JANUARY 1994 the Paul Hamlyn Foundation offered to help the children
of one of the poorer neighborhoods in London see Shakespeare. They would
pay most of the ticket price so the children of Kingsnead Primary School
could see *Romeo and Juliet* performed at one of the finer theaters of London. The
head of Kingsnead, Jane Brown, refused. She did not want the children of her
school seeing Shakespeare, because Romeo and Juliet was "blatantly heterosexual"
(O'NEILL ET AL. 1994:7).

Denying English children the opportunity to see Shakespeare because his
plays are "blatantly heterosexual" created quite a stir. But her colleagues
immediately backed her up, arguing that by keeping the children away from
Shakespeare she was trying to "prevent the children being fed a constant diet
of gang fights and killing." According to one friend, "We want them to see that
you can be a boy and gentle. We want to teach them to be kind to each
other." This line of thinking carried the day, and the children were prevented
from seeing the play.

Welcome to information flow in the 1990s. One English teacher on the
losing side said, "To take some abused, narrow-minded, Californian concept
of political correctness is outrageous." Outrageous it may be, but the decision
stood. And unfortunately, California is not the only place that practices

censorship, nor is political correctness the only justification. This example stands out because it involves a group of English teachers deciding they will bar students from seeing Shakespeare's play because of his heterosexuality. On the plus side, they did not ban Shakespeare's books or burn down the theater. Their friends around the world would not have been so timid.

How bad are worldwide efforts to block information—to stifle, to censor? It is hard to know where to begin. There is clearly no shortage of governments that want to hide the truth, no shortage of people who think their neighbors or their neighbor's children should be kept from some book or play, plenty of teachers who think their job is to hide information, and certainly no shortage of individuals who will do anything to keep unwanted information from their doorstep—up to and including literally shooting the messenger. If this truly is the information age, we seem to be surrounded by people who are not at all happy to have been born to this time and place.

For those who wish to block information flow, there are three places where they can do it: as it is being collected, as it is being transmitted, and as it is being received. All three attacks work quite well. Sadly, there is no shortage of examples to demonstrate how vulnerable information is.

Killing It at the Source

If you can block information before it has even been gathered, you do not have to worry about how far it will spread or how people will receive it. Demagogues worldwide understand this simple principle and apply it ruthlessly. Consider a few of the many forms this blockage can take.

KILLING REPORTERS

In 1993 seventy-five journalists were killed ("At Least" 1993). The International Federation of Journalists is trying to find out what happened to eighteen more who are missing. Journalism is a dangerous profession. Part of the danger is inherent as reporters struggle to be near the action—near the battlefields and near scenes of civil strife. But they are also singled out as targets. A dead reporter files no stories.

One place where this strategy worked remarkably well was El Salvador. In 1982 the Salvadoran army targeted, ambushed, and killed all four members of a Dutch television crew. "It was a time when the El Salvadorian military was reeling under pressure from the international press, and they wanted to send a message, send a message in a deniable way," according to Douglas Cassel, counsel for the United Nations–sponsored "Truth Commission." They made sure no one missed the message. Ann Nelson, a reporter for the *Los Angeles Times* and

Macleans, recalls that the army invited all the other journalists in the country to visit the ambush site to "view the bodies in a degraded and mutilated state, and stripped of their clothing" (FITZGERALD 1993:18).

The reaction of international reporters was predictable—they either left the country or stayed out of risky areas. A media study done by the Committee to Protect Journalists found that within a few months of the ambush, the percentage of television reports from El Salvador devoted to telling the rebel side of the story dropped from 30 to 5 percent (FITZGERALD 1993:18). Dead reporters file no stories—neither do scared reporters.

Unfortunately, governments are not the only threats reporters face. Opposition political movements can be even more deadly. In 1993 four foreign journalists were lured to a meeting with opposition leaders in Somalia, and then hacked to death by an angry mob. A year later an Italian TV journalist and her cameraman were gunned down outside the Italian embassy in the same city. In Angola, Unita, a movement engaged in a civil war that has lasted two decades, is accused of murdering journalists perceived to be critical of the movement.

The most dangerous foe of journalists is building in Algeria as Islamic militants target both foreign and local reporters. By March 1994 they had already killed twelve journalists, including two when they burst into the offices of a weekly newspaper in Algiers, killing two employees and wounding three. The open targeting of journalists and murderous attacks on newsrooms represents a new level of danger. As the death toll mounts, it requires ever-increasing levels of bravery to cover the news.

HARASSING REPORTERS

But you don't have to kill reporters to stop them from getting a story. There are lots of ways of hiding the information they need. Harassing laws are one means. When reporters with Zimbabwe's *Daily Gazette* pointed out in 1993 that companies owned by the ruling party were evading taxes, the government cited the Official Secrets Act and dragged one reporter in for four days of interrogation. In Gambia three government ministers brought a libel suit against an independent weekly, the *Torch*. The ministers lost, but the suit cost so much in legal fees, the paper was forced to close. In Zambia police detained a *Weekly Post* photographer after he photographed police beating a suspect, and put another reporter in jail overnight for "loitering." In Uganda three Ugandan reporters were jailed for defamation in 1990 after they asked probing questions of the visiting Zambian president at a press conference. In 1994 four journalists from the Ivory Coast were sentenced to a year in jail for reporting the government had asked France for $17 million to help cover the lavish funeral of the former president. In the same year China sentenced a reporter to twelve years in prison for "stealing state secrets." His real offense was to publish business news—planned interest rate changes and gold sales—before the government made its official announcements.

Foreign press can be banned as Prohibited Immigrants and kept out of the country. Chris Munnion describes one *Los Angeles Times* reporter who received deportation and PI orders from thirteen African countries. Munnion himself was banned from six. There have been a series of bans in Serbia. On 14 April 1994, all U.S. journalists were ordered out of territory occupied in Bosnia by Serbian-allied troops. Unhappy that UN troops were beginning, finally, to oppose the Serbian onslaught in Bosnia, the Bosnian Serb Information Ministry responded by sending the Americans packing. Not to be outdone, the UN followed up in May with an order banning journalists from an area of Croatia. "We have a gentleman's agreement with the Serbs," said one UN officer. "We promise not to show things that might embarrass them to journalists" ("UN" 1994:17). Among the sights the UN did not want reporters to see, Bosnian Croat tanks destroying the sixteenth-century Stari Most Bridge at Mostar.

Where laws and bans cannot be used to battle reporters, governments can threaten. In 1994 the Zambian defense minister told the local *Weekly Post* it must stop its "careless writing." "Don't excite the army," he told them. "One day they will get annoyed and you will perish." This threat was taken very seriously, coming after the newspaper's offices had been ransacked by youths loyal to the ruling party and a van delivering copies of the newspaper had been stolen and the papers burned. In South Africa, police in the former bantustan of Bophuthatswana stopped a television crew from Reuters who were covering a riot there in 1994, pulled them out of their car, pulled off their bulletproof vests, and beat them with fists and clubs. The police got what they wanted—the crew pulled out of the area and stopped covering the riot.

BLOCKING PUBLISHERS

Journalists work for news organizations—newspapers, radio stations, television stations. If those organizations can be crushed, or prevented from ever starting, then reporters have no employers, no support, no outlet for their stories. There is no news without a publisher. And it turns out blocking publishers is terribly easy.

Here again, the law can be a very effective tool of repression. In Tanzania the government used the Newspaper Act of 1976 to close the weekly newspaper *Baraza* in 1994. Claiming the editor was not qualified, the newspaper published "malicious news," and the paper didn't inform the government when it changed its printing arrangements, the paper was shut down for a month.

In other countries, independent media organizations are never allowed to open. Zimbabwe's President Mugabe has blocked independent radio and TV stations, saying a "station running parallel to our own is a ticklish point because you don't know what propaganda they are going to broadcast." He went on to say that "some things will take time to come" to Africa. New legislation allowing independent broadcasting has been passed in Zambia, Tanzania, and Namibia, but the government has total control over which organizations and individuals will get licenses. It can also control what can be broadcast "in the public interest." This was recently made clear by Tanzania's chairperson of the National Broadcasting Commission, who said, "Since information is power, we want this business (broadcasting) to be conducted by serious people who know the history, culture and development aspirations of our country." So far no licenses have been granted and independent broadcasting remains uncommon in much of Africa.

Not all problems come from governments or the UN. In India, local journalists brought a court case in early 1994 to keep foreign newspapers from setting up in their country. This action stopped both the *Financial Times* and the *International Herald Tribune* from setting up offices in the country. The local newsmen charged foreign newspapers would "threaten the country's sovereignty and corrupt the local culture" ("Foreign" 1994:12). That newsmen would use the government against fellow newsmen indicates how vulnerable press freedoms can be—not even all news people respect them.

Where laws aren't handy to keep news organizations out of a country, economics can be used as a weapon. In Mozambique, Mediacoop, an independent cooperative of journalists, attempted to launch the country's first independent newspaper. The government responded by slapping a 50 percent import levy on the equipment they needed. In Malawi, Life President Hastings Banda was even more clever. The only offset press in the country was owned by a group aligned with the president. Papers wishing to use the press had to pay excessive fees in advance for printing costs. To add insult to injury, the government then demanded a 20 percent surtax on all advertisements. Newsprint is also in short supply in the country and cannot be purchased outside the country for lack of foreign exchange.

USING THE GOVERNMENT PRESS

One group that never seems short of money is government news organizations. But they seem short on news. Walvis Bay is one of the better deep-water ports on the Atlantic side of Africa. Originally claimed by the British, it remained under British control even after the land around it was claimed by the Germans and named German Southwest Africa. It continued to be an administrative island for more than a century. Finally, in early 1994 the South African government turned it over to Namibia. This was cause for a huge "reunification" celebration in Namibia. Dignitaries from around Africa descended on Walvis Bay for the exchange of power. Namibian government press took up residence in the city to broadcast events live over a forty-eight-hour period.

Everything was going according to plan until the day before the celebration, when riots broke out. Stores were looted, guards were beaten, government property was destroyed. The *Namibian*, a local independent, gave most of its front page to the riot, describing what had happened in Walvis Bay. Meanwhile, on government radio and TV, there was nothing. Other local papers gave coverage to the riots and to the lack of government news, claiming a "cover-up." David Lush, a local journalist who has worked for both the government and independent press, had a different view: "It's a bureaucracy. All the people in Walvis Bay have been sent there to cover the celebration. So if there is a riot down the road, it may not occur to them to cover it."

The question of whether government news people are corrupt or just plain incompetent is frequently debated, but the result is the same—news tends to disappear into the bureaucracy and either reappear sugar coated or disappear for ever. Those who claim cover-ups cite Swaziland as a good example. In the 1970s riots occurred right outside the government broadcast offices. Journalists could have looked out their windows and written their stories. But when the evening news came on there was no mention of the riots. Instead, the radio news led with a story about riots in Tanzania! History repeated itself when the state-run media seemed totally unaware of a national strike in 1994. Ironically, one of the strike's demands was for greater press freedom. In Zimbabwe a reporter for a state-run newspaper was very direct about censorship and about not criticizing the ruling party: "That would be biting the hand that feeds you and I wouldn't do that."

The claim for bureaucratic incompetence is made by Bapasi Mphusu, chief press officer for the Botswana Government Press Agency. In complaining about the quality of staff hired for him by the Botswana Civil Service, he said, "Being in government media it is very often you run across someone who calls himself a reporter but has no talent. He was just interested in getting a job. Once hired, it is impossible to fire him." That view of government journalists as government bureaucrats was demonstrated recently during the change of government in Namibia. During the 1989 elections, Sam Nujoma, the candidate from the South West African People's Organization (SWAPO), was invisible on TV. Nujoma was a revolutionary who could not get on the air. The day after the election Nujoma was suddenly all over TV and radio. Since he had won, he was now the new boss of the government press, and they knew what their job was: to give their boss—whoever that might currently be—plenty of air time. The ethics of journalism never entered the picture.

The use of government media to hide news and create news may have reached its most outrageous during Mao Tse-tung's rule in China. In 1958 Mao organized his "Great Leap Forward," which involved the creation of "people's communes." Local leaders made extravagant claims about being able to produce ten times as much food under the new system, often backing up their claims with "Potemkin fields," created by moving the harvest from several fields to one field. So much deception was going on at so many levels that Jung Chang reports, "Those who failed to match other people's fantastic claims began to doubt themselves. Under a dictatorship like Mao's, where information was withheld and fabricated, it was very difficult for ordinary people to have confidence in their own experience or knowledge." The state media got in on the act, with *People's Daily* starting one article with "How do we cope with the problem of producing too much food? Mao himself said, 'The farmers here can just eat and eat. You can eat five meals a day!' " (CHANG 1991:299). But of course nobody ate five meals a day. Communal agriculture failed just as badly in China as anywhere else. The harvest was terrible in 1958, famine struck, and millions starved to death across China.

Government media operated at a much more sophisticated level under South Africa's apartheid regime. "Divide and conquer" being a basic tenet of apartheid, black South Africans were divided into artificial tribal homelands or bantustans with separate tribal authorities. To help create an identity for these separate islands, the South African Broadcasting Corporation took to broadcasting in seven different black languages, each tied to a particular bantustan. Besides reinforcing the existence of mutually indistinguishable black languages, radio further divided blacks by focusing news on the local level. Stations would concentrate on the events and people of the local bantustan to the exclusion of news about the rest of the country or the rest of the world. Surveys indicated the strategy was quite effective. Opinion leaders in each bantustan liked the local coverage. The hiding of news that might have helped black South Africans make common cause was very effectively done.

KILLING NOVELISTS

Journalists aren't the only people who risk their lives gathering information that might embarrass the local president-for-life. Novelists can also be attacked for daring to think and write words that challenge the local orthodoxy. The most stunning example of this, of course, is the case of Salman Rushdie.

On 14 February 1989 Ayatollah Rubullah Khomeini issued a *fatwa*, or religious decree, against Rushdie for Rushdie's book *The Satanic Verses*. The death sentence was also extended to anyone associated with publishing the novel. "We consider Rushdie as a man who tried to destroy Islam, to downgrade Islam and to downgrade the sentiments of more than one billion Muslims," said Jovad Larijani, advisor to Iran's president, Hasbeni Rafsanjani. "So we said only what Islam expects for that man: that he does not deserve to exist" ("Rushdie" 1994:11). While Rushdie, a British citizen born in India, has been able to escape assassination with the help of Scotland Yard's Special Branch, several translators and publishers of his book have been killed or wounded. Iran's Khordad 15 Foundation, a religious charity, has offered a $2 million bounty to anyone who kills Rushdie.

As ugly as this campaign against Rushdie is, it is apparently drawing copy-cat "death sentences." In Bangladesh, Maulan Ayiyul Haque, a local religious leader, has called for the execution of Taslima Nasreen, the author of fifteen books. Haque is upset with Nasreen because "she says that if a man can have four wives, a woman should have the right to four husbands. Even within marriage, she says a woman should have the right to other men. This is against the Koran and Allah, it is blasphemy" (RETTLE 1993:26). Crowds of up to ten thousand marched down the streets of Dhaka demanding that she be hanged. The prime minister of Bangladesh, Begum Khaleda Zia, originally gave her police protection, but he also banned her book, *Lajja*, as detrimental to communal harmony. By July 1994 she had been hauled into court for "making inflammatory statements" while one hundred thousand demonstrators gathered outside the Parliament and screamed for her death. Released on $250 bail, she went into hiding for several weeks before flying to Sweden, where she was granted asylum. Back in Bangladesh the leader of one of the Islamic parties said, "She must not be allowed to return. This will only trigger a new wave of violent protests" (MCIVOR AND MAHMOOD 1994:13). Oddly enough, literary critics seem to agree she is not a very good writer. It is hard to know if she would have much readership if it were not for the controversy that surrounds her. It would appear efforts to silence her are having the opposite effect.

KILLING TOURISTS

Threats against authors are one way to block and devalue uncomfortable ideas. But the prominent are not the only ones at risk from those who want to keep information at bay. In both Egypt and Algeria, foreign tourists have been singled out as targets. At first they would seem an unlikely target. Tourists may seem annoying, or silly looking, but they are hardly dangerous. Yet besides their ability to generate international headlines, tourists are players in the movement of information. They bring with them faces and handshakes and simple words that may contradict the image of foreigners some demagogue is trying to create. And they take away with them images and explanations of local phenomena that may not be flattering to the powerful or would-be powerful.

So they become targets. In Algeria a Russian woman was killed as she shopped. In Egypt tourist boats traveling the Nile are fired on with automatic weapons. Both campaigns have been hugely successful: foreign people, and foreign ideas, are rapidly leaving both countries. More than four thousand foreigners left Algeria in November 1993, when the antiforeign campaign began. In Egypt, tourist visits in 1994 were down one-third to one-half.

There seems no limit to the ways information can be blocked or the forces that want to do the blocking. Those forces have power. And time after time they are successful. On those occasions when information does get past them, they unfortunately have a second chance. For if information cannot be blocked at the source, experience shows us it can be blocked in transit.

Blocking the Information Highway

The year 1976 was a pivotal one in South Africa. It was the year television first appeared in that country. Why television was introduced a quarter of a century after it had arrived in the rest of the industrialized world tells a great deal about the vulnerability of high-technology information systems and even more about the seemingly endless source of cunning available to totalitarian states.

In 1975 the South African government formed the Meyer Commission to investigate the possibility of instituting a state television broadcast system. State-run radio was under strict controls, but this was a new medium and many were nervous about keeping it under control. There was also the question of the expense. While advertising dollars could foot some of the bill, the state would still face substantial costs.

Ultimately, the Meyer Commission came down in support of TV. But their support was not a victory for civil libertarians. Far from it. In arguing their case for broadcast TV, the commission reminded their government that "the simple erection of a small receiving dish in a back yard would enable television-starved South Africans to tune into satellite-transmissions whether or not South Africa was formally locked into the world television grid" (TOMASELLI ET AL. 1989:153). The commission went on to argue that the best way to beat back the threat of these foreign materials was to introduce local TV—TV the state could control. The state followed the commission's cynical advice and introduced TV the following year.

As is demonstrated by states and political movements around the world, there seems to be no technological development or instance of personal bravery that can long keep information free. There are simply far too many means of control. Here are just a few.

BREAKING THE DISHES

As South Africa discovered in the mid-1970s, satellite dishes enable tele-vision viewers to pick up a signal from outside the bounds of the state. No self-respecting police state is going to allow that, and few have been as subtle as South Africa. In 1993 China responded to the presence of half a million dishes across the country by issuing Proclamation 129, banning the manufacture of dishes. Dish owners were picking up a signal from Hong Kong's Star TV that brought them foreign TV, BBC news, and music videos. For the moment, Chinese dish owners have at least been allowed to keep their dishes.

TV viewers in the Middle East haven't been so lucky. In early 1994 Saudi Arabia banned all satellite dishes in the country, even though there were already one hundred thousand in use. They imposed a fine of $133,000 for any-one who dared to use a dish. The Emirate of Qatar had already banned dishes in 1993. In Iran, police seized fifty-four dishes, even though there is no law specif-ically forbidding them. Throughout the region, satellite dishes are viewed as dan-gerous and immoral. To quote Robert Kennedy, deputy head of the Middle East Broadcasting Center, a satellite network owned by Saudi investors, "It is the responsibility of governments to protect their own national and religious cul-ture from unacceptable television programs" (DICKEY 1994:46).

Having "protected" their citizens from unfiltered access to CNN News, Israeli sitcoms, and Turkish soft porn, the governments of the Middle East followed the lead of their colleagues in South Africa. Qatar set up a cable system to carry stations of its choosing. When foreign stations broadcast unwanted sex or pol-itics, government censors simply shut down the signal—instant protection for the people of Qatar. Saudi Arabia is bigger than Qatar and so cannot use a cable system, but it can achieve the same level of control throughout its microwave system. No matter how the signal is propagated, the important point is to get a government clamp on the signal.

If governments are unwilling to "protect" their citizens from foreign infor-mation, sometimes local vigilantes are willing to take on the job. In Algeria fundamentalists have decided that satellite dishes are "diabolic" because they allow in European news and entertainment. Such dishes are attacked, even in the capital city.

CLAMPING THE WIRE

One of the hopes of e-mail advocates is that new computer networks will give citizens a way around totalitarian governments. It is certainly true that every new channel is a new opportunity and that the complex webs of computer net-works pose a particular challenge to government control. But governments can rise to the challenge. Take China. The country is in the midst of developing a large academic computing network to link more than one thousand educational institutions by the end of the century. There is only one twist to this network. Unlike American networks, with multiple electronic routes from campus to campus, all traffic in this Chinese network will have to run through Beijing's Quinghua University. Poon Kee Ho, director of the computer center at the City University of Hong Kong, thinks he knows why. The Chinese academic network will be technically unsound, but with a choke point at Quinghua University government officials "can do what they want to monitor it or shut it down" (HERTLING 1995).

The Chinese government draws another special benefit from their computer network. With links to the institutions of the West, Chinese academics will be able to keep up with Western research without ever leaving the country. This is especially important since, as Education Minister Zhu Kiaxuan complained in March of 1995, two-thirds of the two hundred thousand Chinese students who have gone overseas to study in the last fifteen years never went back to China. With government controlled e-mail available as an alternative information resource, it will be easier to say no to student travel, easier to keep the Chinese in China, where the government can keep a closer watch on them. In effect, the Chinese government has been able to use e-mail as one more lock on the prison gates.

DEATH TO HOLLYWOOD

Not all censorship involves high technology. Some of it is pretty old-fashioned, like blocking the screening of objectionable movies. For instance, one of the first actions of Iran's revolutionary government in 1979 was to ban the sale of all video cassettes. This ban was particularly ironic, since much of the proselytizing done by Ayatollah Khomeini was via audio and video cassettes he produced during exile in France and smuggled to his supporters in Iran. Having seen the power of their approach, his supporters very quickly closed this information gateway after they took power—they didn't want any potential rivals to use the same approach.

Most governments are more selective in the films they ban. A recent favorite for attack was *Schindler's List,* which contained detailed depictions of Nazi concentration camps. In Lebanon, advertisements for the film were seized and the government warned distributors it would confiscate all prints. Jordan similarly banned the movie. Malaysia explained its banning of the film as a kind of protection for Germans. Censors claimed Jews were portrayed as "south hearted" and "intelligent," while Germans were made to look "brutal" ("Schindler's Draws" 1994:16). What kind of description they expected of gas-chamber operators is unclear. Meanwhile, German reviewers seemed less sensitive to their image. One hundred thousand Germans viewed the film the first four days it was shown in their country. This was far more than the thirty-five thousand who saw *Dances with Wolves*, another Hollywood hit ("Schindler's Draws" 1994:16).

In Korea *Falling Down* drew the ire of activists who threatened boycotts and picket lines if the movie was shown in the country. At one point in the movie the mentally deranged leading character attacks a Korean grocer in Los Angeles, making comments about the grocer's greed and destroying much of the store. The Korean national news agency weighed in on the side of the boycotters, claiming, "A problem exists not only with the movie, but with an atmosphere that allows such movies to be made." Apparently criticism of Koreans, even by a deranged character, is unacceptable to many Koreans.

For pure chutzpah the censors of China have to get credit. When the BBC tried to broadcast a film on Mao Tse-tung that contained unflattering material, the Chinese embassy in London attempted not just to prevent a broadcast in China but also to prevent a broadcast in the United Kingdom. The film *Chairman Mao: The Last Emperor* quotes Mao's personal physician, Li Zhisui, as saying, "Women felt honored to have sex with Mao. It was a glorious and natural thing to do because Mao was God and the Supreme Ruler." The Chinese government objected, and as part of its pressure to stop broadcast told the BBC's Beijing corespondent, James Miles, that he would be held personally responsible if the film was broadcast. The BBC went ahead with the broadcast, but China was able to exact at least some revenge. Hong Kong–based STAR TV announced it would stop carrying the BBC in China in an apparent attempt to "mollify Beijing."

CUT AND WASTE

During the 1970s foreigners living in South Korea always knew when *Newsweek* had printed an article critical of Korea—their copy of *Newsweek* would arrive with a hole where the article had been. Readers could then use their imaginations to determine how serious the criticism had been, based on the size of the hole and its location—near the front of the magazine or buried in the back pages. "Cut and waste" censorship of magazines and newspapers continues around the world.

Malawi's censors didn't like an October 1993 *Weekly Mail and Guardian* article about the murder of four Malawi politicians. Copies sold on Malawi newsstands featured a hole where the story had been. During the same month Malawi censors also cut out a story in *New Africa* magazine. In hundreds of instances cutting out single stories was too difficult or time-consuming and Malawi's censorship board simply banned the publications.

FREE SPEECH FOR SOME

1994 saw two talks at Howard University. One was the presentation of Khalid Abdul Muhammad, who said, "I am going to be a pit bull. That is the way I am going to be against the Jews. I am going to bite the tail of the honkies." The second was the scheduled presentation of David Davis, a Jew, whose talk was canceled because college administrators "feared anti-Semitic demonstrations on the campus" ("Politically" 1994:20). There often seems to be a strange inconsistency about who is allowed to speak on college campuses. Sometimes the inconsistencies result from administrators who seem to favor one side or another, but often it comes from students who seem to believe shouting down speakers demonstrates the fervor of their support for the other side.

This hostility to free speech on American campuses can be traced to several incidents. Some argue that it began at Yale in 1963 when Kingman Brewster, then provost and later president, pressured the Yale Political Union to withdraw a speaking invitation to George Wallace. By the 1970s it was William Shockley who was not welcome to present his racial beliefs. At one point Roy Innes of the Congress on Racial Equality (CORE) was anxious to debate Shockley, but campus after campus backed away from letting either man talk. Nat Hentoff, who chronicles censorship in the United States, refers to this as the "Schweitzer syndrome": liberal whites, feeling they know what is best for black people, won't let African Americans stand up for themselves.

Once certain kinds of speech can't be heard on campus, once certain discussions can't be held and certain ideas can't be debated, the campus becomes a hollow place. Reports Deanna Cunningham, a reporter for the student newspaper at San Francisco State, "People are afraid, period. No matter if they have conservative or liberal views. In many interviews, students talked about being afraid to talk about concerns or ideas that could not remotely be regarded as blatantly racist or sexist. Rather, they are afraid to say anything about a controversial topic that they feel could be misconstrued" (HENTOFF 1992:154).

Sometimes the fear is warranted. At the University of Michigan a black student attending a course orientation session said he heard minorities were not treated fairly in the course. The course instructor, also black, heard what the student said and filed a complaint against the student under the university's speech code. The student was required to attend a counseling session and write a three-page letter of apology (HENTOFF 1992). The student came away with a great introduction to the state of free speech at some American universities.

BOOK BANNING

Of the many crimes committed by the Nazis, the one that gave an early sense of the madness of their movement was book burning. That books could be pulled out of libraries and universities, tossed onto piles, and publicly lit before cheering masses was a wholly new face to lunacy. It is unlikely many remembered the words of Henrich Heine, who said in 1820, "Where books are burnt, human beings will be burnt in the end" (BURRESS 1989). One of the horrors of this century is that Heine was exactly right.

People wearing swastikas are back out on the streets. The year 1994 began with dozens of skinheads ransacking an alternative bookstore in Nottingham, England. Wearing swastikas and heavy boots, the men smashed office equipment and tore up books on gay rights. Two shop clerks and a customer on crutches were beaten. In the United States, book burning goes on. In 1974, *Slaughterhouse Five* was burned in North Dakota. *Of Mice and Men* was burned in Pennsylvania in 1977. *The Living Bible* was burned in North Carolina in 1981.

Where books aren't burned in the United States, they are banned, and the number being banned is growing. One survey of schools in Wisconsin showed that 20 percent of school districts had experienced some censorship pressures in 1966. By 1982 the number was 34 percent. A national watchdog group found 43 items had been censored in 1966. In 1975 it was 563.

Why does a nation that has free speech in its First Amendment become such a nation of censors? One cause is an effort to protect children from words or ideas that may harm them. This is the reason behind the frequent banning of *The Adventures of Huckleberry Finn*. The word *nigger* bothers many African American students, who feel the descriptions in the book are disparaging. Some African American students also report increased hazing from white classmates after they have read the book. Religious parents are often concerned by vulgar language in books. Education experts respond that *Huckleberry Finn* can be a boost to the self-esteem of African American students if the book is well taught by a teacher who comes to the assignment fully prepared. And parents concerned about vulgar language should have the right to request an alternative assignment for their children without imposing their concerns on all the kids in a school. But in the majority of cases, censorship prevails over alternatives: 53.8 percent of the time a book is removed from classroom use, is pulled from the library, or is taken from a recommended reading list.

Then there is politics—books pulled not to protect kids from words but to protect a view of America or the world. In 1993 Ginger Gordon and Martha Cooper teamed up to create a book about Kirsy Rodriguez called *My Two Worlds*. It shows Kirsy as she lives in both New York City and the Dominican Republic. It seemed to be a book kids liked and that teachers could use. In fact, Gordon's school district had a workshop scheduled to introduce the book to teachers. Then a group called the Dominican Heritage Committee appeared. They didn't like the book. It "didn't represent Puerto Plata in the most favorable light"

(QUINDLEN 1994:4). The book's sin was that it showed kids working—carrying water and wood. The island looked poor. The committee didn't want kids in New York to see that, so they pressured the school district and the teachers' workshop was canceled.

Whether the root cause is sensitivity or politics, books are being censored in schools all over America. It doesn't matter much whether the objectors are censors of the Left or censors of the Right. Fifty-three percent of the time they win. What is the cost to kids? The books being kept from American children are some of the best ever written. Who can think of a greater irony than the banning of *1984*? Or the censoring of *One Day in the Life of Ivan Denisovich*? What are groups thinking when they try to keep children from learning about the evils of totalitarianism? What are they protecting?

One last incident of book banning before we move on. One more irony. If you were asked to name a group responsible for one of the biggest efforts to ban books in world history, the American Library Association would be the last group to come to mind. Unfortunately, they are responsible for one of the more twisted efforts to keep books out of the hands of kids.

The year is 1987. Over the years a number of American cities have passed resolutions that they will do no business with companies that do business with South Africa. Companies that comply include Simon and Schuster, with its subsidiaries Prentice-Hall, McGraw-Hill, and Macmillan-Scribner's. Book distributor Baker and Taylor also agrees. Companies that go along have good reason to agree: "Public libraries that passed anti–South Africa ordinances had threatened to seek another supplier if Baker and Taylor's parent company continued to do business with South Africa. . . . These included the Chicago public library system, which accounts for $1.8 million of business annually; the Los Angeles Public Library, $225,000; and the San Francisco Public Library, $350,000" (HENTOFF 1992:76).

What were the consequences of the American book ban? As we have previously noted, the apartheid government of South Africa was ingenious in its methods of keeping foreign ideas out of the country. It must have been astonished by its good fortune when U.S. libraries decided to help protect South Africa from outside information. Included in the American ban was medical information. Said one doctor at a primarily black hospital, "Some 80 percent of our patients are black and we serve doctors of all races, so we find it difficult to comprehend why the latest treatment should be denied patients in integrated hospitals wards—in the name of fighting apartheid" (HENTOFF 1992:87).

Schools were also affected: "With the government spending five times more on education for whites than blacks, the book boycott weakens the meager alternative resources for blacks." It should also be noted that the African

National Congress, the group the anti-apartheid groups were trying to help, never asked for a book boycott. While it supported other boycotts, it opposed efforts to block the "inflow of progressive cultural products and ideas." American book banners pursued their ban anyway.

Since public libraries were at the heart of the boycott process, two members of the American Library Association put together a resolution at the 1987 annual meeting of the ALA in which they called for an end to the boycott. The resolution was presented to a membership meeting attended by five to six hundred. Debate took bizarre turns. One former president of ALA claimed the resolution was "a racist document." Other members supported the resolution and the First Amendment, but when the time for a vote came, those who stood in favor were loudly hissed. Those who opposed ending the ban easily carried the day. The ALA would not be accused of racism, nor of support for the freedom of information.

A shudder should have gone through America that summer day. A generation of Americans fought and died to free Europe from book burners. The sons and daughters of that generation seem to have learned nothing from their parents' example. Not even librarians understand what is at stake.

PEER PRESSURE

It doesn't always take a group of politically minded grownups to prevent kids from reading books. Peers can do it quite well too. Ron Suskind of the *Wall Street Journal* tells the story of Cedric Jennings of Frank W. Ballou Senior High in Washington, D.C. Jennings is a bright kid who wants to study, wants to go to college, wants to work his way out of a tough neighborhood. If he succeeds, it will be over the efforts of his peers, who seem willing to do anything to prevent him from learning and succeeding. One tough stops him in the school hallway and threatens to shoot him. A girl copies his work and threatens to attack him if he objects. At a school academic-awards ceremony all winners are jeered. Jennings knows how good students are treated and hides during the ceremony —afraid to get his one-hundred-dollar prize.

Teachers call this treatment the "crab-bucket syndrome." Anyone who tries to crawl out of the bucket is pulled back down by the others. One of the school toughs explains it this way: "Everyone knows they're trying to be white, get ahead in the white man's world. In a way, that's a little bit of disrespect for the rest of us" (SUSKIND 1994:51). So everyone who tries to learn is harassed. Freedom to learn, freedom to read, freedom to move into a bigger world is denied by local toughs with dead eyes and big guns. Meanwhile, Jennings's access to information is barred more effectively than it would be by an ayatollah. He learns about the world at the risk of his life.

BANNING FRIENDSHIP

It wouldn't seem possible that with all the problems the typical American high school principal has, one would have the time or inclination to insert himself into the dating behavior of his students, but 1994 saw a principal in Wedowee, Alabama, try to ban mixed-race dates at the school's prom. He also allegedly told one student she was a "mistake" because she had a black mother and white father. When word of his actions got out, supporters formed a one-hundred-car motorcade to drive through town waving signs and cheering his actions. The school board voted five to two to suspend the principal, Hulond Humphries, while they investigated charges against him. Ultimately he was reinstated and served as principal until arsonists burned the building to the ground in August. At that point he was transferred to other duties, in part because of his on-camera behavior during press coverage of the fire.

In an era when so much of our information comes from people, one would expect schools would be making every effort to connect children with the people around them, whether those people are community leaders, professionals, employers, or kids. If unwilling to help build those connections, one would at least expect schools to stay out of the way as kids made connections on their own. For one thing, the effort to separate people by skin color has been illegal in the United States for over a century. What authority figures think they can gain by pulling people apart is unclear, but the losses are obvious. The interpersonal trust, awareness, and commitments that could last a lifetime can also be blocked by authority figures who like to see people divided. The "teachable moment" came to the high school in Wedowee, but the lesson provided by the principal there had little to do with life in this century.

ISLANDS OF MADNESS

It is no accident that Jim Jones built his commune in the jungles of South America. If you want to control your followers, take them away from friends, relatives, television, and newspapers. Geography helps to create information deprivation. Once you have them alone, the only voice they hear is yours, the only people they see are your followers. They become dependents—children. If they stay there long enough, they begin to believe. If they stay there long enough, they will drink poison and give it to their own children. Jonestown ended when outsiders arrived in a plane, able to take dissenters out, able to bring reporters in. The bubble around the commune was burst. Jim Jones couldn't maintain his island of madness. So he destroyed it all.

Less-famous islands exist all over the world. The Domestic Abuse Intervention Project of Duluth, Minnesota, identifies isolation as one of the principal techniques used in wife abuse. An abuser controls who his wife "sees and talks to, what she reads, where she goes, limiting her outside involvement." Examples they describe border on the incredible. The man who left each morning with his wife's shoes. The man who moved his family to the country and left his wife alone all day with no car and no phone. In case after case, the idea was to separate the woman from friends, relatives, any kind of support. With no one else to turn to, the woman became totally dependent on her husband— exactly what he wanted to achieve. Alone in the countryside the woman has no way to talk through her situation with a trusted friend. She has no way of learning about social services that might help her and her children. She has no options to weigh, no alternatives to select. What she knows about the world comes through her husband—the ultimate filter. He limits her information and limits her choices. It is all part of gaining and maintaining control.

Self-Censorship

Brave people can gather the news, and with enough effort and ingenuity they can sometimes manage to get it past madmen and dictators. At some point the individual becomes responsible for receiving the news. When the information highway comes to your door, you have to be willing to let it in. Unfortunately, there are groups of people who wish to slam their door on the opportunity. A few of the sadder examples follow.

THIS LAND IS MY LAND

The 1990s will probably be remembered as a decade of madness and cowardice. Madness as every demagogue with fifty followers decided to establish his own state, and cowardice as the world not only watched the genocide that resulted, but dared not even give the dead the honor of an honest history. There was nothing clean about "ethnic cleansing." Yet the labels created by war criminals became the accepted euphemism of politicians. Suddenly no one had the courage to shout "genocide" when they saw it.

For those who rush to create these islands of racial, ethnic, or religious uniformity, the justification can always be invented. A classic case was the Volkstaat of South Africa. Once it became clear that white minority rules couldn't be maintained, one group of whites not only reconciled itself to majority rule but actively campaigned for it. But another group of whites wanted nothing to do with a country where they would not have absolute control. In the area around Johannesburg, often referred to as South Africa's "Deep North" because of its political similarities to the American Deep South, whites began looking for new borders, new boundaries that they could control. They invented the Volkstaat—a bantustan for whites.

As the April 1994 elections approached, whites in this area debated what their boundaries would be and debated the political and economic relationship they would have to the rest of South Africa. But the objective they had in mind was clear, and it was best described by Adde Coston, a young mother with a three-year-old daughter who was interviewed wearing her Afrikaner Weerstandsbeweging (AWB) uniform: "I was brought up not as a racialist but believing that whites should be with whites. It's not that I want all the blacks dead, but I don't think we should live together or even across the road from each other" (BESTER 1993:15). Her place for blacks in the new Volkstaat was clearly defined. They could work in the Volkstaat but could not be citizens, could have no say in the government, and would have to be off the streets by 9:00 P.M.

Such a white state would let Coston maintain the relationship she has with her black maid: "She's the right sort, your know. She says they should hang Mandela. I don't let her cook, though. I can't stand the thought of her scratching herself and then touching the food." This bizarre attitude toward their black neighbors and employees lets Coston and her peers overlook some of the realities of their world. No matter how they drew these boundaries of their fantasy nation, there was no way whites would be a majority of the people.

Just prior to the April 1994 elections I drove through this Volkstaat. It is a rural area of small towns. Vryburg proudly announces itself as the "Texas of South Africa." Seventy miles southwest is Kuruman. Large banners announcing the Volkstaat hang over both ends of main street. I pulled over to take a picture of one banner. Every person I could see standing within sight of the banner was black. As I took my picture only one white face came into view—a policeman who walked out of the shadows and stood eyeing me until I got back into my car and drove on. The symbolism of the lone white face wearing a police uniform would no doubt be lost on those who would create this Volkstaat, but the demographics are real—the clear majority of people in the area are black. A tyranny by the minority would have to be maintained.

But legal niceties are seldom a concern for those who would build ethnic islands. They don't want to see people who are different from themselves. They don't want to work with them, to learn from them, to trust them or be dependent on them. And so they exclude all but a sliver of the world's people. If they have enough guns and no conscience about using them, they can often succeed.

CUTTING THE VIDEO LINK

Cutting off communication with one's neighbors and co-workers is easily accomplished—especially telecommunication. Recent TV licensing action in South Africa has demonstrated how vulnerable video information is to individual prejudice. Up until 1993 both television and radio were government operations, tightly controlled by the National Party—the political arm of white Afrikaners. Then the South African Broadcasting Corporation board of directors was shuffled to allow the ANC and other groups to have a voice. The immediate result was a change in programming—a change not welcome to conservative whites. Within months of the change in programming, hundreds of whites had written to complain and to refuse to pay their annual license fee. One viewer complained SABC "is a communist, anti-Christian organization." Another said, "In light of the fiasco of the recent SABC board, which communists and other heathen elements control, I urgently request you to activate necessary rules for my TV set to be sealed. I am no longer prepared to be influenced and polluted by it" (DUBE 1993:11).

So conservative Christians pulled back. They cut themselves off. They chose not to be influenced or "polluted." The information highway might lead to their door, but they were not about to let it cross their threshold.

Conclusion

As we lay optical fiber across the oceans and launch armadas of geosynchronous satellites, it is sobering to remember that our record as information processors is not a good one. Those who seek information are killed. Those who try to transmit it find information blocked at every turn. Those we bring information to are as likely to shoot us as celebrate our effort. Article 19 of the *Universal Declaration* is a straightforward statement of rights. But if these rights are violated by everyone from presidents to librarians, it is clear we have much work to do before any massive changes in technology can make massive improvements in the availability of information. We have met the enemy, and he is us.

Chapter 8　　　　Information Criminals

We know everything about you that we need to know.
　　　　　　　—INTERNAL REVENUE SERVICE

The present is more frightening than any imaginable future
I might dream up.　　　—WILLIAM GIBSON *(credited with*
　　　　　　　　　　first using the term cyberspace)

CENTRAL ALASKA is not easily accessible. Ithabaskan villages along the Yukon River can only be reached by river during the summer and by snowmobile during the winter. Bush pilots make the flight when weather permits. There are no roads to most villages. When the Trans-Alaskan pipeline was laid, a service road was built next to it, cutting straight north to Barrow and the north slope. With the main road in, a few side roads were added as budgets permitted, gradually connecting a few of the Yukon River villages to the oil road and thence to Fairbanks.

One winter several years ago I took that road with two school district administrators. Niki and Alan McCurry. We were on our way to visit the school at Manley Hot Springs. It's not an easy drive. The road is a combination of gravel, snow, and ice, with high winds through narrow mountain passes. We almost didn't make it. The car hit more ice than usual and we slid deep into a snow bank. With night coming on and temperatures at minus thirty and falling, it looked like we were in a survival situation. Fortunately, the car had a winch and four-wheel drive and show shovels, and we were able to dig our way clear in about an hour.

That night we had dinner with one of the teachers at Manley, and during the course of conversation I said it would almost be better to fly in, maybe the road was a mistake. By the pained looks around the table it was clear I had stumbled into exactly the wrong topic. For two hours, in hushed tones, my companions explained the pain.

Two years earlier a madman, a problem case from Los Angeles, had used the road. Oil money had drawn him to Anchorage, where after months of fights, drinking, and drugs, he finally slipped all the way into insanity and killed two people. Escaping in his car, he headed out of town, driving randomly for two days. At the end of the second day chance brought him over the mountain pass, into Manley, and beyond for two miles to the boat landing on the Yukon. The road ended there. He got out of his car, got out his rifle, and shot everyone on the landing. Over the next four hours, he waited at the landing and shot everyone who arrived. The river was far enough away that people in town didn't even know their loved ones were being killed. Only after four hours did one man discover the slaughter and escape before he too became a victim. State police were called, and after a desperate gun battle the man was killed.

For the people of Manly Hot Springs the road to Fairbanks was no longer their link to the outside world. It was an invasion route that had let craziness in and left one person in ten dead or wounded. The road made them vulnerable. The road left their families destroyed.

Fortunately, few people have to experience the horror of that small town. But many more people have been hurt and will be hurt in one way or another as the world links up. Computer systems that were perfectly secure before the Internet are now being sabotaged from half a world away. Neo-Nazis plan strategy via electronic bulletin boards. Pedophiles use computer network to reach children. Thieves steal millions instantly, silently, invisibly. The same wires that carry medical diagnoses and family laughter carry terrorist plots. The same fibers that carry a nation's culture also carry pornography. The road that brings fresh vegetables and schoolteachers also brings madmen with guns.

Links to the world are innocent. The highway doesn't know if it is carrying salvation or slaughter. It can be used for either, as can airports, satellite dishes, and optical fiber. Each link gives us opportunity and vulnerability. The extent of the vulnerability is growing. Safeguards are limited. The dangers need to be more fully explored and protections extended before communities begin responding with the electronic equivalent of those South Florida towns that have placed barriers across their roads. They now have fewer ways of getting out of their neighborhoods, but criminals have fewer ways of getting in.

Information-age criminals strike in many ways. Obviously we don't have the space to look at all the ways information crimes can be committed, but we can look at five categories: invasion of privacy, theft, vandalism, fraud, and hate. Each category of crime has its own destructive forces on the complex web of information available to us. Ultimately, information crime can make the entire system too dangerous to use and block access for all of us.

Invasion of Privacy

The 1994 Winter Olympics began with one of the more bizarre episodes in the history of the Olympics. American figure-skating champion Nancy Kerrigan was attacked by a masked man as she completed a training session. Struck in the knee with an iron bar, she was too injured to compete in the Olympic trials and almost missed the Olympics. Days later police began checking on the entourage of Kerrigan's main competitor. Here is one account of how they did their work:

> Since the first phone tip to Napoleon, the FBI had been tracking phone records and other documents tying the men named in the woman's account to the assault. FBI sources indicate that in the two months before Christmas, Smith phoned Eckardt 31 times; in the month of December alone he phone Gillooly's parents' home at least 15 times. FBI sources say that Stant actually flew to Boston on 30 December to attack Kerrigan before she ever got to the figure-skating championships. But he apparently found the winter weather unsuitable for mayhem. Five days later he checked into the Super 8 Motel—under his own name and recorded by videotape—in Romulus, Michigan, near the Detroit airport. Stant took a room with a water bed and killed time watching movies like *Hollywood Fantasies* and *Girls of Beverly Hills* and calling Oregon and Arizona through the motel switchboard.   (STARR ET AL. 1994:40)

Not a pretty story, you say, but what's all this got to do with the computer as an information source and information medium? Plenty. If you reread the *Newsweek* passage, try scratching out "FBI sources" and replacing it with "phone company records" or "computer databases." As the men accused of this crime discovered, it is virtually impossible to go anywhere or do anything without leaving a computer record. Pick up the phone—a record is made. Pass over your credit card—a record is made. Board a plane, watch a fight or a movie on pay-per-view, pay your taxes, buy a house, visit your dentist, apply for a passport, have your tires rotated. It is getting harder and harder to find occasions when there is *not* a record kept. In *1984* George Orwell had visions of state control brought about by watchers—you could watch TV and it could watch you. He may have understood the goals of the police state, but he totally misunderstood technology. Who needs armies of people watching people when trivial computer programs and minuscule storage devices can effortlessly record every move you make?

For most middle-class Americans, the daily mail brings a daily reminder of how much is known about us and routinely passed around. The credit card offers from companies that already know our credit limits. The magazine offers from publishers that seem to know our interests and hobbies. The political literature from groups that seem to know our predisposition. Every day's junk mail is a garish warning: we know about you. And they do. How can so much be known about us? Just look to customer lists, government forms, and electronic communications.

CUSTOMER LISTS

Want to know who's gay in America? Strub Media Group of New York City has created a list of ninety thousand gay men and thirty thousand lesbians. How does the company know? It asked businesses—gay guest houses, bookstores, and magazines. Want to reach the religious Right? No problem. Ten prominent fundamentalist churches have happily sold the names of their donors to a list company in California, which can now sell half a million names labeled "Christian Zealots" (LARSON 1992:69). In each case, the people you gave your business to turned around and sold your name.

Those businesses are trying to learn more about their customers so they have more information to sell. Consider three telephone companies. Bell Atlantic, Nynex, and Pacific Telesis began work in 1994 with Michael Ovitz's Creative Artists Agency to put together a package of services to come into the home. Besides video shopping and information retrieval services, the phone companies would offer entertainment shows. One of the features of this new system would be powerful software: "The software that manages delivery of the programming will be able to monitor what a customer watches and suggest similar viewing fare in the future" (EDUPAGE 27 October 1994). Any business wants to know as much as it can about its customers, and ideally such a system would let the phone companies do a better job of supplying what customers want and eliminating what they don't want. But the average couch potato can be excused for being a bit squeamish knowing that some huge corporation with the latest computers is keeping a record of every show he watches.

How about your shopping? Much has already been said about the records UPC codes enable. More needs to be said. Citicorp has a mailing list of 511,227 "weight-conscious" shoppers. Where did they get the list? They tracked the food purchases of customers who had joined "frequent shopper" programs (LARSON 1992). Once in the program, every purchase they made was recorded and categorized.

Food purchases aren't the only things monitored. Waldenbooks has a preferred reader program. It too enables the store to record the titles and subjects of books customers select. It turned out to be very handy in the Persian Gulf War. Within ten days of the war's start, the store had sent special mailings to all readers who had shown a previous interest in the program. What kind of person voluntarily gives a company that kind of personal information? Millions of people. Says Erik Larson in his analysis of privacy issues, "We consumers bridle at the thought of carrying a national identity card yet for the promise of a few cents off our grocery bills gladly carry an ID card assigned by our grocers" (LARSON 1992:135).

Even computer experts can sometimes be surprised by the extent of the record keeping going on. One of the joys of Internet access is the chance to "surf" from one gopher server to another, one mail list to another, listening in briefly and then moving on. Most users assume they have complete anonymity and can just be a fly on the wall as they travel the electronic world. Most users would be wrong. Commercial enterprises might well want to keep and use those e-mail addresses. Each time someone logged in to see what was going on at a site established by some company, the company might record the address. It would be much like Sears knowing the name and address of every person who walked through their store to browse.

What can surfers do about their electronic trail? Very little. The best advice seems to come from an old network hand: "I think it only prudent to assume that any site you visit on the net could keep a log of your visit; and that as time passes, more and more sites—particularly commercial sites—will do just that. Browse carefully; the junk mail 'you will' receive may be at stake" (HEDLUND 1994).

GOVERNMENT FORMS

But Mastercard transactions aren't the only trail we leave behind. There are government forms we must all fill out. But who will protect us from our own government? The Internal Revenue Service has been making the most news lately with its blatant misuse of taxpayer data. At Senate hearings in August 1993 and July 1994 it became clear that hundreds of IRS employees are browsing through tax records of neighbors, friends, relatives, and celebrities. Between 1989 and 1994 the IRS investigated more than 1,300 employees for unauthorized access to taxpayer records and penalized 420 (GLENN 1994).

With all this electronic window peeping, the IRS has very little built in to their computer system that might pull down the shades. Congressional testimony by James Hinchman of the U.S. Comptroller General's Office sums up the problems with the IRS computer systems: "An internal systems security study commissioned by the IRS in 1993 pointed out that one of the greatest risks to security is from employees. Nevertheless, a December 1993 review by IRS' internal auditors found that there were virtually no controls programmed into the

Integrated Data Retrieval System (IRDS) to limit what employees can do once they are authorized IRDS access and authorized to input account adjustments" (HINCHMAN 1994:10).

Not only does the system have no access controls, but it also has no audit trail that would record who has been in a taxpayer's account. The computer system is not set up to catch browsers. Meanwhile, the IRS is moving ahead on its new project, the "Golden Eagle" tax return. In apparent seriousness Coletta Brueck, project manager for the IRS' Document Processing System, offered this description of the new filing system she wants to implement: "We know everything about you that we need to know. Your employer tells us everything about you that we need to know. Your activity record on your credit cards tells us everything about you that we need to know. Through interface with Social Security, with DMV, with your banking institutions, we really have a lot of information. . . . We could literally file a return for you. This is the future we'd like to go to" (LEVY 1994:218). This may not be the future all the rest of us would like to go to, but it is one the IRS is working on. In the meantime, investigations of illegal browsing by IRS employees continue.

The Census Bureau has also shown the limits of its privacy protections. The most famous breakdown came in 1942, when census data was used to round up Japanese Americans and send them to internment camps. While the Census Bureau never provided exact names, it came close: "They would lay out on tables various city blocks where the Japanese lived, and they would tell me how many were living in each block" (LARSON 1992:53). It is doubtful the Japanese Americans who dutifully filled out their census forms in 1940 considered those forms would be used to aid their incarceration.

It is also doubtful many of us understand how connected the Census Bureau is to direct-mail companies. For starters, the Census Bureau heads have frequently come from marketing companies. Since 1969 bureau heads have come from jobs such as director of marketing at Ford, manager of a political polling firm, a market research manager for Sears, a past president of the American Marketing Association, and senior vice president of Market Opinion Research. With such backgrounds it is no surprise that the bureau has worked with a number of direct-mail companies to provide census data or to retabulate data in a manner more useful to marketers.

Once major project undertaken by the Census Bureau was the breakdown of census data by zip code. The breakdown wasn't part of any official compilation; it was performed specifically to make selling to Americans easier. A consortium of companies paid $250,000 for producing the actual computer tapes, then turned around and made huge profits selling the census tapes to other companies. The tapes became the basis for much more sophisticated targeting of consumer groups. Needless to say, none of this use of citizen data is mentioned in the Constitution.

But the Census Bureau isn't the only government agency that sells citizen information. In Wisconsin, the Department of Motor Vehicles is in the business of selling the names and addresses of drivers. One survey in Wisconsin found that more than one hundred companies used state agency lists to sell products or keep track of such things as the number of drivers in a car-insurance policy-holder's household.

Besides the nuisance of having your name available to everyone with a product to sell, there are recorded instances of burglars using license-plate information to identify targets. Worse was the situation of a woman who had been raped. When she learned that the man who raped her was about to be freed from prison she asked that the state delete her address from the license plate file available to everyone—including, potentially, the rapist. The state said she could put in some address other than her home, but there had to be some address in the file. Apparently, "there was nothing else the state could do for her" ("State Collects" 1994:19). One option, that the state stop selling DMV records, apparently never occurred to them.

COMMUNICATION PRIVACY

Then there is communication privacy. Here the threat seems overwhelming. For starters, consider Alana Shoars. The e-mail coordinator for Epson America, she was instructed to create an electronic "tap" on all mail that moved from the company's mainframe computer to the MCI Mail Communication Service. Essentially, she was ordered to write a program that would copy all mail that employees sent to the outside world. She objected and was fired (SHIEH AND BALLARD 1994).

The case raises two important issues about electronic communication: technical ease and legal distinctions. First, Epson American (and the rest of the corporate world) would never be in a position to eavesdrop on digital communication if it weren't so easy to do so. As digital traffic moves from one place to another it sits briefly in a "router," a computer that determines where the message is to go and starts it on its way. A message may encounter a number of routing computers during its passage. Any of those computers can quickly make a copy of a message and send the original on its way. All that is required is a small copy program and storage space for the messages being copied. With computers becoming faster and storage becoming cheaper, the barriers to copying drop to nothing.

With technical barriers gone, the only protection becomes the law. Here there is less protection than most people realize. To begin with, up until 1986 digital (data) communication was treated differently than analog (voice) communication. While a phone couldn't be tapped, electronic communications were uncovered by the law. The Electronic Communication Privacy Act gave some protection in 1986, making it a crime for an electronic communication service to knowingly disclose the contents of a communication to any third party. So now AT&T, MCI, and Sprint couldn't make copies of electronic communication. But what about the originating company? Can it listen in? *Yes.* The "ECPA applies only to persons or entities providing service to the public and not to employers who electronically monitor or disclose electronic communications transmitted by their employees" (SHIEH AND BALLARD 1994:60).

So workplace privacy is unprotected. In 1993 Representative Pat Williams introduced the Privacy for Consumers and Workers Act to give employees some protection, but even that act leaves plenty of openings for employer monitoring. Employers have the right to monitor new employees routinely for the first sixty days, or to monitor any employee during their first five years if the monitoring is part of a group of employees. Employers have to notify employees that monitoring is occurring, unless the employer suspects the employee is engaged in unlawful activity. In short, a wide range of workplace monitoring is still perfectly legal under the Williams Act.

Questions of privacy are also emerging with electronic discussion lists. With tens of thousands of such lists in place, and new lists springing up daily, these have become important vehicles for conversation. Some are used by organizations as supplements to newsletters, others more closely resemble academic journals with carefully measured, elaborately worded expositions, still others appear more like hallway conversation—there is a basic thread, but there is also plenty of personal gossip. Whatever the character of the information posted on the lists, the question now being raised is whether the contents are public.

As can be expected, the issue arose in one of the more political discussion groups. A feminist philosophy list with 650 members is managed by Linda Lopez McAlister of the University of South Florida. She already restricts access to the discussion by interviewing all prospective members about their interest in feminist philosophy. Only those cleared by her are allowed to read the discussions posted on the list. Now her list is debating whether to throw two people off the list. One is Frederic Sommers, the husband of Christina Hoff Sommers. Since his wife is a critic of feminist scholarship, there is concern that he is showing his wife some of the messages on the list. The other potential exile is Liz McMillen, a reporter for the *Chronicle of Higher Education* who printed some of the messages sent to the list.

For McAlister the issue is privacy: "There is something about being an object of voyeuristic scrutiny that is uncomfortable. I think it is an inhibiting factor to know when you are putting something out on the list that the next thing is that a reporter for the *Chronicle* might call you" (DELOUGHRY 1994:A22). On the opposite side of the issue is David Carlson of Texas A&M University: "I don't see how any public institution is going to allow its faculty or staff to maintain little private domains in which they let people on and let people off."

Ultimately the issue may move from one of ethics and law to one of practical implementation. Can a list in which 650 people have access to all messages really expect that not one of the 650 will show messages to outsiders? What about a list of 1,000? 10,000? To quote Carlson again, "Those who suggest that material on their mailing lists will not be seen by ideological enemies or by journalists are kidding themselves. And the greater problem is that they may be kidding their subscribers." Electronic discussion lists may be a great new vehicle for the exchange of information, but there appear to be few practical ways to protect the privacy of participants.

Information Theft

Like many leading companies, Waterford Glass in the Republic of Ireland has turned to automation to improve the quality of its product. Much of its glassware is produced by computer-controlled machines. Those machines are able to achieve a consistent quality that makes Waterford an acknowledged leader in its industry. But the machines also make Waterford vulnerable to a new kind of theft. In December 1984 a box containing twenty-five computer disks disappeared from the Merlyn Park factory in Galway. On those disks was all the information needed to control glass-making machines. Since that date, quantities of bogus glassware have been turning up in the United Kingdom and United States. The glassware looks like Waterford glass and meets the same quality standards. It should—it is being turned out by the same production process used at Waterford.

The original computer disks were eventually recovered, but copying such disks is a trivial activity even a child can do. So the number and location of all the possible copies is simply unknowable. What is known is that the collected intelligence of generations of Waterford employees was coded onto computer disks that then walked out the door. Is the original information still at Waterford? Yes. Does it have the same value? No. Much of the value of the manufacturing information on those disks was its exclusivity. Once everyone had the information, the original value dropped substantially.

The difficulties in identifying that a theft has occurred, and in quantifying the amount of the loss, has made information theft a difficult crime to combat. How do you stop a crime you may not notice? How do you explain to a judge and a jury that taking a box of twenty-five disks is a theft of more than twenty-five dollars' worth of disks? To quote Cornwall, "The largest estimates for computer crime include the consequences of industrial espionage. How on earth can anyone measure these losses? The main area of penalty for victims is in loss of business opportunities—the new product that will now have an unsuccessful launch, the proprietary process that will now be cheaply copied, the exclusive mailing list now in the hands of a competitor—how do you put a realistic figure on any of these?" (CORNWALL 1987:53).

The Business Software Alliance in Britain has put a very specific figure on one kind of theft—software piracy. Beginning on 1 November 1994 they set a bounty on piracy—thirty-nine hundred dollars. Any disgruntled (or former) employees who want to turn in their companies can dial a well-advertised toll-free number. By one estimate half the software being used in Britain is unlicensed (EDUPAGE 11 October 1994). Of course this means that half the software in Britain is paid for, a level of honesty fairly unusual in the world. Microsoft's vice president for Asia estimates that "virtually all applications software sold in China is counterfeit" (EDUPAGE 11 November 1994). China is the unfortunate norm for developing nations. Throughout the Third World, copying software is standard practice. The cost to American companies alone is estimated at $800 million annually in China alone.

The copying of compute software can be quite sophisticated (and profitable). One Chinese company, Shenzhen Reflective Materials Institute, was found to have produced 650,000 fake holograms that could be used to pass counterfeit Microsoft products off as authentic. Microsoft sued in a Chinese court and won—several hundred dollars. After protest the fine was raised—to $5,000. Microsoft is appealing and asking for $20 million (BORRUS 1994). Meanwhile Chinese software pirates are counterfeiting American software and selling it all over the world.

The motivation for such thefts may be greed for some and claims of poverty for others. The effects on the original software producers may be clear—loss of millions or billions in sales. A more subtle problem is the impact all this has on Third World software houses. It is hard enough to compete with the Microsofts of the world, but what chance does a local software engineer have when every business in town is getting its software for free? Of course the governments that allow software theft to go on see their countries as perpetual consumers who need to get the best price possible, legally or otherwise. The idea that they might someday be producers of software or other intellectual materials never occurs to them. So they destroy their local producers at the same time they cheat foreigners, a lesson learned by every Third World musician who has ever tried to sell tapes or CDs.

Speaking of music theft, now that music is digital, it can make the rounds over the same computer systems that are used to pirate software. The Recording Industry Association of America has already identified a number of computer bulletin boards where music is posted (PORT 1994). It can be copied and played on today's multimedia computers just as easily as computer games. As networks become more interrelated, it will be increasingly easy for a single pirated copy of software, music, or movies to be stored at any one network server and be copied illegally by computers all over the world.

As we close on the subject of information theft, it is worth at least mentioning that not all theft is as subtle as copying tapes or pirating software or CDs. There still is old-fashioned theft. The IRS found that out for itself when it set up its electronic tax filing system. In 1993 twelve million Americans filed electronically. The point was to save $20 million in paper-shuffling costs, and make friends for the IRS by churning out refunds in as little as two days. It may have been a great idea, but there were enough security holes in the program to draw sharks. One Pennsylvania tax preparer thought he had died and gone to heaven. He filed 431 returns for nonexistent people and collected $1.1 million (REISS 1994). The IRS found more than twenty-five thousand fraudulent returns and has no way of knowing how many they missed. One thing they do know— half of the people collecting false returns took the money and disappeared. Recovering from them will be impossible.

The IRS built an electronic highway to their office only to find criminals driving through the gate. Waterford put their expertise on a disk only to have it walk out the door. Microsoft invested millions in products others will sell for a profit. Our information, our products, our networks are vulnerable now to thieves we may never see, thieves who may take far more from us than the thugs who go after our payrolls or after goods scattered on our loading docks.

Information Vandalism

At 2:25 A.M., Thursday, 3 November 1988, Cliff Stoll got a phone call from NASA. "Hi Cliff." It was Gene Miya at NASA's Ames Laboratories. "No apologies for waking you up. Our computers are under attack" (STOLL 1990:334). As it turned out, so were Stoll's computers and two thousand other computers around the United States. All were major research machines plugged into the Internet. All were being ordered in endless circles by a "worm program," a silly program that does no real work other than to duplicate itself endlessly, forcing the host machine to do nothing other than execute its infinite loops.

Stoll was famous in 1988 for having identified a group of German hackers who had used the Internet to access U.S. military computers around the country. They then sold the information they gained to the East German and Soviet regimes. Caught by Stoll, the hackers were arrested by the German authorities, convicted, and sentenced to probation. Their leader now writes network software for a company in Hannover. The lack of punishment for their crime is typical for cases of this kind. But at least they were stopped.

This new attack on American computers was something different, not done by foreigners or spies. For two days in 1988 the main research centers of the United States were in chaos due to a program written by an American— Robert T. Morris. Not some teenager bumping his way through puberty, Morris had studied at Harvard and Cornell and was the son of another Robert Morris, the one who heads computer security at the National Security Agency (NSA). Morris used his computer at Cornell to link with one at MIT, using his access privileges to the Internet as a means for destroying the same network. One of the best and the brightest, he used his Ivy League opportunities to bring down every research center in the United States.

Ultimately arrested and convicted, Morris was sentenced in 1990 to three years' probation, four hundred hours' community service, and a fine of ten thousand dollars. The fact that he totally escaped jail time is normal. If anything, the fact that he was even prosecuted is unusual. Jay J. Buck Bloombecker (1994:15), director of the National Center for Computer Crime Data, has figures that would surprise most. He cites these figures for annual prosecutions for computer crimes in California:

Year	Number of Prosecutions
1986	29
1987	53
1988	27
1989	16
1990	13
1991	13
1992	31

If prosecutions are rare, jail time is even more unusual. Of the 129 individuals convicted of computer crimes in California during the seven years listed above, only 9 computer criminals ever went to jail. Prosecuting, convicting, and jailing computer criminals is not easy. First, they have to be caught, not an easy task when the crime can be executed by remote control. Then a district attorney has to decide the crime is worth the effort to prosecute, not an easy decision at a time when people walk the streets with Uzis. Then a case has to be won. Bloombecker is direct about the difficulties involved: (1) The cases take too long; (2) there are so few of them each seems to require starting all over;

(3) expensive experts are often needed to assist in investigation and prosecution; and (4) victims bear considerable costs for the trial—they must wait, produce evidence, and testify. As a result, it is very easy to see why law enforcement (and victims) would choose to let the criminals go and invest their resources in producing a better "fire wall" to protect their computer systems against the next criminal. But the damage from information vandals is real. In the case of the Morris worm, two thousand computers nationwide were infected: "Those machines were dead in the water—useless until disinfected. And removing the virus often took two days" (STOLL 1990:348). Since the machines involved were not personal computers sitting on desktops, this is not a matter of simply stopping the work of two thousand individuals. These were system machines, serving as controllers for two thousand local networks. Tens of thousands of scientists were affected.

Now, of course, people are very aware of how vulnerable they are. For it is not the monster without that threatens them—it is the Harvard graduates within that destroy for kicks. One response is to simply stay away from networks. A number of times in the late 1980s IBM simply cut off all electronic contact to universities. It was too dangerous to let university network traffic come across the electronic drawbridge. IBM is not the only corporation that has seen the vandalism occurring outside their walls and decided the risk of participating in the Internet community was greater than the reward.

Will there be less vandalism in the future? That appears unlikely. The Defense Information Systems Agency says hacker attacks on military networks now run two a day, more than double the rate for 1994. There are now even for-profit hackers. During the Persian Gulf War a group of Dutch hackers called High Tech for Peace approached the Iraqi embassy in Paris offering to foul up the U.S. military networks for a million dollars. Hussein turned them down (FIALKA 1995:A12).

As the Internet brings more and more people together, it brings more cultures together, each with its own values and agendas. A Canadian computer scientist who was visiting one of the black townships of South Africa was excited when he met a young man who had learned a great deal about computers. To his shock the boy began a recital of his skills by telling how he had already created a virus. That boy isn't the only youngster in the world who believes international communication is an avenue for destructive energy. In places where the dominant ethic has been to "get" some group of privileged people, the information highway is one more avenue of attack.

Describing workers in South Africa, the Canadian said, "Most employees have the attitude they should take the system for what they can. Copying software from the office is done without a second thought, yet it is just as much stealing as is taking home office equipment. What if this attitude spills over into the Internet?" (GOLDSTRUCK 1994:26). If a Harvard graduate could sit in his office at Cornell and willfully bring down the scientific network across the United States, what are we to expect from bright kids across the world who have not even a nominal allegiance to this country or its institutions?

Electronic Fraud

The pundits already have a name for it—I-way robbery. Consider, for example, the scam artist who posted a number of messages on an investments bulletin board. Having established himself as an "expert," he then offered his services as a money manager. At least one retiree trusted him and sent him ten thousand dollars. The money instantly disappeared.

Hiding your real identity can be used in other electronic scams as well. A public relations officer for ETC Industries found a great way to build interest in his company's stock. He started posting messages on the Prodigy online service: "Thirty-five cents moving to $2! $1 million profit! A stock primed for breakout!" (FLAHERTY 1994:16). Who was to know he was connected to the company? How would they know? How would they even know his real name? In this case, it took securities officials two months to put a stop to this manipulation.

In November 1994 the Federal Trade Commission began playing a role in policing the information highway, going after Chase Consulting, a company advertising on America Online's network that it could "repair" credit for ninety-nine dollars. The FTC forced the company to give back all the money it had taken through the scheme: "The commission wants to make it clear that advertisers on the information superhighway will be held to the same standards as advertisers in other media" ("Online" 1994:A4). Maybe so, but it won't be easy. During one two-week period in 1994 the Prodigy online service had over fifty-six hundred messages posted on investment topics. The sheer volume makes identifying fraud and tracking down abuses nearly impossible. "Regulators," notes Gram, "are not going to be able to police these networks any time soon" (1994:24).

As bad as securities fraud may be, it is not the worst example of online fraud. Surely that "honor" goes to pedophiles who have started using computers to get next to children. Their approach is clever. They browse electronic bulletin boards, post general messages, try to make initial contact with children. Once the conversation has been started in a "public" forum like a bulletin board, they begin more direct electronic mail with likely victims. Because they are invisible, pedophiles can pretend to be any age and to have any identity. How are their victims to know they aren't really just other fourteen year olds who want to complain about their parents and talk big about going off on their own? By the time the child actually sees his or her electronic "friend," the child has given away every secret, told the adult all he needs to know to lure the child away from home.

"Pedophiles are like anyone else. They're becoming more high-tech and using it to their advantage," says one law-enforcement expert experienced in such cases. Says another, "This whole information superhighway is wonderful, but it's loaded with dangers" ("Paedophiles" 1994:12). They should know. One of the experts had just brought charges against a twenty-three year old who used a bulletin board to find children. He raped two boys he met through e-mail and tried to recruit two teenagers to kidnap young boys for him. E-mail is a perfect avenue for such criminals. It is one of the few places where they can have lengthy conversations with children. The children feel safe because they are in their own homes. The criminal feels safe because no one has seen him with the child. It is a situation made to order for criminals, and they are taking advantage of it.

Hate by Wire

Ingo Hasselbach is a former skinhead jailed by the East Germans. When Germany was reunited he moved on to join the neo-Nazi groups then forming all over the country. He led raids in Lichtenburg against Gypsies and in Rostock, Hunxe, and Molln against refugees. His groups firebombed homes and beat people to death. To him the smashing of the Berlin Wall was an opportunity to get help for his Nazi activities. With the Wall gone, he had amazing new contacts: "With the help of our new contacts with the West, we founded the first right-wing party in the GDR. They taught us how to draw up a party platform, supplied us with propaganda materials and educational literature which we didn't have in the East. We had joint meetings with Nazi parties from America, Denmark, Spain, and the Netherlands" (THEIL 1994:54).

Freedom of movement means freedom of movement for all—the loving and the hate-filled. For Hasselbach, freedom of movement meant access to training in hatred. But the ability to travel to such "experts" isn't the only gain Nazis have made in a united Germany. They now have access to modern communication technology: "With mobile phones, computer mailboxes, there's a whole network being created in Germany. The police know what's going on, but they're powerless against modern communications" (THEIL 1994:54).

Communication technology is international, and the new tools available to the Nazis can reach well beyond their friends across Germany. It can reach to their allies in the United States: "The American Nazi Party in Lincoln,

Nebraska, plays a huge role because all the propaganda, all the material, can be legally produced there" (THEIL 1994:54). So the German Nazis become like any other international corporation. They have suppliers all over the world, all linked by modern communications. E-mail über alles.

Summary

Information crime existed before satellite communications and continues to be available in the low-tech variety. Fraud has always been with us, yet the digital era does bring a new aspect to crime—an increase in our vulnerability. The more that is known about me, the more that can be used against me, whether by overzealous corporations or by government agents. The more pathways into my home, the more access criminals have to my children. The more electronics in my office, the more easy I am to watch. At the moment paranoia not only seems healthy, it may be overdue.

The largest danger may be that we decide that the possible advantages of connecting to the outside world are more than offset by the dangers. This is already a decision made by a number of corporations that do not want to run the risk of traveling on public thoroughfares frequented by bandits. So they use private thoroughfares—their own networks. These electronic highways may not be as visible as private interstates, but they are every bit as real, as are the consequences. Closed information systems violate every tenet of the information age, but closed information systems are what we will have until predators can be kept off the public systems.

Part III

Reception Problems

Chapter 9   World Education

*When I have control of Native Education, I will reform it
so Natives will be taught from childhood to realize equality
with Europeans is not for them.* —H. VERWOERD

WINDHOEK TECHNICAL HIGH SCHOOL is a beautiful place. Surrounded by well-kept lawns, its courtyards feature gardens of flowers that bloom most of the year. The school is in a section of town called Academia. You turn left onto Plato Street, right on Socrates, go past Descartes and Sartre, and there you are. This is the white part of Windhoek. All blacks were forced to move five miles north to Katatura in 1959. But it didn't originally matter how distant it might be for black students—when the school was built, blacks couldn't attend.

The school enrolls several hundred students who take courses in math, building, electronics, mechanics, mechanical drawing, computer studies, and science. Students work hard and are successful. Companies from all over Namibia and South Africa try to hire their graduates at very high wages. Many students go on to university to study engineering or technical subjects. In 1992 two of the three highest scores on the national exams came from their school. It is an impressive place to visit. But it is also a little frightening. Four years after independence and majority rule, the student body is still all white. You can walk into any classroom and find a room full of blond boys all wearing identical gray uniforms. On first glance it looks like a meeting of the Hitler youth. Black students will not attend. They believe a technical education makes one subservient.

Meanwhile in America, it is Saturday morning. In between Road Runner cartoons up pops a commercial. It features a fourth- or fifth-grade classroom. At the front stands a short, bald, middle-aged man wearing glasses and an argyle sweater. In a voice devoid of life he begins his lecture with the words, "Our solar system" and turns with a pointer to a drawing on the chalkboard. The minute his back is turned one student pulls out a box of cookies and passes it around. Immediately the kids are all up and dancing to music while lights flash and confetti drops from the ceiling. It is a party! They laugh and talk, eat cookies, and dance. Then the teacher turns back to the class. They instantly sit, the music ends with the confetti. Totally ignorant of what is happening in his classroom, the teacher asks, "Are there any questions?" The boy with the cookies asks with a knowing smile, "Could you repeat that?" The zombie teacher turns back to the board and the party resumes.

In Korea it's New Year's Eve 1974. A Peace Corps volunteer in South Korea, I work in a health center in a rural county seat on the Yellow Sea coast. Two friends and I make the rounds of the local wine houses. We have already stopped in two or three places, surrounded by the crowds—it appears the entire town is out celebrating. Then we get to a small place on a back street that is empty except for two patrons. It is deathly quiet. I walk in but realize after a minute that my two friends are still out on the street. I look back to see my friends peering around the door with their mouths open. The two patrons of the back-street wine house are high school teachers. I don't understand what that means, so I urge my friends in. My friends won't go in. These men had been their teachers, and you don't drink or smoke in front of a teacher. It doesn't matter that my friends had finished high school, graduated college, and had responsible jobs—these men had been their teachers and that relationship lasts for life. So we stand outside and watch while the two old men have their annual drink and the wine house owner stands and fumes—for as long as these teachers are in her house, no former students will enter. Given the teachers' age and the size of the town, that means she is going to have a very quiet New Year's Eve.

Three stories of education, each showing a different corner of the world. One shows a culture based around race war, one shows a culture based around consumption, one shows a culture based on hard work and respect. There are many other education stories to tell, many other reasons for the wide differences between countries and between schools. Unfortunately, most of the stories are about problems. The truth is, even a decade after Alvin Toffler popularized the term *information age* in his *Third Wave*, a minuscule few are prepared to participate in the age. While an exuberant few "surf the third wave," the vast majority are drowning.

Ignorance by Design

The National Party's rise to power in 1948 ranked as a watershed in South African politics. Essentially, a revolution at the ballot box. White voters with ties to England and the Commonwealth lost. White voters aligned with the Dutch Afrikaners won. It was the Boer War fought over again, and this time the Afrikaners won. F. W. Malan, the new prime minister, lost no time taking charge and dividing up the spoils. He saw the election as winner take all, and the Afrikaners took every ministry, every place in the civil service, every policy position. They knew what they wanted in the "new" South Africa, and they drove for it in every aspect of society. Apartheid was under way.

Apartheid was systematic, it was organized, and it effected every aspect of every citizen's life. That included education. Within a year of taking power, the Afrikaners set up a working group to organize the new educational system. By 1951 they had their plan—Bantu Education. The theory was simple, if unbelievably ugly. Dr. H. Verwoerd made his objectives as Minister of Bantu Education clear: "When I have control of Native Education, I will reform it so that Natives will be taught from childhood to realize that equality with Europeans is not for them. People who believe in equality are not desirable teachers for the native. Education must train and teach people in accordance with their opportunities in life, according to the sphere in which they live" (AMUKUGO 1993:57).

Education for inequality was the law of the land. The place for blacks was to be at the bottom of the apartheid ladder. Education would be used to help prepare blacks for their appointed position. What would they be taught? The Odendaal Commission, which extended Bantu Education into South Africa's colony of Namibia, listed these skills for black children (AMUKUGO 1993:61–62):

1. Religious knowledge and good manners.
2. Literacy in his native language as a means of communication and of preserving pride in his national traditions.
3. Literacy in the official language as a means of communications with Europeans, as an aid in economic matters and in gaining knowledge of the outside world.
4. Knowledge of hygiene for the protection of health.
5. Knowledge of technical skills.
6. Social patterning of behavior and values which make one a good member of the community, a good parent, and a useful citizen.

Religious training was a double victory for the Afrikaners. Not only did it help them feel the righteousness of saving savage souls, but it helped create a docile population. Teaching children their native language may seem generous, but it was actually part of a very effective strategy to divide blacks against one another. With multiple languages, blacks couldn't communicate with one another. They could only speak with those of their "nation," usually an area of soil so infertile no white farmer wanted it. Literacy in the official language meant workers could take orders. Knowledge of hygiene made the list on the assumption that blacks were inherently dirty and needed special education in this area. Technical skills really meant using hammers and shovels. Social values were clear indoctrination.

Such was the purpose of education under apartheid. As it turned out, even these meager goals were never reached. Part of the problem was money. In 1953, when Bantu Education went into effect in South Africa, the government spent 13 cents on each black child for every dollar it spent on white children (17 rand per year vs. 128 rand). When you can only spend one-eighth as much on schools, books, and teachers, you don't get much. Unfortunately, things only got worse. By 1982 the government was only spending 12 cents on black children for every dollar it spent on white students (CHRISTIE 1985:98).

Money shortages meant huge classes and unqualified teachers. In 1983 the pupil-teacher ratio for blacks was forty-three to one. For whites it was eighteen to one. At one point (1971) the pupil-teacher ratio was fifty-eight to one (CHRISTIE 1985:115). Given such teaching loads, coupled with low salaries, qualified teachers were few and far between. Only 2 percent of teachers in black schools were university graduates in 1979, whereas 32 percent of teachers in white schools had graduated. Eighty-two percent of the teachers in black schools had never completed high school! No teachers without at least a high school diploma were employed in white schools.

Unqualified teachers, crowded conditions, lack of books, desks, and basic materials, all had the obvious effect. Students quickly stopped coming to school. In 1982 there were just over one million black first graders in South African schools. By fourth grade the number was only half a million, by sixth grade, less than a quarter million, with only seventy-two thousand attending grade twelve. In other words, only 7 percent of black students who started school made it to twelfth grade. For whites it was 65 percent. Bantu Education was working exactly as intended.

South Africa's policies were the law of the land in its colony of Namibia, and the effects were the same. In 1975 the colonial government spent nine times as much on the education of white students as on blacks (615 rand vs. 68 rand) (AMUKUGO 1993). This had the same effect on student-teacher ratios—forty-two to one for black schools, eighteen to one for white. And the hardships had the same effect on school persistence. While 43,285 Namibian blacks attended first grade in 1974, only 185 persisted to twelfth grade (.4 percent). The persistence rate for whites was 40 percent—one hundred times better! In parts of the country things were even worse. In the North, where most of the population of Namibia lives, 1977 saw only two black children graduate from high school.

Given the Bantu curriculum, there was a general sense that even if students endured all the hardships of long walks to distant schools and tried to learn from unqualified teachers with huge classes and no textbooks, what was the point? As one critic put it, "At the end of the . . . seven year primary course, the pupils knew nothing beyond reading, writing, and basic arithmetic, the Bible, and how to care for white people's homes, gardens, and farms" (AMUKUGO 1993:64). Maybe that's part of the reason why only 17 percent of black students finished primary school.

Things were no better in Rhodesia. Ian Smith and the Rhodesian Front Party seized power in 1965. For the next fifteen years they controlled the country, and like their friends to the south, used education as a way of preserving white privileges. Their Ministry of Education made the new policies clear in 1966: "An academic education has little relevance to the work needs, or even the life needs, of the African community and if there has been in the past too much emphasis in the primary schools on a literary education at the expense of practical training, and the inclusion of desirable work habits, so at secondary school, there has been too much emphasis on academic studies at the expense of prevocational preapprenticeship training" (AMUKUGO 1993:143).

These policies were supported by new quotas. Only 12.5 percent of black primary school learners were to enter academic secondary schools, while another 37.5 percent were allowed to attend new technical schools. These new schools were linked to agricultural extension services, so the basic curriculum was agriculture, carpentry, building, bricklaying, woodwork, commerce, and bookkeeping. Fifty percent of black students were to be excluded from any additional education unless they cared to use correspondence colleges at their own expense.

White Rhodesians need not have worried that too many black students would seek an academic education. By 1971 only 43 percent of black schools even offered a full seven years of education. And instead of 50 percent of black primary school learners going on to some form of secondary school, only 19 percent moved up: 5 percent to academic secondary schools and 14 percent to the new technical schools. Put in bolder figures, "Of every 1,000 African school children, about 337 completed primary education, 60 enrolled in secondary schools" (AMUKUGO 1993:154). Even there numbers are optimistic, since 25 percent of black children in Rhodesia never even started school. Given the numbers of children who never attended school and the numbers who quickly dropped out, 70 percent of the black population was either illiterate or semiliterate.

Recovery from educational discrimination is not an easy matter. In 1980 Ian Smith's government was forced from power and Robert Mugabe took over. Rhodesia became Zimbabwe. The new government set specific educational goals, including "free and compulsory primary and secondary education for all children, regardless of race." Between 1980 and 1985 they made great strides to achieve those goals. Primary enrollments increased 160 percent, secondary enrollments 500 percent, with concomitant building programs that increased Zimbabwe's primary schools by 73 percent and secondary schools by 538 percent. It was an impressive beginning.

Unfortunately, the costs for this growth were staggering. Educational expenses between 1980 and 1985 increased more than fivefold. Yet even with this huge increase there were significant shortcomings. Attendance jumped, but still not to 100 percent. As of this writing, primary school attendance is still not compulsory in Zimbabwe. Nor is it free. As recently as 1990 the Ministry of Education announced: "Although primary education is tuition free, parents are, however, required to pay [into the] general purpose fund which varies according to school type, and contribute towards the construction of schools in partnership with local communities" (AMUKUGO 1993:159).

In short, the burden of fully educating all its citizens was more than the government could bear alone. It simply didn't have enough money. As it turned out, it also didn't have enough teachers. So it turned to unqualified teachers. From 1974 to 1985 the number of primary school teachers jumped from 18,483 to 56,691. Unfortunately, only 22,000 of them were fully trained. As a consequence, 60 percent of primary teachers are now untrained. At the secondary level there are now five times as many teachers. The result: 45 percent of secondary school teachers don't have the training they should.

By any standard, Zimbabwe has come a long way in a short period of time, but it came from such a miserable position it will be decades before education there is what it should be. Namibia has had even less time. Finally granted independence in 1990, it has only had four years to repair the damage of decades. The government has poured money into schools. Well over one-fourth of the nation's budget goes for education. Donors from around the world have tried to help. They have built or equipped schools. Both the Peace Corps and World Teach have supplied significant members of teachers and teacher trainers. New teachers are being graduated in large numbers by teacher training colleges, and current teachers are undergoing massive retraining.

But educational systems don't change overnight. In the 1993 tenth-grade national exams, only 17 percent of students passed the mathematics test. Small wonder, given the instruction they have received. For current teachers upgrading their license, one of the courses they have to take is Mathematics A. The twenty-unit, year-long course only gets to addition in unit six, subtraction in unit seven, and multiplication in unit eight; fractions are in unit fourteen, and measuring lengths in unit eighteen. The course finishes with the area and volume of simple shapes. This is the mathematics studied by the teachers *upgrading* their licenses. Many had been teaching for decades knowing even *less* math than this. Remember that under apartheid, math was an academic subject of no use to people being trained for a lifetime of servitude. So instead they got Bible studies and personal hygiene. Math was for whites.

Now it is South Africa's turn. With the movement to majority rule complete, apartheid is finally dead and educational institutions can begin giving a complete education to all. But it won't be easy. When the average teacher-student ratio in Lebowa or Kwa Zulu is one to forty-nine and less than one teacher in five has graduated from high school, there is a long way to go. And while Namibia and Zimbabwe have relatively small populations, South Africa is a nation of forty million. A few hundred Peace Corps volunteers would be invisible there. Any efforts assume that political and criminal violence quiets down and the economy stays strong enough to support a substantial educational budget. Miracles can happen and both individuals and nations have been known to move mountains when the times were right, but South Africa is looking at the Everest of educational problems. The racists who took power in 1948 had no idea how huge a problem they were leaving their grandchildren and the grandchildren of their neighbors. They are about to find out.

For those of us lucky enough to live in more settled parts of the world, educational issues are framed in different terms—do our schools measure up to the schools in the next state or the schools in a competing country? We aren't forced into a curriculum of subservience. The issues now are subtler, but still significant as we try to measure up to our trading partners and emerging nations try to measure up to us. A quick review of quantity and quality measures shows just how much difference there is between nations in their response to educational options.

The Quantity of Education

There has been much discussion in the United States recently about the length of the school year. People point out that our chief economic competitors send their children to school 240 days per year while ours only attend 180 days. Some communities have moved to close the gap, but differences are still significant. However, the length of the school year is only one measure of quantity. Children around the world have vastly different school experiences based not just on the number of days in the official calendar but on the number of days and number of years they actually attend. Let's begin with some international comparisons of attendance data.

ATTENDANCE

Driving through northern Namibia can be a frustrating experience. The most significant local industry is cattle raising, and around any bend might be a herd of cattle being raised right on the highway. Each herd, usually six to fifteen in number, is watched carefully by a boy around age ten. Tending that herd is his job—all day, every day. If he has a brother of a similar age they may share the work, alternating herd tending and school attendance, but often the boy herds cattle full time—his days of school attendance ended after just three or four years. His nation is full of boys and girls just like him. According to the Namibian Ministry of Education, there are eighty-six thousand children enrolled in first grade in the country. There are five thousand in twelfth grade. Sadly, in countries the world over, there are similar figures.

Here are some international comparisons on school attendance (DOE 1992a:409):

Country	Percentage Attending Elementary	Percentage Attending Secondary
Algeria	94	61
Ivory Coast	75	20
Egypt	97	81
Ghana	75	39
Nigeria	70	19
Tanzania	63	4
Afghanistan	24	8
China	100	44
India	98	43
Japan	100	96
Pakistan	38	20
France	100	97
Germany	100	100
Poland	99	81
United States	N/A	89

What is remarkable about the figures is the range. Japan, noted for its strong schools, leads the world, with a high school completion rate exceeding 90 percent. Then there is the developing world—places where one child in ten or only one in twenty even finishes high school.

For developing nations a second attendance measure is significant—the percentage of children who finish sixth grade. This is a meaningful measure. By the end of sixth grade a child is reading independently, has a good foundation in arithmetic, some knowledge of science, geography, and history, and has internalized the daily disciplines of schooling. In short, a sixth-grade graduate is employable for certain jobs. At the same time, poor countries often restrict access to secondary school, either by fees or by tests. So a fair comparison of developing nations would be the percentage who complete sixth grade. Here Afghanistan, at 24 percent, is at the bottom, followed by Ethiopia and Pakistan at 38 percent, and the Sudan at 49 percent. But many developing countries are into ranges of 70 and 80 percent. And there have been big improvements since 1970. Ethiopia has gone from 16 percent to 38 percent grade school completion. Kenya moved from 58 percent to 93 percent. India went from 73 percent to 98 percent.

Unfortunately, not all countries have moved in the right direction. According to official figures, Zaire has dropped from 88 percent to 78 percent grade school completion since 1970. But one school official says even the 78 percent figure is just wishful thinking: "Today it is impossible to get statistics on students and teachers. All the figures you will be given are made up. The state no longer exists in this country" (NGONGO 1995). With the collapse of the civil service in Zaire, civil servants, teachers among them, go unpaid. Many quit; others teach only if paid directly by students. Students who can afford it carry not only their books to school, but also rice, flour, smoked fish, gasoline, and even secondhand clothing to pay their teachers. And what of the students who can't afford to pay their teachers? Education stops.

TIME ON TASK

The number of years a child is in school is the most important quantitative measure of learning, but there are others. We could also look at the number of days in the year and the number of hours in the day. These are international variations on the number of days per year of instruction (DOE 1992b:17):

Country	Days of Instruction
China	251
Korea	222
Taiwan	222
Israel	215
Japan	210+
Italy	204
Soviet Union	198
England	192
Canada	188
Spain	188
United States	178
Hungary	177
France	174
Portugal	172

HOMEWORK

Here is a quantity measure the average twelve year old may not want to talk about, but it clearly plays a part in education. Homework not only extends the school day but allows students to recast the material in their own terms—to reread when necessary, to seek help privately, to internalize fully. Here, for some selected countries, are the percentages of high school students doing two or more hours of homework a day (DOE 1992b):

Country	Percentage
China	44
Korea	41
Hungary	58
Italy	79
Canada	27
Ireland	63
United States	29

We will discuss the atmosphere for education later, but one point is pertinent to homework—how it is done. For the huge portion of the world's population, homework is as difficult as it was a century ago in the United States—no lights, no heat, no desk or paper. At the other extreme is the Japanese mother who actually helps with the homework. Teachers in Riverdale, New York, saw the difference when Japanese parents all bought two sets of schoolbooks—one for the child and one for the mother, who would learn the material herself so she could help her child (WHITE 1987). So even in something as apparently simple as homework, one hour here doesn't equal one hour there. The quality of the hour will vary with technology and culture.

EXTRA SCHOOLING

Surely as there's a middle class, there are parents who want to give their kids an extra advantage. Besides straight teeth and ten speeds, we give them summer school and piano lessons. While not often talked about in educational planning, these extra hours of school add up. As in so many other cases, however, they don't add up equally. For developing countries, summer school is nonexistent. Part of this is a victory of climate. When the temperature exceeds one hundred degrees every day and there is no air conditioning—or even electricity for fans—heat wins out over good intentions. Even if heat were not an issue, schools that can't afford to hire high school graduates as teachers, and never have enough textbooks, don't have the money for summer school. The 160 or 180 days of the school year is all the school these kids are going to see.

On the other extreme is the Japanese. These children may be enrolled in any of three kinds of supplementary school. How many Japanese children are engaged in this extra schooling? One source estimates that 60–70 percent of all junior high students are attending one of these schools at least two or three afternoons a week, for two hours each session. For many students these extra sessions occur not just in the late afternoon and evening but Saturday afternoon (they have regular school Saturday morning) and Sundays (DUKE 1986). All this is in addition to the 240 days Japanese children attend regular school—60 more days than American children even before all this extra schooling is added.

The experience of American children varies widely. Some are little different from their Third World peers. When the school day and school year ends, their connection to formal schooling is cut. Yet there are also children who attend summer sessions or college-enrichment programs, visit Stanley Kaplan or Sylvan Learning Centers, or go on family vacations with an obvious educational component—the trips to museums, Washington, D.C., and various national parks. The result is that while some of America's children come back to school in September with a three-month experience in soap operas, others come back with a smattering of French, a personal experience with national monuments, and a firmer grasp of the multiplication tables. The distinctions are often stark and have played a part in some of the calls for year-round schooling.

The Quality of Education

We have already seen that in countries such as Namibia, Zimbabwe, and South Africa, where education was used to separate people, the result was not only huge differences in the amount of education certain class of children received but also huge differences in what those children were taught and by whom. Simply put, political policy not only limited the quantity of education, but the quality as well. Differences in quality exist elsewhere in the world as well. Some of these differences result from economics, some result from educational policy. Whatever the cause, the differences can be stark. We will look at four principal areas of difference: teachers, resources, methodology, and curriculum. Appropriately, let's begin with the most crucial component of quality—the teacher.

TEACHERS

We change textbooks every seven to ten years, change teaching methods once a generation, and change our curriculum whenever the legislature is in session or the principal has been to a conference. What we don't change is the fact that we expect education to consist of a room, some children, and a teacher. The right teacher can find excitement in even the most politically correct textbook, can salvage any methodology, and can outlast any politician or administrator. But what's the right teacher? There may be many attributes that define a teacher as such, but I will focus on two—talent and training.

TALENT. The question of who goes into teaching is an interesting one because it seems to vary over time and from place to place. In much of the developing world the teaching profession has a lock on talent because there are so few alternatives. In Africa the mass of people are engaged in subsistence farming or drift into the cities to perform unskilled labor. With industrial production in decline for two decades there is very little call for business or engineering skills. At the time of independence there was a need for college graduates to take over the civil service from expatriate Europeans, but those positions are now filled or even overfilled. So a bright teenager reviewing the opportunities may see teaching as the only alternative. Teaching offers steady employment, a passable salary, and a position of respect in the community. Besides, what else is there?

An American teenager is faced with a very different situation. Job cycles come and go, but in general there is a wide range of opportunities—for both men and women. Teaching offers job security, long vacations, and a work day that gets mothers home at the same time as their children (usually), but it has its disadvantages too. Salaries are low in relation to competing professions. College freshmen have to know they will earn a minimum of five thousand dollars less than their college roommates if they choose teaching as a career (u.s. census 1993):

Career	Average Starting Salary in 1992
Teaching	22,171
Engineering	34,620
Accounting	28,404
Business	27,156
Liberal arts	27,324
Chemistry	30,360
Math	29,473
Computing	30,888

Besides low salaries, we have weekly exposés on the trouble in our schools—descriptions of attacks on teachers, descriptions of incompetent teachers—and anytime that settles down we have contract negotiations that pit teachers against the community and bring out the worst in both. A bright eighteen year old could be forgiven for wanting to forget the whole thing. And they do. We know from college-entrance examinations that future teachers are far down the list in their SAT scores (byers 1984). One study of bright high school students who had rejected teaching summed up the problem: They were concerned about "job autonomy, working conditions, availability of jobs, social status of teaching, opportunities for advancement, and salary" (TINCHER 1986). The best and the brightest Americans want more money and more respect than they will ever see in teaching.

The situation is very different in Japan. Here, too, career opportunities are extensive, but teaching compares quite favorably with any of them. In 1987 starting salaries for Japanese teachers were $19,000 to $20,000 (U.S. teachers were averaging $17,600 at the time) (WHITE 1987), two thousand more than other government sectors, and within a dollar or two of the income for the famous corporate "salaryman." With that very adequate salary goes both respect and opportunity.

Respect comes from tradition. As Merry White puts it, "The prewar teacher was the embodiment of virtue; the concrete knowledge the child might absorb was secondary to the moral virtue acquired by emulating the teacher" (83). The tradition has changed with the times, but much of it remains. Students begin each class by rising to say, "Teacher, please do us the favor of teaching us." Students go to their teachers' homes over the New Year's holidays to pay their respects. In some cases they will return years later to pay their respects to former teachers.

Teachers are not only accorded respect but have opportunities not available to the average salaryman. One is creativity and independence. While teachers follow a prescribed curriculum and use approved textbooks, they still have the classroom to themselves and can exercise more independent control than is found in some other professions, where constant consensus-making forces loyalty to a group. This independence also shows up in very practical matters. While the salaryman is forced by peer pressure to not only work unpaid overtime with his peers, he must follow the overtime with extensive socializing that keeps him away from his family. Teachers can avoid both the overtime and the drinking.

Given the salaries, respect, and freedom, it is no wonder the best and brightest Japanese youths want to be teachers. But few of them have the opportunity. Japanese teacher education programs can only accept one-fourth of the applicants. They take the best of the best.

TRAINING. Teacher training varies as much as teacher selection around the globe. To begin with, remember that most of a teacher's training comes long before college. Teachers are the products of the very schools to which they return. These schools produce strikingly different results. To illustrate some of the differences, here is just one comparison published in 1982, showing how the world's fourteen year olds vary in their knowledge of science (INKELES 1982:214–215):

Country	Score (1–40 scale)
Australia	24.6
Belgium	21.2
England	21.3
Finland	20.5
Germany	23.7
Hungary	29.1
Italy	18.5
Japan	31.2
New Zealand	24.2
Sweden	21.7
United States	21.6
Chile	9.2
India	7.6
Iran	7.8
Thailand	15.6

These fourteen year olds from 1982 are now young teachers. As we can see, they come to their careers with very different levels of science knowledge. Our immediate observation is that these children fall into two groups: those from industrialized nations and those from the developing world. With the exception of Italy, the science scores of all the industrialized countries ranged from twenty to thirty-one, and with the exception of Thailand, the science scores of all the developing nations fell below ten. The gulf is wide and obvious. And if anything, the differences are worse than they appear on the table. For while 95 percent of children are included in the scores of industrialized nations, only 25 percent of the children of Iran and India are included, because only 25 percent of their fourteen year olds were still attending school in 1982. So one could read the table to say that in 1982 the educational elite of Iran or India knew one-fourth as much science as the average Japanese student. Not a happy circumstance for the developing world.

Some of these children went on to become teachers. As we have seen in the cases of Zimbabwe, Namibia, and South Africa, in much of the developing world these fourteen year olds may have received little additional training before taking over a classroom themselves. Maybe they went on to finish high school, maybe they did not. Maybe they went on to a teacher training college, maybe they did not. In either case, a decade later they were teaching, taking their 7 percent science score with them.

For the elite of the developing world, a teacher training college awaits them. What are the colleges like? I had an opportunity to visit the Teacher Training College at Ongwediva in northern Namibia. With an enrollment of 767, it graduated 359 teachers in 1994. Prospective students must have graduated high school or, if they only finished tenth grade, must already have two years' teaching experience. In either case they must also pass a written English and mathematics test and sit for an interview. Professors having only bachelor's degrees themselves teach an average of twenty-six hours per week. Students are bright, cheerful, and eager. Everything looks perfect until you walk into a science lab and discover there is only one microscope and no chemistry equipment or chemicals. There is no computer on campus. The library is a single room—twenty by thirty feet—and while filled with eager students, is virtually denuded of books. If these students were typical of their developing world peers and knew one-fourth the science of their Japanese counterparts when they were in ninth grade, there is little in the labs or library that will help them close that gap.

RESOURCES

While a creative teacher can do a lot with very little, teachers still need something to work with. As with every other aspect of education, the resources teachers have available to them vary dramatically from place to place.

Consider Russia and the remnants of the Soviet Union. Schools in Moscow are equivalent of urban schools in the United States. But out in the countryside fewer than half the schools have indoor toilets. This in a country where winter temperatures hit thirty to fifty below zero. Even rudimentary electrical service is hit and miss in a land where darkness may fill most of the day. This lack of electricity also means microcomputers or other modern teaching aids are a problem. While computers are plentiful in Moscow high schools, when the state created an informatics course and required it of all high school students, the vast majority practiced typing on a cardboard drawing of a keyboard and wrote programs and "ran" them by taking them to the teacher, who mentally ran the program and told students if their output was correct. Most students graduated from the course without ever seeing an actual computer, much less using one.

Similar disparities exist across the United States. Some schools in this country not only have plentiful computers for students, but are introducing telecommunications. Texas has taken the leadership here with their TENET (Texas Education Network) being used to link classrooms with people and resources around the world. Students can get daily updates from NASA or contact students in classrooms around the world. TENET is already being used to give students special opportunities in science, history, current affairs, geography, and foreign languages. Students have direct access to far more information and far more current information than would ever be available in a textbook. Meanwhile, other states, especially rural states, have few phone links to their schools and use the few computers they may have for endless drills. Students at either end of this extreme may spend the same number of hours in school each day, but the educational opportunities they have during those hours are wildly divergent.

CURRICULUM

What we teach also varies across the world. For starters, there are the subjects themselves—which get taught and for how long. Then there is tracking—who gets put in what class and at what level. There is also the political component—the number of hours used by the government to push its aims.

Let's start with the simplest area—courses and teaching times. Below is a chart of subjects and "units," or "hours," each should receive (LAWSON 1988). Actual class-period lengths vary from place to place, so comparisons aren't exact, but the figures should provide a general sense of what is taught where:

Location	Native Language	Math	Science	Social Studies	Physical Education	Art	Foreign Language
Maryland	4	3	2	3	1	1	0
Texas	4	3	2	3	1	0	0
France	3	4	3	4	1	0	4
Japan	4	4	4	4	4	2	4
Germany	4	4	4	4	0	0	4
Zimbabwe	4	4	4	4	0	0	4

The core of the curriculum around the world seems set. Everyone agrees that the native language should be taught, plus science, math, social studies, and a foreign language. The only country that seems to stand out at all is the United States, where high school students are required to take less science and math and no foreign language. But with the exception of the United States, the rest of the world seems to have a pretty unified idea of what should go on in high school.

TRACKING. Where more fundamental differences lie is in who should get what courses in what form. Here we have wild extremes. On one side we have Europe and the United States, where tracking is widespread; on the other side we have Africa and Japan, where tracking is minimal.

In virtually every country in Europe, students take a common core of courses through seventh or eighth grade, and then split into two or even three tracks. Germany is the best-known example. Children here have identical education through the first two years of junior high school. At the end of the second year, parents (not teachers) make the decision about which track their children will follow. There are three. Currently 19.8 percent go on to the Gymnasium—the academic high school leading to university admission. Enrollment in full-time vocational schools is 22.9 percent—with the chance of being admitted to selected university programs—and 57.3 percent enter part-time vocational schools (MILLER 1982).

Tracking in the United States is far less organized than in Europe. We are all familiar with the two basic tracks—college-bound and not college-bound. Lately a third, or vocational, track is emerging under pressure from employers. Often labeled tech prep, this track tries to combine academic coursework with job experience. The actual quality of the technical training tends to vary dramatically from one school to the next.

While Europe and the United States separate students by one means or another, Japan does very little tracking. Japan has discussed tracks but is reluctant to move to a form of education that reduces a child's options for later success. There is also a general agreement from employers that they will provide whatever technical training new employees will need. This still leaves the problem of what to do with children who have limited academic abilities. Some distinctions are addressed by having high schools with their own admission tests, so that students are somewhat tracked according to ability by the high school that admits them. Nevertheless, over 96 percent of students attend and graduate high school of some sort, and the primary focus of all high schools is academic.

There is almost no tracking in African high schools either, but for very different reasons. First, only a small number of African students ever attend high school, so ability tracking is not needed. Second, vocational training is associated with colonial policies. For instance, the white minority government of Rhodesia (now Zimbabwe) set up "F2" secondary schools. These were to be vocational schools with agricultural farms in the rural areas and an industrial focus in urban areas. Since the white government would only allow 12.5 percent of black children to attend academic secondary schools, these F2 schools were seen as an attempt to deprive blacks of an education that might enable them to attend universities and take on positions of power. Furthermore, the rural F2 school had such an agricultural focus that it was viewed as a way of keeping blacks out of the cities by denying them skills that could get them urban jobs. With its Marxist orientation, the majority government, when it took over the country in 1980, tried to launch a program of "Education with Production." This was immediately opposed by parents, students, and teachers, who thought it resembled the old F2 schools. The result was a de-emphasis of technical subjects.

This has been the pattern across Africa. In 1950, 22 percent of African secondary school students were in vocational schools. By 1975, when most countries had become independent, the figure was 8 percent. During the same time the countries in Asia and Eastern Europe were increasing their vocational schools. As we saw at the beginning of this chapter, often African students pass up excellent vocational schools, such as the Windhoek Technical High School, but the racist legacy is long-lasting. Convincing students and their parents that vocational education is not subservient education is nearly impossible.

HIDDEN TRACK. While the curricular tracks available to children vary dramatically across the globe, what does not vary is the presence of unofficial tracks—pressures on certain kinds of students to take particular kinds and levels of classes. Nowhere in the world is there genuine equality of opportunity.

One hidden track is principally for racial and ethnic minorities. John Ogbu of the University of California at Berkeley has studied the education of minority students in the United States, Britain, Israel, India, Japan, and New Zealand. He finds a consistent pattern in all six countries. In every case, minority students trail the majority in school enrollment, literacy rates, classroom performance, graduation rates, and IQ tests. The reasons for the reduced performance are many. In India, the Harijan minority was denied any schooling until early in this century. In Israel, oriental Jews attended different schools from the dominant Ashkenazim until 1948. Japan's Buroku were formally excluded from schooling until early in this century and are still somewhat segregated. The Maoris of New Zealand have experienced exclusion, then inclusion, and are now being treated more separately. The West Indians of Britain are not formally separated from whites but are largely taught in poorer schools with black majorities. The historical exclusion of black students in the United States is well known.

Besides an ugly history and large-scale current poverty, what these minorities also share is a view of the world at odds with schooling. If they identify themselves as part of a minority oppressed by a majority, then the majority-controlled school can be seen as a player in that oppression. As Ogbu puts it, "The strong distrust for the schools makes it difficult for the minorities to fully accept school goals and rules. To the extent that children are aware of this relationship and of adult perceptions of the schools, it is that much harder for them . . . to accept school goals and regulations and to persevere and perform to the maximum at their school tasks" (OGBU 1982:275).

Not that minorities are the only ones tracked into reduced opportunity. Friszman's studies of education in Eastern Europe showed that while everyone was equal under communism, rural kids were somehow less equal. In Poland, 39 percent of rural children who wanted to attend secondary school were unable to. Those who did get into a secondary school were largely tracked into basic vocational schools. Only 12 percent of them were able to attend an academic high school, compared to 29 percent of the urban children. This is repeated at the country's universities, where only 14 percent of total enrollment was rural in background (FRISZMAN 1982).

The third major group to be tracked in negative directions is females. The National Science Foundation has gathered extensive data that shows the removal of American girls from math and science classrooms. From a rough parity with boys in sixth grade, by twelfth grade girls are a small minority— a minority that gets smaller every year in college. On occasion, someone will point to the uniquely American system of high school electives as the problem. Make every student take the same classes, they would say, and the destructive American system of peer pressure won't be able to force girls into stereotyped roles.

Unfortunately, the experience of Japan and Russia shows the problem is more complicated than that. Neither country allows electives among core subjects or separate courses for girls and boys. But differences still crop up. In Russia boys and girls may finish high school with similar backgrounds, but then they go separate ways. At one leading university, men represented 86 percent of physics students, 67 percent of geology majors, and 67 percent of applied math majors. Women were the majority in chemistry, biology, and economics. In Japan, girls are tracked with more subtlety. White tells us families are less likely to pay for expensive private school lessons for their daughters. Although they want their daughters to go to college, they see problems if the girls go to the best schools: "Girls who enter Tokyo University, the pinnacle of academic success, may find themselves completely ineligible for marriage, because Tokyo University males (and all others) prefer to marry presumably less independent women from a less exalted institution" (WHITE 1987:155).

It appears impossible to find an educational system anywhere in the world that gives all children an equal opportunity. Hidden tracks are waiting to push many of them onto the sidelines.

Cultures of Education

One final aspect of education has to be described. As we mentioned at the beginning of this chapter, education occurs within a culture. In Korea, we have a culture that reveres teachers. In the United States, teachers are frequently laughingstocks. Other aspects of the culture play roles as well.

THE POLITICAL HOUR

If there is another universal to school systems around the world, it is that for some period of time, usually one to five hours per week, and under some label, usually civics or history, whatever political or religious organization runs the school will demand its time to strut its stuff. The class should be entitled "We Are the Best," for that is its content across the globe. In the developing world the class usually describes the heroic struggle against the colonists. In the former Communist Bloc the class covered the miracle of Marxism.

In Florida a group of fundamentalists have taken charge of a district and stated publicly that American civilization is superior: "Instruction shall also include and instill in our students an appreciation of our American heritage and culture, such as: our republican form of government, capitalism, a free enterprise system, patriotism, strong family values, freedom of religion and other basic values that are superior to other foreign or historic cultures" (WALKER 1994c). It must be marvelous to live in Florida. To not only be the best in the world, but the best in the history of the world. What a pinnacle. Good thing Florida has the world's lowest crime rate, lowest teen pregnancy rate, highest literacy rate, highest per capita income, and longest life expectancy in the world, or teachers in that district might be uncomfortable with the official version of "the truth." But they aren't any more uncomfortable than their colleagues around the world, all of whom are required to use class time for this year's version of "we're number one."

The one exception, oddly enough, seems to be Japan, where the official motto is, apparently, "We're dead last and the future looks terrible indeed." Rather than being given the usual rah-rah treatment, Japanese children are regularly given the raspberries. The problems of Japan they are told, are many, but the focus is on three general areas: the country's small size, its lack of natural resources, and its vulnerability to disasters such as earthquakes and monsoons. There is some truth in this. Japan is a small, mountainous country with little room, its resources in coal and fish are being depleted, and earthquakes are frequent. But there is also a political component. Essentially the message is, it's tough being Japanese, and the only way we will make it is if we all pull together.

This message is brought directly into schools. They have regular earthquake drills complete with padded hats. There is a practical side to this of course, but it is also a reminder of Japan's fragility. The message comes through in required readings—typically involving someone who has encountered and persevered over amazing impediments. Helen Keller is a common subject. It comes through in sports participation, where children on a team report to school at 7:00 A.M. six days a week plus holidays. It comes through in elementary school textbooks, in a book about work that makes no description of middle-class office workers but concentrates exclusively on fishmongers, rice farmers, wood cutters, and factory workers—tough jobs that require endurance and patience (DUKE 1986:142). The message is loud and consistent—life is hard here and only perseverance will bring success.

Japan's political message is, of course, a distortion. It is no more at the bottom of the world than Florida is at the top. But in both places and everywhere else in the world, facts are colored to meet the goals of those in power.

FAMILY

Writing barely a decade ago, Keith Watson describes the breakdown of the family in England and its effects on the classroom: "Of a class of 30 children in an English classroom . . . at least 12 will suffer from the trauma of marital breakdown, 9 will come from families where there has been at least one divorce and remarriage, between 12 and 15 will have mothers out at work, 2.5 will have one parent chronically sick, 3 (an underestimate) will have fathers unemployed" (1984:187).

Bad as that sounds, there are teachers all over America who would trade their classrooms for those in England in an instant. So "12 will suffer from marital breakdown." You mean, they might ask in envy, 18 out of 30 have parents who are married? And 3 have unemployed fathers. Does that mean 27 have employed fathers whom they see on a regular basis? In an America in which less than 50 percent of minority children are born to married mothers and in which whites are rapidly moving toward that figure, *family* is becoming an increasingly obscure term.

It would be nice to think that while America had lost its head, maybe the rest of the world was doing better, but that seems not to be the case. Figures on teen pregnancy and single parenthood establish an uncomfortable trend. In much of the world, children have less parenting available to them.

DISRUPTIONS

Schools are not isolated from the world around them. What happens outside the walls echoes inside. This has been demonstrated most recently in South Africa. Through the decades of struggle for majority rule, protests and rallies were a common occurrence in some parts of the country. They played a role in securing majority rule, but there was a price. In those parts of the country where political activity was strongest, such as Johannesburg, the pass rate on the national high school exams was just 28.4 percent the year before elections. In rural South Africa, where political activity is much less, the pass rate was 64.98 percent. Describing the rural schools, one deputy principal said, "Most pupils want to be at school. There is a student's representative council but it concerns itself with school matters. The remoteness of the area means teachers can't attend rallies or demonstrations" ("Rural" 1994:6). Remoteness meant serenity, which meant learning occurred.

The figures from South Africa remind us of how fragile a learning environment is. The political activists of Johannesburg didn't set out to disrupt schools. But a day out for this rally, an evening out for that demonstration, classes that slide into political arguments, and suddenly the interest in studying chemistry or algebra is gone. But the students' opportunity to learn is gone too. They will only be fifteen once. The base of skills that didn't get built that year will create a deficiency that will be visible a lifetime.

Summary

Education is a complex system. Much work is being done around the world, but it is too often fragmented, based on partial visions of the problem, like blind men identifying the elephant. In the United States many efforts are going into increasing the qualifications of teachers. That may be good, but for every corporation that pays an award to an outstanding local teacher, there's another corporation putting ads on Saturday morning TV that say "teachers are dweebs." Besides, any eighteen year old who can read a newspaper can see that choosing a teaching career is a good way to get beaten up and have her car vandalized.

So it goes with each piece of the puzzle—curriculum, resources, methodology, and environment. People work on one piece of the puzzle but ignore the others, or work on one piece while other forces are working in the opposite direction. So we end up with very different results. Some countries have a comprehensive effort that is producing good results, other countries aren't keeping up. A child unlucky enough to be born into one of the latter countries may find that if he or she ever does get a chance to listen in on the global conversation, she cannot understand what is being said.

Chapter 10   Psychology

I . . . stopped when it was apparent that I couldn't get
anybody to listen.

       —ROGER BOISJOLY *(Morton-Thiokol engineer*
       who tried to stop the Challenger *launch)*

AT 11:38 A.M. ON 28 JANUARY 1986, shuttle flight 51-L—the *Challenger*—lifted off from Cape Canaveral. It was a cold morning, thirty-six degrees Fahrenheit, far colder than for any previous shuttle launch. On board were seven astronauts: Francis R. Scobee, commander; Michael John Smith, pilot; Ellison S. Onizuka, mission specialist; Judith Arlene Resnick, mission specialist; Ronald Erwin McNair, mission specialist; S. Christa McAuliffe, payload specialist; and Gregory Bruce Jarvis, payload specialist. In seventy-three seconds, all seven would be dead.

Within milliseconds of ignition, gases from the right solid rocket booster began pouring through a loose joint between sections of the booster. Smoke from this area was already visible less than one second into the flight. At 58 seconds flames from the hot gases were burning visibly. For about 5 seconds the plume grew in size, with flames aimed directly at the huge external fuel tank. At 64.660 seconds the hydrogen tank portion of the external tank was breached. Cryogenic liquid hydrogen rushed from the tank directly onto the burning gases from the booster rocket. At 72.201 seconds the shuttle began to break up. The lower attaching strut between the right solid rocket booster and the external tank broke. The solid rocket booster began twisting counterclockwise. At 73.124 seconds the hydrogen tank exploded, causing disintegration of the intertank and the liquid oxygen tank. The *Challenger* exploded in a huge white fireball (PRESIDENTIAL COMMISSION 1986).

Millions of schoolchildren all over the country were watching the launch, because the first teacher-astronaut, Christa McAuliffe, was aboard. Her mission assignment was to broadcast lessons from space. The children sat shocked in school auditoriums as they watched the pieces of the shuttle arc down into the sea. The lesson they learned was that the shuttle was dangerous and that people could die in an instant.

There were more lessons for adults. Most were shocked to learn that space flight could not be considered "routine." Business and military groups had been told that the shuttle represented a reliable vehicle for putting payloads in space. Shuttle flights were to be the equivalent of commercial airlines, with twenty-four flights scheduled each year (U.S. CONGRESS 1987). The shuttle would demonstrate America's mastery of space and compete with commercial challengers such as Europe's Ariane rocket.

But some of the most troubling lessons came as the Presidential Commission (also referred to as the Rogers Commission, after its chair, William Rogers) reviewed engineering documents. They discovered that the leak between sections of the solid rocket booster—the leak that led to the *Challenger* explosion—had been a source of concern for years. As early as 1977 engineers at the Marshall Space Flight Center were highly critical of the design for the solid rocket booster. Nevertheless, Morton-Thiokol received the contract for the solid rocket boosters and used the joint design.

But the engineers at Marshall were correct in their estimate of the joint problem. Damage to O-rings was found on most flights, beginning with flights in 1984. Then came the first low-temperature launch. Flight 51-C was launched 24 January 1985, when the temperature was fifty-three degrees Fahrenheit. This was the lowest temperature to date for a shuttle launch, and it demonstrated a new danger. Stiffened with cold, the O-rings sealed even worse than on previous flights, and there was "blow-by"—evidence that hot gases had passed the primary O-ring and charred the grease between the two seals. The engineers at Morton-Thiokol now knew that cold was a problem.

For that reason, engineers were especially worried the following January about flight 51-L, the *Challenger*. Temperatures at the launch site had dropped into the low twenties, far below the temperatures of any previous shuttle flight. A group of Morton-Thiokol engineers convened a meeting on 27 January to discuss the problems caused by such unusual cold. They called the Kennedy Space Center at Cape Canaveral to get more information about the weather and to warn their liaison there that they considered the cold a problem for the O-rings.

Engineers at the Kennedy Space Center were so concerned that they set up a conference call for the afternoon between the Marshall Space Flight Center, Kennedy Space Center, and Morton-Thiokol. That conference began at 5:45 P.M., was broken off, reconvened at about 9:00 P.M., was recessed at 10:30, and reconvened in its final session at 11:00 P.M. The dialogue of that extended conference was later examined in detail by the Presidential Commission, which examined the *Challenger* disaster. Here is part of the testimony to the Presidential Commission by Roger Boisjoly, an engineer at Morton-Thiokol, about what happened during the conference:

> Those of us who opposed the launch continued to speak out, and I am specifically speaking of Mr. Thompson and myself because in my recollection he and I were the only ones who vigorously continued to oppose the launch. And we were attempting to go back and rereview and try to make clear what we were trying to get across, and we couldn't understand why it was going to be reversed. So we spoke out and tried to explain once again the effects of low temperature. Arnie actually got up from his position which was down the table, and walked up the table and put a quarter pad down in front of the table, in front of the management folks, and tried to sketch out once again what his concern was with the joint, and when he realized he wasn't getting through, he just stopped.
>
> I tried once more with the photos. I grabbed the photos and I went up and discussed the photos once again and tried to make the point that it was my opinion from actual observations that temperature was indeed a discriminator and we should not ignore the physical evidence that we had observed.
>
> And again I brought up the point that SRM-15 [Flight 51-C, January 1985] had a 110 degree arc of black grease while SRM-22 [Flight 61-A, October 1985] had a relatively different amount, which was less and wasn't quite as black. I also stopped when it was apparent that I couldn't get anybody to listen.
>
> (PRESIDENTIAL COMMISSION 1986)

Morton-Thiokol's management recommended going ahead with the launch and signed an assessment of the problem, stating that "if the primary seal does not seat, the secondary seal will seat" (PRESIDENTIAL COMMISSION 1986). With this memo in hand, the Kennedy Space Center and Marshall Space Flight Center also recommended launch of flight 51-L. The secondary seal did not seat and the *Challenger* disaster resulted.

How can managers make such a mistake? They had evidence from past launches. They had their own research data available to them. They had engineers in the room with them saying do not launch. Yet they launched anyway.

First, before we add to all the blame that has been heaped on individual managers and NASA, it is useful to remember that they were engaged in an inherently risky business. Systems like the *Challenger* are incredibly complicated and prone to error. In his book on engineering disasters, *Human Error* (1990), James Reason reminds us that several aspects of technology contribute to the risk:

1. Systems are more automated. The operator is more removed from the process they nominally control.
2. Systems are more complex. Failure of one unit can have multiple effects on other units.
3. Systems have more defenses against failure. But the defenses are also complex and prone to unexpected failure.
4. Systems are more opaque. People who manage and run the systems are less and less aware of what the systems actually do.

In short, modern systems will fail, and we should adjust our expectations accordingly. But having said that, the *Challenger* seems a unique disaster in that a group of engineers were convinced there would be trouble, told their managers there would be trouble, yet the shuttle was launched anyway. Lifesaving information was ignored.

In past chapters we have seen that information can flood an area but be ignored because people are willfully ignorant. Their politics makes them dumb. They burn the books or disable the satellite dishes or keep kids home from Shakespeare. Politics will do that. But the *Challenger* wasn't a political problem. Nobody died from political correctness. This was a different kind of event entirely. Here experts acted not as if they were blinded by belief, but as if they were hypnotised. Only later, when they had a chance to look back, did they seem to wake up.

This hypnotism is a significant barrier to information flow, and as we shall see, the *Challenger* wasn't the first disaster it has caused. These are situations in which the best and brightest have all the information they need to make the right decision but they ignore the crucial data. How can this happen? There are many ways. We will look at just five.

Human Information Processing

We have a new science—cognitive science—which has had a couple decades to pull together and examine mountains of research on how people think, speak, see, reason, and listen. And in general, the news is not very good. We seem to come flawed from the factory. Begin with the fact that there is more going on in the world than we can hope to process. Whether that world is the larger social, scientific, political world, or even the immediate room in which we are seated, we simply cannot attend to all the information available to us. So we filter. We screen out enormous amounts of information.

Take a simple example. Two people are sitting in a restaurant talking. Other people are in the room, but the two are engaged in conversation. If asked later to describe any of the people, or even to tell how many people were in the room, they couldn't do it. Nor could they say much about the restaurant or even the table at which they sat. But say a person at another table gets up and begins walking in their direction. They will both look up, follow the person's motion, and possibly stop their conversation. Why notice the person now? Because a person in motion, especially motion in their direction, is a threat. Random motion or distant motion may be screened out, but motion toward a person will be noted. Our species has learned when it is important to channel its limited information-handling ability. We don't want to be eaten.

Ignoring the overwhelming majority of what goes on in the world around us is hardly admirable. Unfortunately, it is not our worst characteristic as information processors. Research tells us we not only ignore most of the world's information, but what information we do take in, we twist.

Some of the earliest research in this area was conducted by Leon Festinger of Stanford University. He showed that our values can determine what information we will see and what we will ignore. His classic book, *A Theory of Cognitive Dissonance* (1957), provides a number of examples that are relevant here. His theory is simple: people strive for consistency. If they encounter inconsistency, or dissonance, they will try to remove it either by changing their views or by *avoiding situations and information that increase dissonance*. In short, we happily turn a blind eye to information that doesn't match our values.

In one of his better known examples of this kind of information filtering, Festinger describes an experiment with new car buyers in Minnesota. Shown newspaper ads that had been printed in the weeks after they had purchased their car, subjects were asked to note which new car ads they could remember seeing. Of the ads they had seen, which had they gone on to read? By a substantial margin, the ads these people could remember seeing, and the ads these people had taken the time to read, were ads for the cars they had bought. Why were they almost twice as likely to read ads for the model of car they had bought than for other models? The theory says they were glad to have information that confirmed the correctness of their purchase and didn't want to see information that might indicate they had made a mistake.

Think you are an exception, the one truly objective person in a world full of zealots? Consider the following passage:

> Every Saturday night four good friends get together. When Jerry,
> Mike, and Pat arrived, Karen was sitting in her living room writing
> some notes. She quickly gathered the cards and stood up to greet her
> friends at the door. They followed her into the living room but as

usual they couldn't agree on exactly what to play. Jerry eventually took a stand and set things up. Finally they began to play. Karen's recorder filled the room with soft and pleasant music. Early in the evening, Mike noticed Pat's hand and the many diamonds. As the night progressed the tempo of play increased. Finally a lull in the activities occurred. Taking advantage of this, Jerry pondered the arrangement in front of him. Mike interrupted Jerry's reverie and said, "Let's hear the score." They listened carefully and commented on their performance. Then they all went home.   (ANDERSON 1977)

The passage is simple enough. Anyone can understand it. It's about a group of musicians, right? They get together, follow a score, play. Very simple. Except a significant number of people don't think it's about musicians at all. They think it is about card players. They play cards, keep score. Is that what the passage is about? How could two different people come up with totally different interpretations of the same passage? Who is right and who is wrong?

Rereading the passage you should find that either interpretation works fine. Both are fully justified by the language and the events that take place. Both are, in fact, "right." What is odd is that people generally take one view of the passage and totally overlook the other possibility. If they read it to be about card players, it was obviously about card players. No other interpretation seems reasonable to them. When Richard Anderson's research team asked readers about other interpretations, 62 percent said another interpretation had never occurred to them. Another 20 percent only became aware of another interpretation when they began answering multiple choice questions.

Why is it readers take one view or the other? Why do some people see card players and other musicians? And why do they only see one interpretation? Cognitive science currently uses schema theory as its best explanation for how people interpret events around them. Schema theory begins with a model of human memory. Facts or experiences are grouped or clustered around topics or "schemata." These clusters may contain images, events, and processes. A frequently used example is the restaurant schema. If asked to recall what a restaurant is, research indicates we not only call up an image of a restaurant's exterior but also recall the process by which we order, eat, and pay, the kinds of people who work in restaurants, and the kinds of food we normally find there. So a schema is a rich collection of information, all of which seems instantly accessible to people once a topic, such as "restaurant," has been mentioned.

Schema theory serves especially useful in explaining why people can understand each other even though our typical conversations omit much of what would seem to be crucial information. For instance, if a person said, "I went to Marie's Diner last night, but after ten minutes I got up and left," a listener could well respond, "Yes, I heard the service is bad there." If you think about this conversation, and about most conversations you hear, the speakers leave out as much as 90 percent of the information critical to determining what went on, yet speakers and listeners still understand each other. In the conversation about Marie's Diner, the first speaker tells of getting up but never talks about sitting down. The speaker and listener assume that when one goes to a restaurant, one goes to a table and sits. When the speaker describes leaving after ten minutes, the listener assumes it is because of bad service—that a waiter or waitress should have come to the table during that time and taken an order.

What makes such an abbreviated conversation possible is that both speaker and listener share an understanding of restaurants—what they look like, what one does there, what employees are expected to do. A fair amount of research shows that people do in fact demonstrate such understandings. They are useful not just in conversations but in our understanding of the world. We see a restaurant and know what to do when we get inside. We share similar understandings for "school," "hospital," "grocery store," and so on.

But what happens if we encounter something new or ambiguous? The test passage above was written so that words such as "score" could be read in more than one way. Avid card players see the word and pull up their "card schema." With it comes images of where cards are played, who plays them, and how they are played. The passage seems to match up well with the card schema, so it seems obvious that the passage is about cards. To musicians, "score" fits another schema. It brings up another set of people and activities, and, as it turns out, the rest of the passage matches up. Two different schemata are called up, tested, found to match, and used to create two totally different interpretations of the passage. Each reader not only feels their interpretation is right, they can't even image a different view.

Had the passage been part of a conversation, with one person describing the previous nights activities, it might continue with a listener responding:

"I like playing too. You'll have to have me over sometime."
"We'd be glad to have you. How about next Wednesday?"
"I'll be there."

Next Wednesday could be very interesting. Depending upon how the listener interpreted the original conversation, he might show up at the house carrying either a tuba or a deck of cards. Only then would the two discover whether they really understood each other or were happily sharing two totally different conversations.

Confusing violins and pinochle seems comic, and we can all recall conversations that had to be interrupted midstream when we suddenly realized the depth of our confusion, but interpreting the world from a base of experience might not be funny at all. To see just how tragic alternative interpretation can be, we need look no further than Rodney King.

The videotape of the police beating Rodney King, shown daily on television, was electrifying. The nation watched the police beat a black man as he lay on the ground alongside a highway. The meaning of the tape was obvious. Unfortunately, while the interpretations of the tape were obvious, they were not unanimous. It became chillingly clear that the white Ventura County jury saw a totally different tape than the African American residents of South Central Los Angeles. Each group saw the same tape. How could they possibly have such different reactions to it? Schema theory provides a very simple answer.

White jurors watched the tape. They saw a black man and pulled up their "black male" schema. In their schema black men are frequently criminals. The fact that this one was surrounded by police reinforced that view. Bring a criminal, he would confront or disobey the police. To the jurors, his actions matched that expected behavior. Police also have a role in the "black male" schema, and jurors saw them behaving as they expected. In the end, they saw on tape what matched their expectations. They saw no criminal behavior on the part of police.

The citizens of South Central Los Angeles also saw the tape. They saw the white cops surrounding Rodney King and called up their "white cop" schema. Every baton blow, every kick, matched up with their schema. The cops behaved as they expected them to. Rodney King behaved as they expected him to. Everything matched up with the behavior they expected—white cops brutalizing a black male. The citizens of South Central saw documented evidence of criminal behavior from police.

That different people and different cultures have widely different experiences means that the same information will have different meanings. It will be taken, and twisted, routinely, because that is how our species works. We are not neutral observers. The information we have access to, the little bit we don't consciously ban or unconsciously ignore, we twist to fit our experience/expectations/prejudices. Welcome to the information age, where the blind lead the bigoted.

Groupthink

Irving Janis is known for his reflections on political disasters. How can it be, he would ask, that a group of highly educated, well-informed, well-intentioned leaders can make decisions that turn out to be so amazingly stupid? Yet such decisions occur again and again in administration after administration (and corporate board room after corporate board room).

His classic analysis is of a fiasco well known to every middle-aged American—the Bay of Pigs. On 17 April 1961, a brigade of fourteen hundred Cuban exiles, aided by the U.S. Navy, the U.S. Air Force, and the CIA, invaded the southern coast of Cuba. They lasted three days before surrendering. Two hundred men died, and the invasion force never got off the beach. Survivors spent two years in Cuban jails before being ransomed by the United States for $53 million in food and medicine. Political damage for the United States was almost as bad. It was clear the invasion was U.S. led from the start, and American attempts to pretend otherwise just branded a generation of U.S. leaders as liars. For President Kennedy, who had been in office just four months, the failure and the lies dashed many of the hopes that had been raised by his presidency. As one critic said at the time, "Nixon or Kennedy: Does it make any difference?" (Less difference than the critic might have known, since Nixon was the man who initiated the invasion plan when he was vice president under Eisenhower.)

Before the first day had ended it was clear that everything the U.S. leadership had assumed would work would not. They believed no one would know the United States was behind the invasion. That assumption proved false before the exiles even hit the beach. In the weeks before the invasion a number of people had leaked the plan to the press. There were so many people involved in so many places it was naïve to assume leaks wouldn't happen. So, as it turned out, before the first shot was fired, U.S. involvement was already an established fact.

Kennedy's planning team also assumed the Cuban air force was weak and could be knocked out using obsolete B-26 planes whose markings had been removed. Old planes made it look more like these could be exile planes, but old planes also have engine trouble. So did these. Only a small portion of Castro's planes were destroyed, while half of the B-26s were shot down. Cuban planes were able to drive off all resupply efforts for the invasion, and to attack the exiles as they lay exposed on the beach.

The team believed the exiles had high morale. It turned out they did fight well, but there were many problems within the invasion force, including a mutiny at one of the training sites in Guatemala. No information about that mutiny or other problems ever made it to White House discussions.

The team assumed Cuba's army was weak. As it turned out, the U.S. bombings tipped them off to approaching trouble, so they had patrols out. One patrol happened on the invasion vanguard. Within hours the Cuban army was on the scene with howitzers and rocket launchers. Tanks arrived on day two. By then, the fourteen hundred invaders faced an army of twenty thousand.

The team assumed and expected that news of the invasion would encourage local resistance to the Castro government. But here again the bombings warned the Cuban government that trouble was coming (assuming they hadn't read about the invasion preparations in the American press). In Havana alone, the police rounded up two hundred thousand suspects (JANIS 1982). Nationwide, resistance was minor and totally disorganized.

As a last resort, the team assumed that the invasion force could retreat to the Escambray Mountains, where they could join up with other resistance forces and be a permanent thorn in Castro's side. Had anyone of the president's team looked at a map of Cuba, they would have seen the Escambray Mountains were eighty miles from the Bay of Pigs, across swamps and jungles that would have made escape to the mountains nearly impossible if there had not been a single soldier in their way. Covering eighty miles through that terrain while under fire was simply not possible. As it turned out, the invaders never crossed the first mile.

The invasion was based on six assumptions. An error in any one assumption would cause real problems. It turned out every assumption was wrong and the invasion never had a chance. The best and the brightest were wrong about everything. Two hundred men died and the Kennedy administration began its tenure in office with an epic failure.

How do bright people make such colossal blunders? Janis presents six causes:

1. The illusion of invulnerability.
2. The illusion of unanimity.
3. Suppression of personal doubts.
4. Self-appointed mindguards.
5. Docility fostered by suave leadership.
6. A taboo against antagonizing valuable new members.

The belief that one is invulnerable must be a constant problem for occupants of the Oval Office. To hold such power, to be surrounded by such talent, to be preceded by such historic figures. How could anyone in that room consider the possibility of failure? To quote a government figure of the time, "It seemed that, with John Kennedy leading us and with all the talent he had assembled, nothing could stop us" (JANIS 1982:35). Who could sit in that room surrounded by those famous men and believe in the reality of Cuban tanks, or the reality of broken B-26 engines?

It must have been an awe-inspiring sight—a large group of exceptionally talented men arriving at a unanimous decision. And it must have seemed nearly impossible. After all, these were strong-willed, highly independent individuals. Yet these were individuals surrounded by men of equal talent. High school valedictorians can be impressed by high school valedictorians, and Pulitzer Prize winners can be speechless in a room full of Pulitzer Prize winners. Historians tell us Dean Rusk asked penetrating questions about the invasion plans when back at the State Department but was silent at White House meetings. Such silence was common and was taken for agreement. Each silent man assumed he was the only one who had doubts.

Besides a sense that there was unanimity, how else could doubters be silenced? Arthur Schlesinger mentions the "virile poses" assumed by CIA representatives who presented the invasion plans. Once testosterone entered the room, doubters wanted to show they were just as manly as the CIA folks. Because expressions of doubt might be interpreted as expressions of personal weakness, they were suppressed.

The rare person who was willing to express a doubt, first had to make it through a gauntlet of "mind-guards." Robert Kennedy told one doubter, "You may be right or you may be wrong, but the President has made his mind up. Don't push it any further. Now is the time for everyone to help him all they can" (JANIS 1982:40). The president may not have considered suppressing information much of a "help," but his supporters felt that way, so information was filtered.

Not that President Kennedy was blameless. Records of the time show that his leadership style stifled contrary views. Kennedy invited Senator J. William Fulbright to a group meeting on 4 April 1961 and allowed Fulbright to present his dissenting opinion. But after Fulbright had stated his case, rather than calling for any discussion of Fulbright's ideas, Kennedy moved the meeting to a poll of positions. Each person was to say whether he was for or against the invasion. Even that poll was never completed. A reality check was in the room, but Kennedy's actions as leader minimized the impact the dissenter could have. He followed an agenda that admitted only limited dissent.

To make matters worse, Kennedy's group seemed to go out of its way to be kind to the CIA because they were holdovers from the Eisenhower administration. They were not part of his group. He was trying to bring them into his group and so subjected their ideas to less criticism than he might otherwise have done. He wanted Dulles on his team. To get him there, he was willing to treat Dulles's projects with special reserve.

Do the problems of groupthink occur outside the White House? Of course. Illusions of invulnerability go back over millennia. As conquering generals paraded through the streets of Rome on their way to receive their laurels from the emperor, a man ran along side their chariot repeating, "You are not a god, You are not a god." Whether the general could hear the man over the cheers of the multitudes is open to question. At least the effort was made. As

CEOs fly from city to city in corporate jets, dine at the White House, sit in offices decorated at huge costs, and listen to the polite words of consultants from Harvard and Stanford, who is in the room to say, "You are not a god"? How could any mortal believe in vulnerability when the view from the corner office is so spectacular?

Cultural Blinders

Paul Fussell is the author of one of the finest books ever written about war. *The Great War and Modern Memory* presents a view of World War I that is more complete, and more humane, than virtually any other book available. Among the book's many contributions is a look at the way culture changed with the war. He reminds us that in 1914 Britain had not had a major war in a century, and there had been no war on the Continent since 1871: "No man in the prime of life knew what war was like. All imagined that it would be an affair of great marches and great battles, quickly decided" (FUSSELL 1975:21). That view was reflected in the early depiction of the war. Fussell describes a popular recruiting poster of the time showing a boy in the future asking his obviously troubled father, "Daddy, what did *you* do in the Great War?" Social and moral pressures to join in the war were real. "Glory," "honor," and "courage" were key words. They resonated through the culture. People used them without self-consciousness. "Out of the world of summer, 1914, marched a unique generation," Fussell notes. "It believed in Progress and Art and in no way doubted the benignity even of technology. The word machine was not yet invariably coupled with the word gun" (1975:24). One poem of the time refers to a military charge with the line "Play up! Play up! and play the game!"

When not thinking about honor, glory, and commitment, the talk was of war as a kind of sport. And to the soldiers of the time, sport was not just a metaphor. We know that in 1915 the First Battalion of the Eighteenth London Regiment kicked a soccer ball before them as they attacked the German lines. In the Battle of the Somme, "Captain Nevill, a company commander of the 8th east Surreys, bought four footballs, one for each platoon, during his last London leave before the attack. He offered a prize to the platoon, which, at the jump off, first kicked its football up to the German front line." His company actually tried it. Captain Nevill was killed instantly. Two of the footballs survived.

In retrospect, worries about honor and the kicking of soccer balls through no-man's-land strike us as naïve, childish, or just plain crazy. Eleven years after the war Hemingway was writing, "Abstract words such as glory, honor, courage, or hallow were obscene beside the concrete names of villages, the number of roads, the names of rivers, the numbers of regiments and the dates." Obscenity we understand well; honor eludes us. In the years after the war and before poetry disappeared completely from our culture, the poetry was of T. S. Eliot, who described a land of waste, hollow men, stuffed men.

Hemingway and Eliot remain dominant voices of our times, even if we hear them as distant echoes. Whether it is descriptions of the atrocities of the World War II, the obscenities of Vietnam, or the insanity of Rwanda or Bosnia, we still see with the war-weary eyes of the men dragging themselves out of the trenches in 1918. It is a view we now find "right." Any other view is unacceptable. Spielberg has learned from the reactions to *Schindler's List* that depictions of heroes are not welcome to many. To even describe one hero, one act of courage, one man of honor, is seen as a slur on the memory of all who perished. Heroism cannot be described in our age; only degradation can be presented, only horror.

That the current view of the world may make us less gullible, more appreciative of the depths to which our species can fall, the view is valuable. To the extent the view disallows any thought of honor, courage, and, yes, glory, we wear blinders that hide much of what we are or could be. We may need to be worried men; we don't need to be hollow men. Those who would describe heroes should be given that chance. But we have become so mesmerized by hate and hurt, it may be generations before artists are given that chance. When artists do start presenting heroes again, and more important, having heroic portrayals accepted by the public, we may well look back and wonder why our views were so black for so long.

Technology Fixations

Theodore Levitt's criticism of American railroads has to be common knowledge to everyone who has ever taken a business seminar. His analysis is crushing and oft-quoted: "They assumed themselves to be in the railroad business rather than in the transportation business" (1975:1). They narrowly defined their goals and so stood by while trucking, airplanes, and automobiles overwhelmed them. Their businesses were suffocated, not by lack of effort, but by lack of vision.

While this criticism is true, it is worth just a moment to consider the other side of the story. It is true railroads defined themselves in a fairly narrow way. It is also true that obsessing on trains is not like obsessing on root beer floats or bowling alleys. Levitt is kind enough to provide a quotation that nicely sums up the view railroad men must have had: "By the turn of the century it [the railroad industry] was an institution, an image of man, a tradition, a code of honor, a source of poetry, a nursery of boyhood desires, a sublimest of toys, and the most solemn machine—next to the funeral hearse—that marks epochs in man's life" (LEVITT 1975:10). Railroad men might be forgiven for limiting themselves

to "just" being in the railroad business. In their day they were in the most exciting business their species had yet imagined.

Levitt's final criticism of railroad men is that they had a "product orientation rather than a customer orientation." This is surely true, but it was one hel-
luva product. Mere mortals might be forgiven if they stood in the engine of a
fast-moving freight train and had trouble giving much thought to other ways
they might transport customers and their goods. They were surely hypnotized
by the technology they had developed, but it is hard to blame them.

It seems equally hard to cast many stones at Steve Jobs and his friends in
Cupertino. Yet they are clearly the next best example of technological hypnotism. In their impressive article "The Computerless Computer Company," Rappaport and Halevi point out that Apple only briefly had an edge as a computer
manufacturing company. What made it special was its operating system—its use
of the mouse and icons and menus. Apple had an easy way for mere mortals
to use a complex machine. That operating system would have been a billion-
dollar product with huge profit margins if Apple had just licensed it (several years
after the appearance of this article Apple is trying to do just that, but it seems
to be a case of too little too late). But Apple wanted to sell computers. And the
profits went to the ultimate computerless computer company—Microsoft. As
Rappaport and Halevi put it, "The missed opportunity was vast. Put simply, Apple
could have been Microsoft—a fabulously profitable computer company whose
software defines the desktop computing environment" (1991:72).

But who can blame Apple? Their computers are beautiful. They are historic.
They have a loyal following most cults only dream of. How could any of the Apple
CEOs possibly stand at the end of an assembly line, watch machine after
machine round that final corner, and say, "Let's stop all this and get into the software business." So with hordes of cheering fans screaming their adoration, the
company heads for a questionable future.

The problem for computer companies is the same problem faced by the railroads. How can you participate in the most exciting enterprise of your era yet
somehow retain enough detachment from it to see what is coming next? The
information is there. You don't need a gigabyte network to bring in the articles
with fresh ideas, or satellite communications to get the phone calls. What is
needed is the will to look away from industries experiencing explosive growth
and profits so huge no CEO could spend his share in a lifetime. Who can turn
his back on a winner? Who can look beyond current technology, when current
technology has been so good? The railroads couldn't, Apple couldn't. It will
be interesting to see if Microsoft can. Will Microsoft change when the technology moves on, or will they sit creating ever more dazzling icons for screens
people have stopped using?

Speaking of sitting while the world moves on, individuals are just as prone as corporations, and often for the same reasons. One recent example comes from the world of research universities. Imagine the surprise of the American Council of Learned Societies when their 1985 study of library use showed that 38 percent of professors at research universities who responded to their survey had never used their university's computerized card catalog. Fifty-two percent had never done a search of the new online indexes to journal articles. Only 5 percent were frequent users of these new indexes (JONES 1994). Here we are worried about "information glut" and what to do about the number of scientific articles doubling every three or four years, and we find out that 52 percent of our leading professors have already solved the problem—they just never look for articles online.

The usual response to such statistics is to label such professors as "technophobes" or just old and slow. But it helps to think for a minute about this group. Professors at the top research universities are the elite. This is the group that produces the Nobel Prizes and jets around the country doing consulting. These people often bring in far more in research dollars than their universities pay them in salaries. In a sense, all this makes them the railroad men of the universities. They are doing exciting work. They may well be amazed by their success. Fascinated by their day-to-day activities, they may be less technologically phobic than they are technologically satisfied. After all, they must have done something right to get to their current positions. So they don't all move to the latest information access strategies (many, of course, do). They, and their corporate cousins around the world, become victims of their own success. They stare too long at the beauty of what they've got and miss what's coming. Maybe that makes them hypnotized. Maybe that just makes them human. In either case, the technology moves on and they don't.

Protecting Fantasies

What if the world brings us information at odds with our prejudices? Festinger tells us we will just ignore such information—we won't even see it. Festinger may be right in most circumstances, but he ignores a more disturbing reaction. One response to troubling contradictions is to eliminate them. This has apparently happened already once on the streets of Milwaukee. In 1993 two boys, one fifteen, one sixteen, armed with sawed-off shotguns, confronted Christine Schweiger and her ten-year-old daughter Monique in the parking lot of a fast food restaurant. Forcing Schweiger to her knees, they demanded money. At some point the sixteen year old, who was holding a shotgun to Schweiger's head, took offense at something Schweiger said, or did, or some expression on her face. He fired his shotgun from point-blank range.

Captured later, he told police, "I'm the big man. I got the gun. Why does she have this attitude?" It's hard to know what a sixteen-year-old boy means by "attitude," but it appears his justification for slaughtering a mother of three is that she wasn't "properly" respectful. He saw himself not just as a man, but as "the big man." He may have done nothing in his life to earn respect, but he believed he had a gun and therefore deserved some special status. Schweiger's answers, her movements, maybe just the look on her face contradicted that view. So he killed her. At its most primitive, this was a terrible act of information exclusion. He didn't need to hear a different view, he didn't need to reconsider his self-image, he could just pull the trigger. This may be an extreme and nauseating example of information denial, but it is not totally unheard-of for our species.

Summary

At the end of every information pipeline is a person. That person may bring some dazzling abilities to the interpretation of the incoming information, but the person also brings a host of limitations. We know the person will unconsciously filter out any information that contradicts his beliefs and interpret ambiguous information in a way that is consistent with his experiences. If we put the person in with a group, the group will exclude information and selectively value the information that does get in. Whether a group or individual, they will entertain information in light of their cultural values, values often formed so many generations ago none can remember the reasons for them. And, of course, when we give them tools, they may be no more happy with the new tools than they were with new information.

This is not to say that humans are hopeless information processors. While we have spectacular failures like the *Challenger*, we have spectacular successes too. Dozens of space launches have occurred safely before and since that disaster. But the *Challenger*, and the Bay of Pigs, and all the other prominent mistakes of our age remind us that information access does not automatically equal information use. Just ask a railroad man, or any employee of a computer company that was briefly on the cutting edge. The information we choose to ignore can be painfully visible in no time at all. Yet we continue to ignore it.

Chapter 11   Noise

Exit access is that part of a means of egress that leads to an
entrance to an exit.
         —*Fire-prevention pamphlet for homes for the elderly*

In 1789 Ephraim Kirby began publishing *Connecticut Reports*, thus enabling the legal profession to have access to court decisions. By 1798 U.S. Supreme Court decisions were being regularly reported, followed by other federal legal information in 1804. By 1820, there was so much being published that "practitioners were already complaining that they could not keep up with the digests, statutes, and court reports that seemed to be pouring from the presses" (BLOOMFIELD 1988:36). So here we have it—the first recorded case of information glut. Nearly two centuries ago people were already complaining that they were getting too much.

In 1995 it was Clifford Stoll's turn to remark on the problem: "The information highway is being sold to us as delivering information, but what it is really delivering is data. Numbers, bits, bytes, but damned little information. . . . What's missing is anyone who will say, hey, this is no good. Editors serve as barometers of quality, and most of an editor's time is spent saying no" (WALD 1995:4).

Stoll is right about the crush of unsubstantiated, inaccurate information flooding the digital systems, but he misses the point about information in general. Whether the source is America Online, the *New York Times*, or the company e-mail system, we face too much false information. The editors he praises just aren't doing their job. Too many lies and silly ideas come through dressed up as truth. We learn to be distrustful of all information, and ultimately just stop listening.

How did we get here? There seem to be plenty of people to blame, includ-ing ourselves. Let's start with the easiest target—our government.

Noise by Design: Government Information

In the early months of 1994, South Africa prepared for civil war. On one side was the vast majority of South Africans, led by Nelson Mandela's African National Congress and F. W. De Klerk's National Party. They, and a handful of smaller parties, formed the Transitional Executive Council, wrote a provi-sional constitution, and worked out an election procedure that would take South Africa from white rule to majority rule.

On the other side were reactionary whites, some Zulus under Mangothso Buthelezi, and some semi-independent enclaves (bantustans), including Bophuthatswana. They formed the Freedom Alliance, threatened to break away from the rest of the country, and promised to boycott any election. The breakup of South Africa seemed so real, one of the blacker jokes of the day was, "We don't need to travel, Bosnia is coming to us." Both sides were heavily armed, scores of people were being killed each week as people battled in the street, and the situation kept getting worse.

In March it all came to a head. Civil servants went on strike in Bophuthatswana, demanding their pensions and supporting the ANC. Local police initially beat the demonstrators but soon began going over to their side. The Bophuthatswanan army was called in, and its white leadership called for a reactionary white army (the AWB) to join them. Whites donned uniforms, grabbed guns, and headed for Bophuthatswana. Meanwhile, the South African Defense Force mobilized and started heading for Bophuthatswana too. The AWB got there first and started shooting demonstrators. At this point the lower-ranking members of the Bophuthatswanan army rebelled against their white leaders and turned on the AWB. Fighting raged in the streets, the South African army arrived, and it looked like the civil war had begun.

For those in Namibia, a country on the northern border of South Africa, a country ruled by South Africa until 1990, the events were riveting. A large number of South African citizens live in Namibia, many more Namibians have family or business connections in South Africa, and the Namibian army was actively planning how to respond if the war spilled over its border. These were desperate times.

Yet you would never know it from listening to the government radio. That night, as countless families turned up the radio for news on the war, the lead story was this: "Buddy Wentworth, deputy minister of Education and Culture, today dedicated a six-classroom addition to a school in Ovambo." The story went on to describe the school and to quote Wentworth about the benefits of education. Several similar stories followed. Only late in the broadcast was there any mention of South Africa, and that was just a one-line mention that three whites had been killed. The government-owned radio stations had nothing else to say about South Africa.

Imagine, if you will, turning on the evening news while Canada is at war with itself and thousands are fighting in Toronto, only to hear Dan Rather begin his broadcast, "And in tonight's top story, Donna Shalala, secretary of Health and Social Services, dedicated a new hospital addition in Dallas today. The new addition has forty-seven rooms. Said Secretary Shalala, 'These rooms will be very important to the sick people of Texas.'" With one minute to go in the broadcast, Rather says, "Meanwhile in Canada, civil war has broken out in several parts of the country. Well that's all for tonight."

The Namibian Broadcast Corporation has one of the most technically advanced newsrooms in the world. Right outside the room are huge satellite dishes that bring in CNN, a South African channel, and a French channel. Data from the dishes is linked to a local area network that gives every journalist in the room instant access to both visuals and wire service text. News comes into their newsroom. It comes in multiple channels, it comes in full color, it comes in twenty-four hours a day. Unfortunately, government-sponsored trivia comes out.

It is not only common for African governments to own the only television and radio stations in the country, it is only just since 1995 that it was legal for anyone other than the government to operate a station. So for Africans (and many others around the world), radio and TV mean government news.

What does it mean to have major information channels controlled by the government? At its worst, it means lies presented as facts. But it often means ego trips presented as news. The Namibian Broadcasting Company does not have air time to cover a war across its border; it needs every second to show how various ministers spent their day, closing with a shot of the president getting on board his private jet to fly off to meet with other exalted figures. It is as if somebody decided the company newsletter could masquerade as the daily newspaper.

THE LANGUAGE OF POLITICS

Where governments haven't appropriated news channels to present a constant diet of happy faces and earnest officials, they can still do their best to block journalists. We have already looked in chapter 6 at some of the more violent strategies governments can use. But violence isn't the only tool governments have to keep people from understanding. Let's look at the use of language. Orwell said, "Political language has to consist largely of euphemism, question begging and sheer cloudy vagueness. . . . Political language . . . is designed to make lies sound truthful and murder respectable, and to give an appearance of solidity to pure wind" (LUTZ 1989:9).

For pure wind, one might start with the U.S. Nuclear Regulatory Commission (NRC). After writing a series of articles on problems with the Oyster Creek nuclear power plant in New Jersey, reporter David Vis of the *Press* in Atlantic City began to see a pattern in the language use of the NRC. Soon he began to collect examples of "NRC-Speak." The table below includes some of his best selections (LUTZ 1989:254–255):

English	*NRC-Speak*
Alarms are going off	System monitoring indicators are affected
A machine broke down	A failure mode has been identified
In an accident people would die from nuclear radiation	The design of the plant would allow immediate high consequences to people living downwind
Management blew it	Management attention and initiatives to meet and address these concerns have not been entirely successful

Faced with the language load being dumped on them by the NRC, the average person could be excused for scratching his head and just wandering away. One suspects that's exactly what the NRC would like.

GOVERNMENT COVER-UPS

Where weasel words won't hide the truth well enough, one solution is to lie. There seem to be endless examples of governments covering up what they have done with outright lies. Americans are learning now of the massive and often bizarre nuclear tests funded by the American military in the 1940s through 1970s: retarded teenagers fed radioactive meals, hospital patients injected with plutonium to see how long it took their bodies to excrete the element, patients at a free prenatal clinic given a radioactive iron isotope so researchers could chart the absorption of the iron, and of course the many thousands of soldiers who were involved in nuclear blasts. These activities were hidden for decades and are only now being revealed under a new administration.

But governments do not just lie about their more lethal activities. We are learning now that the Soviet Union lied about much of its fishing activity to hide its massive violation of international fishing treaties for over forty years. As one example, the Soviets told the International Whaling Commission that their fleets had killed 274 rare humpback whales in 1961–1962. Their real figure was 1,568 for just one fleet. One result of these lies is that scientists trying to determine the size and viability of various whale species were using wrong numbers in their calculations. All their research was twisted by the deception. The long-term effects on the world's whale population are still being determined.

Currently, governments around the world seem to be involved in self-deception and lies about AIDS. Usually taking the attitude that "it can't happen here," the countries of Asia have been very slow to admit the size of their problem. In Africa the problem is known to be huge, but even there governments do their best to bury their heads and bury information. Namibia may be one of the more silly examples. Public figures showed Namibia to be a safe "island" in Africa, with only 5,524 AIDS cases in a population of 1.5 million. This is an infection rate far below its neighbors. It was also old data. A 1991–1992 government survey actually showed an infection rate of 4.7 percent, a huge increase in infection levels. But this data was not shared with the public. Insisting that there was no cover-up, the minister of Health and Social Services claimed the current data was not sent to the press because the cost of a fax is "too expensive." The press was only able to get the correct figures seventeen months after the government completed its survey. For seventeen months the public—and policy makers—were able to live an illusion.

GOVERNMENT ERRORS

Even when governments aren't lying, they can produce a flood of "facts" that are just plain wrong. Let's look at one example, the U.S. inflation rate. Critics have claimed for years that the American number is high. It assumes people don't shop for discounts, or that products costing more are the same products, when in fact the reason for price increases may be additional features. Using a formula that more closely represents the nature of products and the behavior of buyers, these critics claim real U.S. inflation was 2 percent in the fall of 1994, not the official 3 percent. What difference does 1 percent make? Begin with cost of living adjustments to Social Security. Then add corporate raises: "Some 76 percent of corporations use the CPI [Consumer Price Index] to help determine how much to increase their salary budget." Then add consumer behavior: "People's expectations don't just come out of thin air. Information that relates to job security and inflation-rate prospects has a significant cumulative impact on people's decisions" (MANDELL 1994:111). What does all this add up to? A $5 billion rise in the federal budget deficit annually, plus another $10 billion in incorrect business and consumer decisions. Clearly, it is worth the effort to state an accurate inflation rate. Once that is done, the government might look at trade figures, business investment, consumer savings . . .

Blinded by the Blizzard

It would be nice if we could blame all noise on the government, but the fact is much of it comes from our colleagues around the office. Consider just two examples.

THE ENDLESS IN BOX

One source puts 1994 business expenditures for network hubs at over three billion dollars. Add another ten billion for network routers and other networking software. What do you get for that kind of money? Twenty-eight million electronic mailboxes in the United States alone (STEWART 1994a:44). Mailboxes mean mail. At Sun Microsystems, employees generate a million and a half internal messages *per day*. That turns out to be 120 messages per employee per day. Can *any* employee read all those messages, least of all executives who get far more than the average number of e-mail messages while still getting phone calls (and voice mail—11.9 billion messages left nationwide in 1993 [TETZELI 1994]), faxes, memos, even old-fashioned letters?

The network builds corporate democracy so any employee can e-mail the boss. But no network yet guarantees that the boss will have the time to read any of the messages pouring in. Says one analyst, "That ten-page salesman's report, the one that was edited down to a few lines on a chart? Now you get the whole ten pages, *plus* the chart. There's no way to turn it off. The dangers are obvious. The urgent drives out the important; others impose on your time; everyone's a critic, especially the uninformed. Your mailbox swells with 'FYIs' where you don't care and 'what do you thinks' where you don't know" (STEWART 1994a:56).

So what's a manager to do? Stop reading e-mail. The technology is barely in place to speed this new form of communication, and already executives have seen they can't deal with it. They are already being told, "You can't—you mustn't—read it all, or you'll end up doing what SynOptics' Andy Ludwick calls 'managing by flitting around' " (STEWART 1994a:56). The best current advice is to just "dip into" all the e-mail hitting corporate in boxes to look for trends and to hear from divergent points of view. The rest of the mail is ignored—there is just too much of it.

GOPHER TO THE UNIVERSE

While the data coming at us from our peers may be overwhelming and uneven in quality, at least the network gives us access to the great databases of the world, right? True, but a few cautions are in order. If there is such a thing as too much of a good thing, we must be pretty close. Consider a little traffic information (BERNERS-LEE ET AL. 1994:81):

Transfer Method	November 1992	March 1994
HTTP	80 megabytes	700 gigabytes
Gopher	30 gigabytes	700 gigabytes
FTP	2 terabytes	7 terabytes

HTTP (Hypertext Transfer Protocol), Gopher, and FTP (File Transfer Protocol) are all approaches to transferring blocks of information over the Internet. Each has its own uses. But what matters here is that each is growing into numbers far out of the understanding of average people. HTTP finished 1992 being used to transfer 80 million bytes of information each month. Eighteen months later, this approach is being used for 700 billion bytes. FTP starts the period with 2 trillion bytes and ends with more than seven. By any measure, the information highway is already getting crowded.

Main computers that do searches for data on the Internet (Veronica searches) are routinely filled. Getting time on one takes patience and creativity. Yet the traffic is growing. Search speeds and delivery times can be expected to decline as overwhelming traffic brings the net to its knees. Complains one frequent user, "I can't find anything anywhere, and when I do, the site tells me too many people are using it already." He continues, "At some point in time there will simply be too many people with too much information too poorly indexed to be of any use to anybody" (SNYDER 1994:94).

Unprofessional Information Professionals

If workplace noise is getting out of hand, at least once home we get "real" news, written by professionals, right? Yes, but good intentions don't always mean real news. Even "hard" news can be full of noise.

LAZY REPORTERS

Rush Limbaugh makes a very good living bashing the American press. Susan Faludi may be less well paid, but she too has her complaints to make. These two may have nothing else in common, but they do agree on one thing: if you pick up a paper you are likely to encounter a fair amount of nonsense. Each tells a different story from an opposite end of the political spectrum.

For Limbaugh and conservatives, the problem is the homeless and the numbers oft cited in the 1980s. Mitch Snyder, the well-known homeless advocate, is usually cited as the original source. In his book with Mary Ellen Hombs, *Homelessness in America: A Forced March to Nowhere,* and in frequent television interviews, Snyder claimed there were two to three million homeless people in America. In short, one American in a hundred was sleeping in the streets. Given the ugly scenes in many urban areas, people in major cities could well have believed such a huge number was possible, but people would have been wrong. Part of the problem is extrapolating from one small neighborhood to the entire country. Another problem is our difficulty handling large numbers. The number "one million" is literally incomprehensible to more than a tiny fraction of adults. To demonstrate our problem with large numbers, schoolteachers will sometimes have students gather one million pop cans or one million gun wrappers. Teachers almost never repeat the activity, because they discover how much time and room it takes to gather one million of anything. They go to retirement knowing one million is an impossibly large pile of smelly pop cans. The rest of us see one million as just another number except it has lots of zeros after it.

Having no real experience with large quantities, we use the words but have no more understanding than if we were speaking Zulu. The problem comes when we try to act on these unknown words. Snyder wanted to impress on the political leadership that this was a serious problem requiring immediate action. The problem comes when the numbers are repeated, as they were, by journalists. Now the number is not part of a lobbying effort but a "fact," laundered through the newspaper or television station doing the reporting.

And the number was wrong. How wrong depends on definitions, but clearly there are not that many homeless in America. People who have actually tried to do counts have come up with the number three hundred thousand, or about one-tenth the number presented by advocates (BECKER 1994). This is not to say that homelessness is not a problem. Clearly the three hundred thousand Americans without permanent shelter face real hardships. But resolving a problem begins with understanding it. A problem for three hundred thousand is fundamentally different than a problem for two or three million.

This is where media critics come in, because it appears few if any of the journalists quoting Snyder ever questioned the number. Maybe journalists shared the same weakness as the rest of us and simply didn't understand how large a number was being cited. Maybe they shared his aims and "liked" the number. Or maybe, faced with a deadline and the requirement to "do something on the homeless," they got their footage, built in a short interview with a photogenic spokesman like Snyder, and moved on to other things. If so, they left political leaders in a real bind. As "two to three million" moved from off-the-cuff remark to established fact, social service administrators were left to solve a problem that was presented very differently than the facts reveal. The unwillingness of reporters to determine the accuracy of that first number confused the homeless issue for a decade.

Susan Faludi believes reporters' lazy acceptance of statistics is part of a conscious attack on women. She has many examples of malfeasance by her journalist peers, but one example will suffice—marriage data. In 1986 Lisa Marie Petersen of the *Stamford Advocate* was doing background research on a Valentine's Day article on romance and called Neil Bennett, a young sociology professor at Yale. He had been doing some research on marriage and gave her some preliminary data. His study showed that educated women were having trouble with the "marriage market." "Never married college-educated women at thirty had a 20 percent chance of being wed; by thirty-five their odds were down to 5 percent; by forty, to 1.3 percent" (FALUDI 1991:9). Petersen put the numbers in her story, her paper put the story on the front page, the Associated Press put the story on the wire, and papers around the world used it.

The only problem is that the numbers are apparently wrong. Two researchers at the U.S. Census Bureau looked at the numbers that were being presented to the public and did their own analysis. One of them found thirty-year-old college-educated women had a 58–66 percent chance of getting married, the odds were still 32–41 percent at age thirty-five, and still 17–23 percent at age forty. The other analyzed the original Yale research and found a flaw in their model. The two sides were invited to a convention of the Population Association of America to present their analyses, but the expected debate never occurred. The Yale researcher just stated that his analysis was preliminary; the Census Bureau statistician had been told by her superiors not to make references to the Yale study. Three years later the Yale study was actually published, but without the marriage data.

So how does an unpublished study make so many headlines? Part of the reason is the source. Says Petersen, "We usually just take anything from good schools. If it's a study from Yale, we just put it in the paper." Part of the reason is gullibility. That a study is unpublished means that no one other than the authors have reviewed that data or debated their analysis. Part of the reason is impatience. It took three and a half years for this particular study to be published and for the statistics in question to disappear in the final version. Why wait so long when there are numbers at hand now and they seem so interesting? To this list of reasons Faludi would add a conscious or unconscious backlash against women, especially educated, "uppity" women. That education kills a woman's chance for marriage presents a powerful threat to women who would seek to better themselves. No doubt there are many who would have reasons to promote numbers, even preliminary, unproven, numbers that support such a threat.

But what of Lisa Marie Petersen, the initial cog in the wheel that delivered such pain and such misinformation to her readers? A twenty-seven-year-old single college graduate, she had every reason to think through the implications of the "study," not just for her readers, but for herself. Instead, she got her data and printed it. After all, it was from Yale. Besides, this way there was no need for troublesome phone calls to other researchers in the field, no need to even identify other researchers in the field. She had heard from Yale—case closed. Easy for her, not so easy for the millions of readers who trusted her.

RATINGS RACES

If you live in St. Louis, you are probably scared. There is every reason to believe crime has run amuck there. It would certainly appear so from the ten o'clock news. According to a count done by the *St. Louis Post-Dispatch* during the week of 10 July 1994, "crime or violence accounted for 24 percent of the 14-plus minutes each station devotes to general news on the 10 P.M. news" (LEVINS 1994a:1). Lead stories included a child molester on one channel, a pipe-bomb victim on another, a serial rapist, an infant dead in a motel . . . Spin the dial and look at bodies on every channel.

The only good news for St. Louis residents is that they don't live in Chicago. There one study found Chicago's three network affiliates give crime 60 percent of their newscasts. If television news devotes 60 percent of its time to crime, there must a lot of it, right? One viewer of St. Louis TV summed up the general view: "It seems like everybody's shooting everybody else" (LEVINS 1994b:B1). That viewer and others interviewed had a very distinct response to what they were seeing on TV—they stayed out of St. Louis. Should they have? There certainly is more crime in the world than people would like, but is it really the major issue TV makes it seem? Not if you listen to the FBI. Here are the crime numbers they report ("Uniform Crime Reports" 1993) (+ indicates an increase; – indicates a decrease):

Years	Violent Crime	Property Crime	Murder	Robbery	Burglary
1991–1992	−.1%	−4.6%	−5.1%	−3.3%	−6.7%
1988–1992	+18.9%	−2.5%	+10.7%	+19.3%	−10.8%
1983–1992	+40.9%	+5.7%	+12%	+21.8%	−12.7%

Is crime too high in the United States? Yes. Is it getting worse? Well, it did for nearly a decade. Violent crime jumped over 40 percent (rate of crime per one hundred thousand inhabitants) from 1983 to 1992. But that trend seems to be stalling, or even turning around. Murders dropped over 5 percent from 1991 to 1992, and violent crime in general is down marginally.

But there are those who dislike the FBI's numbers. The Census Bureau interviews one hundred thousand households annually for its National Crime Victimization Survey. Begun in 1967, the survey is considered important to criminologists because it gets at crimes that may not have been reported to police and is not affected by changes in the forms police send in to the FBI. So the survey (BROWNE 1994:14) looks at crime from the victim's point of view and provides a constant base of reference. What does it say about crime?

Year	Number of Victimizations
1973	36 million
1983	41 million
1992	34 million

Over the nineteen-year period household victimization rates have increased in two categories: simple assault and motor vehicle theft, but rates have decreased for rape, robbery, aggravated assault, theft, burglary, and larceny. How could this survey show declining crime while the FBI shows crime only beginning to level off? One explanation is that people are now reporting more crime. The FBI knows about more crime than it did before. But even with more people taking the time to report crimes, reported crime is leveling off or declining.

So why would crime take up 24 percent of the TV news in St. Louis, 60 percent in Chicago? Harry Levins offers seven explanations for his colleagues' love affair with crime coverage:

1. TV competes with itself as a medium. This is a business. Getting viewers to turn to your ten o'clock news rather than to a rival station is not easy.
2. TV needs pictures. Crime scenes teem with visuals: flashing lights on emergency vehicles, wide eyed witnesses, weeping relatives.
3. TV abhors abstractions. Discussion, talk, analysis—all require a person explaining, discussing, presenting information. But such scenes show "talking heads," little action. Talking heads get zapped by channel changers.
4. TV craves immediacy. To keep each newscast fresh, stations need new news. There is no time to go back and talk about what yesterday's news actually meant.
5. TV often lacks context. On television news, sixty seconds is a long time. Who has time to explain why this event occurred or what it may mean?
6. TV rations its time. If there is no time, keep it simple. Most murders can be reported briefly: good guys, bad guys, dead guys, and back to you, Steve.
7. TV shuns specialties. TV reporters are expected to cover a range of stories, from the political to the economic to local crime. Having

> no special background in a kind of story, a reporter is drawn to the
> simple. Crime coverage is easy. You drive the truck out, and you set
> up the camera so the police yellow tape is showing. It's not hard
> work; there's no investigation involved. You ask a few questions
> and that's a wrap.

So crime and TV are made for each other. This is a view shared by Walter
Cronkite: "The consultants [have] convinced all these stations that they have
to have action in the first 45 seconds—any old barn-burning or truck crash on
the interstate would do. There is no attempt to cover any of the major stories
of the town in depth—the school board and city hall and that sort of thing"
(ROTTENBERG 1994:36). So television gives us crime stories. But then maybe it
isn't just TV. Levins also did a count of crime stories in his own newspaper. Fully
26 percent of Sunday news was crime-related. It would appear TV isn't the only
medium that abhors abstractions or craves immediacy.

IGNORANCE

Assuming that news media *wanted* to cover something more substantial than
the latest street crime, journalists would first have to understand what they were
trying to cover. This can be a problem. Sometimes the harshest critics of American journalists are foreign journalists. Chris Ndivanga was one of a number of
African journalists invited to intern in some of the major newspapers in the United
States in 1994. Brought over at the expense of the United States Information
Agency, it was hoped he would learn about news gathering and newspaper production. He learned all that, but he also learned his American counterparts were
clueless about Africa.

"I soon realized that for convenience's sake I would have to assume a new
nationality," Ndivanga said. "No longer a Namibian, but an 'African.' Otherwise I had to explain every moment where and what Namibia is" (1994:8). He
continued, "A professor at the Department of Journalism and Mass Communication at Rutgers University in New Brunswick, New Jersey, kept referring to
us as South Africans even after I had written Namibia and Zambia on a piece
of paper for him" (8). Students at the college seemed just as confused. Since the
elections in South Africa were in the news, students wanted to know, "Are you
guys not going to vote? This was after we had been introduced as Namibian and
Zambian."

Ndivanga also learned a lesson in what kind of news makes the rounds.
Desperate to learn soccer scores from back home, he could find no coverage
anywhere, no scores in any papers. When he raised the issue with an American editor, he was told, "We reported about that plane crash," referring to the
crash that had killed the Zambian national team years earlier. About the new

team that came from nowhere to make a serious run at the World Cup, there was nothing. Bad news was reported; good news was ignored. A ferry capsizing off the Kenyan coast made the news, as did refugees in Rwanda. "This was the trend," said Ndivanga. "When a negative event—crisis, war, famine, et cetera, was reported on one channel the others were sure to pick it up. The next morning it would be in all the newspapers" (1994:8). The reporters may not have known where Namibia was, or understood that not all Africans are South Africans, but they do know one thing about Africa—that is where bad news comes from.

POLITICAL EXPEDIENCE

No one talks about it much, but one reason reporters get their facts wrong is that people who have the facts hide them. There are no shortage of examples of occasions when professionals of one political persuasion or another withheld information because of political leanings. Take a recent, and powerful, example—motherhood.

When is it best for women to have children? While magazines throughout the 1980s were replete with articles about older parents, much less was said about research pointing to the difficulties older women have in becoming pregnant. The longer they waited, the greater the chance they were taking that they would never have children. The evidence was available. One French study in the early 1980s showed success rates for artificial insemination worsened as women aged. An editorial in the *New England Journal of Medicine* declared, "If the decline in the fecundity after 30 is as great as the French investigation indicates, new guidelines for counseling on reproduction may have to be formulated" (MARANTO 1995:56).

It might have been a good time to sound a warning, but it was also the Reagan era, and "to announce during the Reagan years that the ideal time for a woman to have children was in her twenties was to align oneself, however unintentionally, with the 'pro-family' advocates who argues that a woman's proper place is in the home tending little ones" (MARANTO 1995:56). So rather than see information go out that might lend support to a political opposition, all the talk was of the opposite—the virtues of waiting. One 1989 *New Yorker* article took the idea to its logical extreme, praising women who "are intent on pushing old age back as far as they can push it. They are a tough, feisty, indomitable group of women who are redefining what it means to age in the most profound way they can—by having babies who will enter kindergarten after their mothers have celebrated their fiftieth birthdays" (MARANTO 1995:58).

With the popular press full of articles like that, no wonder one pregnancy counselor said, "Infertility is a shock at any age, but it comes as a particular shock to women of my generation." The shock arrived because the facts were politically inconvenient. So the facts were downplayed or ignored by people who should have known better.

Relishing the Inane

While it is easy to blame the government, our co-workers, and the professional media for giving us candy-coated half-truths and out-and-out lies, the truth seems to be that much of the nonsense we get, we get by choice. Consider two humbling examples.

TABLOIDS ARE US

Each month 200,000 people buy *Harper's Magazine*; 500,000 buy *Atlantic Monthly*. These may seem like big numbers, but they are nothing compared to the *Star*, which sells 11.2 million copies a month. The *Star*, and its cousins, the *Globe*, the *National Enquirer*, and the *Sun*, are what Americans are really reading. What are they reading about? Let's take a quick look at issues from the last week in October 1994.

The *Star* had twenty-five stories, including seventeen on performers, two on Princess Diana, three on O. J. Simpson, and one on Ted Kennedy. There were only two stories not about celebrities: one on the benefits of garlic on health and one on government waste in moving the statue atop the Capitol Building.

The *Globe* had twenty-nine stories, including eighteen stories on performers, two on Princess Diana, and one on O. J. Simpson. The only other subjects to make the issue were diet (two), rich dogs, a religious cult, a destructive husband, a principal who saved some students from a gunman, and a kid who lives with lions.

The *National Enquirer* had twenty-six stories. Twelve were about performers (including two pages of best-dressed women), plus the obligatory O. J. Simpson story and complaints about Lee Iacocca by his wife. Beyond three stories on health and one on beauty secrets, the only reference to the world of regular people included stories on parents "evicting" their seven year old, a sheriff putting prisoners in tents, a bus being hijacked by a drunk, a man who builds match houses, bosses who are jerks, a man arrested for selling flowers without a permit, a man known for hoaxes, and a guidance counselor who gets slum kids into college.

The *Sun* had more diversity in its twenty-seven stories. They included an interview with a Russian astronaut who had been kept for twenty years by space aliens, an old-folks home visited by Jesus Christ, a ghost who cleans out refrigerators, a man who married a sheep, and a rock in Death Valley that kills people. It also explained that a recent airplane crash was caused by the fact that the flight number—427—added up to 13. In a momentary lapse of unreality, the magazine also printed a comparison of Big Mac prices around the world.

People commonly joke about the bizarre stories in the tabloids, but these (with the exception of the *Sun*) are really very narrow publications. They ignore politics, business, sports, education, and religion. Nothing outside the United States is covered other than Princess Diana. Despite the banana facials and skin-diving dogs, these are actually very staid, very restricted magazines. They almost assume membership in a club—people who know who Tracey Gold is and are happy her health has improved. For members of that club, the tabloids provide a steady diet of news about a very restricted range of subjects. Outsiders may see it as a diet of mostly empty calories, but club members are happy to spend $1.25 to learn which of their heroines were best-dressed this week.

ALT.BIZARRE

But it is just *those* people, the working poor, who read about Princess Diana while watching their clothes dry at the laundromat, right? The truly connected, those worthy enough to have a computer hook-up, often at taxpayer expense, are using their access to the information highway to get real information, right? Unfortunately, it doesn't take more than a short cruise down the highway to realize the laundromat can be even more bizarre in cyber city.

How about a news group on Usenet called "alt.alien.visitor." Newcomers to the group can read the Frequently Asked Questions (FAQ) to get a list of alien races, names of experts in the field, and titles of various books and magazines on the subject. To help with definitions, it also provides an explanation of the various types of encounters with aliens. Then readers can turn to the day's discussion. Some describe their experiences with aliens. But there are skeptics online too: "People who try to talk about being abducted and the like are called loony by insensitive skeptics, just like in the real world" (NOACK 1994:90).

If participants are bothered by the hostility, they can always switch to "alt.out-of-body." One reader, John Stormm, says, "Sometimes I catch some tall tales, but it's the honest reports I am looking for, which I compare to what I already know on the subject; and I try to glean more, if possible." Fellow Internet user Dave Ritchie not only likes the out-of-body group, but prefers it to other sources of information on the subject: "[It is] a lot more personal than just reading a book" (NOACK 1994:90). You also get to save the $1.25 you would spend on the newsstand version. Better yet, it is far more wild than the supposedly bizarre tabloids. Pick your group:

alt.bigfoot
alt.paranet.abduct
alt.paranet.ufo
alt.paranormal.channeling
alt.religion.satanism
alt.vampyres

Compared to some of what is available on the Internet, the supermarket tabloids are just plain boring. Welcome to the "information" highway, where you can access the bizarre and inane at the speed of light.

So what is it eleven million readers and millions of computer nerds want from the information age? Noise. One wonders why governments work so hard to hide information from us. We have what we want—hairstyles and bigfoot.

Summary

At the moment we seem so taken with the ability to communicate fast, we have forgotten why we communicate in the first place. Surely at a minimum we should expect the information we put on the optical fiber to be correct. Instead, we broadcast the trivial, the exaggerated, the mangled. We have e-mail that stacks up unanswered, discussion lists that lose readers as fast as they gain them, and megabytes of data that no one can find or use because even the best Veronica search can't uncover what the data is really about.

We have noise. It may be government noise, it may be inane noise, or it may be important data buried in noise, but it is noise nonetheless. The fact that it comes to us at the speed of light bounced from satellite to optical fiber and back doesn't change its character. It is noise, and it grows ever louder. Given the difficulty we have as information processors, the last thing we need is more noise. Yet that is what we have. And it may be what we want.

Part IV   Solutions

Chapter 12   Reasons for Hope

I T'S NOT EASY to write about the information age while in Africa. As I write this, the euphoria over the peaceful transition to majority rule in South Africa is still with us, but so are the pictures of Rwanda. Today's paper had a picture of two small children who had been hacked in the neck with machetes and left in a pile of dead adults for a week. Both survived but wore bandages far larger than a child that age should ever see. A block away from me is the street that bears the name of Namibia's president. It is a Saturday, but up and down that street stand young men hoping some employer will pick them up, even if only for a few hours. Almost all will go home having stood in the sun for eight or nine hours without making a cent.

In such an environment breathless descriptions of satellite networks seem silly, as do discussions of how many shopping channels will be part of the new four-hundred-channel TV. It would be easy to deride the whole concept of information access as just one more frill of the wealthy nations, like cars, blue jeans, and three meals a day. And there is the danger that in much of the world, maybe most of the world, access to information will be a frill, the average person remaining brutishly poor and blindly obedient. That could certainly be the destiny of much of the developing world. It could even be the destiny of much of the United States.

But after twelve chapters of often very bad tidings, let me close on a hopeful note. And there are reasons to hope. Just the other side of all the men waiting for a day's wages is a small university where eighteen year olds sign onto the Internet each day and exchange news and personal greetings with eighteen year olds in St. Cloud, Minnesota, and Stevens Point, Wisconsin. The talk this week was of the South African elections. Other weeks it has been health care or college life. The content of the discussions seems less important to the Namibian students than the opportunity to reach out. To talk to a real American is important to them. Nothing may come of these discussions that can be reflected in Gross Domestic Product, or even in political developments, but a few dozen students who can reach beyond stereotypes is significant.

There are other hopeful signs as well. In keeping with the rest of this book let me present them as stories—success stories.

The Red Carpet of Sarajevo

In February 1994 Serbian gunners opened fire on the crowded Markdale Market in Sarajevo. One mortar shell scored a direct hit, blowing sixty-eight people to pieces and wounding two hundred more. Gordana Knezevic, deputy editor of *Oslobodenje* (Liberation), Sarajevo's largest daily newspaper, sent reporters out to cover the attack: "When I heard the blast, I sent the first journalist out. He came back vomiting, so sick he couldn't report. So I sent another, and he came back absolutely shocked. We had a big problem pulling ourselves together that day" (RICCHIARDI 1994:20).

Vlado Staka finally managed to write the story. "It was impossible to pass through the marketplace without walking in blood that day," he said. "When I arrived, I tried to interview some of the survivors, but people were too stunned; they couldn't talk. So I stood in a corner for five hours watching and recording the scene—the twisted faces, the screams, the words people were saying" (RICCHIARDI 1994:20).

After witnessing the scene for five hours, Staka walked back to the newsroom and filed his story: "I remember there were bloody footprints in our newsroom when we finished work that night. It's interesting how blood can look and feel greasy, like paint. I went home and flipped out. For 48 hours, I wasn't rational. Even now, when I talk about it, there is a cramp in my guts. I am eating myself from the inside over this. Sometime I don't know how close to being a madman I am" (RICCHIARDI 1994:20). Staka, who lost forty-five pounds during the first two years of the siege of Sarajevo, is at least alive. Five other employees of the paper have been killed. One reporter was shot while covering the destruction of Zvornik. A photojournalist was killed by shrapnel as he took pictures of Sarajevans waiting in line for water. A secretary was killed by a sniper as she left the office. Twenty-five employees have been wounded, and ten correspondents are missing in Serb-controlled territory.

Dead reporters and blood on the newsroom carpet aren't the only problems *Oslobodenje* faces. Just getting the paper printed has gotten impossibly hard. Pre-war circulation was sixty thousand. But then Serbs started shelling the newspaper's buildings. Four times the buildings have been set alight by Serb shelling.

During one attack the top story of the building burned. Reporters moved to lower floors and kept writing while firemen battled the blaze. One fireman was killed by snipers as he battled the blaze, but at 6:00 A.M. the fire was out. The presses started rolling at 6:05.

Press runs have dropped to a low of thirty-five hundred, but the presses have run every day, even if that means running on whatever paper is around, including poster paper in pink, yellow, and green. Importing newsprint is like importing anything else—it has to make it through the Serb gauntlet. Some paper makes it, some doesn't. In the meantime, the newspaper patches its buildings together as best it can and prints on whatever paper it can find. Reporters write by candlelight and go for weeks without phones or fax lines or international wire services. What international news they get for their paper comes by radio—the BBC or Voice of America.

So far the paper has survived. Long-term survival of its staff may be another matter. "For me, the worst was seeing children without limbs, without eyes; helpless little beings," says Staka. "That scene struck me the hardest. When I covered the massacre in the market that day, I saw a mother crying, begging the police to let her into the crime scene. Then, she saw her husband. They spoke no words at all; they just exchanged looks and she knew instantly that her son was dead." The psychological burden of witnessing such scenes can be unbearable: "We all try not to have conflicts with our families, but our nerves are so raw. The victims of my job are my wife and daughter" (RICCHIARDI 1994:22).

Reporter Senad Gubelic copes differently: "I don't feel anything any more. Every day I ran across from *Oslobodenje*. Every day I heard shells exploding; I saw people dead on the streets. After a few months, I felt numb." Why go through such agony to keep a newspaper going? "For us, it was the ultimate sign of resistance," explains editor Gordana Knezevic. "When Sarajevans couldn't find bread, they could find our newspaper." Says a reporter at Reuters, "The people were falling into a dark hole; they were desperately trying to stick to any of their habits. They could go out in the morning and get their newspaper, and for a few moments, pretend they were leading a normal life" (RICCHIARDI 1994:22).

Professional pride was another reason given by reporters: "There were a few things that made us obliged to do it. We began as a liberation newspaper 50 years ago, so there was the tradition. We also had a responsibility to the profession, and we had to maintain our own self-respect. We saw hundreds of our foreign colleagues coming to write about a war that was affecting our families, our city, or country. How could we stop doing it?" (RICCHIARDI 1994:22). So they continue, and so far five have died, twenty-five have been wounded. And each day they walk through more blood.

These are very brave people, but in their effort to keep information flowing, they may face even greater long-term problems. One continent south of them, the story of Kevin Carter shows that the burdens for reporters can build to a level even Pulitzer Prize winners can't survive.

Kevin Carter won the Pulitzer Prize for photojournalism in 1993. After walking for days through the Sudan he came to a refugee camp where thousands were starving to death. As he watched, a baby, starving and exhausted, collapsed near the edge of the camp. A vulture swooped down behind the baby and waited. Carter captured the scene in a picture that was seen around the world.

What happened after he took the picture was the topic of controversy in media circles. According to one story, "he broke open a pack of cigarettes, sat down and cried for four hours." A friend asked what he had done about the baby: "He looked at me in bewilderment and said, 'Nothing, there were thousands of them' " (BERESFORD 1994:21). That he had walked away from a dying baby created discussion worldwide and a fair amount of criticism. It was not criticism that he had to listen to for long.

In the months that followed he was battered by other forces. Back in his native South Africa he rose early each morning to cruise through the black townships, where political rivals battled daily. It was an exhausting effort to dodge the bullets that flew between the two sides and sometimes in his direction. When a gang of young men chanted "One settler, one bullet" in his direction, Carter started swinging and ended up back in the office with a black eye. Days later he and dozens of journalists followed a group of newly trained South African troops into a township. In the fight that ensued, the troops opened fire on the journalists, killing two—one standing next to Carter.

Weeks later Carter was in Mozambique on assignment for *Time*. It was a difficult assignment, but he got his pictures and got on the plane home. It was only after he was back home that he realized he had left his exposed film on the plane. There is no way of knowing whether this lost film was the motive or whether it was just the last straw in a burden of too many memories, too many pressures, but several days later he got into his car and rigged the exhaust so it poured into his window. He died less than a year after gaining his Pulitzer.

In one sense the story of Kevin Carter demonstrates that journalism is simply beyond the abilities of mere mortals. Taking pictures of reality, they are then criticized for not fixing that reality. To obtain glimpses of danger, they face danger themselves, frequently dying in the process. They live a journalistic ideal in a world that is real. They shoot pictures; the world shoots back bullets.

But it was a battle Carter survived for years, one the staff at *Oslobodenje* still fight. The fact that people like them are willing to take such risks to get information and deliver it to the rest of us gives us hope that the information age may yet be something more than shopping channels and sound bites.

An Honest Man

Jesse Jackson has as many critics as fans, but on 27 November 1993 he made more fans by proving himself one of the bravest men in America. That was the day he gave a speech that included this statement: "There is nothing more painful to me at this stage of my life than to walk down the street and hear footsteps and start to think about robbery and then look around and see it's somebody white and feel relieved. How humiliating" (MINER BROOK 1994).

This was clearly not an easy statement for Jackson to make. It came after a series of incidents in which his house was robbed and four people were gunned down on his block. Crime touched him and his family personally and he responded. What may have surprised his critics was the response. Where lesser men might have attacked the police and other easy targets, Jackson was willing to go a step beyond and begin to address black-on-black crime. He moved into a subject that had been taboo. And because he had done so, it was now acceptable for others to join the discussion and take on the problem more forthrightly. From this point on, black-on-black crime could be discussed openly.

Fortunately, time after time, we have had some leader summon the strength to come forward and step into the vacuum of silence. Whether Arthur Ashe and Magic Johnson on AIDS, or Gloria Steinem on relationships with men, or Ronald Reagan on his troubles with Alzheimer's disease, our recent history is filled with people who were courageous enough to take the first step, so that others would be free to follow. For information flow this is critical. Political dogma delivered at the speed of light, bounced from satellite to satellite, is still political dogma. Its information value is zero. An idea that can't be expressed, a topic that can't be discussed, is like a room in the house that can't be entered. Everyone knows it's there, and the longer they pretend it is not, the more disgusted and embarrassed everyone feels.

Much of the clamor against political correctness is motivated by fears that yet more topics will become taboo, more ideas unutterable. Orwell's *1984* and its description of a shrinking language still holds power more than a decade after this novel of the future was to have taken place. Yet there always seem to be people honest enough and brave enough to take on political and linguistic fashions and enter an area that has been off limits. As long as this is the case, our communication systems will have messages worth communicating.

An Honest Web Page

Speaking of honesty, one of the weaknesses of the World Wide Web is the fact that the vast majority of pages present sales pitches. These can be pitches for corporations as they rush to put their sales brochures online, entertainers happy to "share" the schedule of their upcoming appearances, and individuals who turn the Web into a kind of electronic vanity press. This use of the Web may result in fewer dead trees and savings on corporate mailing charges, but it minimizes the information value of the medium.

A dramatically different approach has been taken by Zambia. They have a home page (www.zamnet.zm) that should be a model for the rest of us. Is there sales information on their page? Sure. They have a complete tourist guide on line with such routinely pretty prose as, "Discover Zambia, a land of many contrasts. . . . Prolific wildlife, birds in abundance, fertile valleys, spectacular waterfalls, huge lakes and winding rivers, swamps and wetlands, hot springs and vast golden plains. Famous for their friendliness, Zambians are ready to welcome you to their beautiful country. The standard of lodges caters for all, combining rustic comfort and excellent cuisine with all the conveniences of modern hotels. Grand Travel can tailor make an unforgettable journey through Zambia for you at the lodges of your choice."

If you wished, you could take out "Zambia," insert the name of any state in the union (or any island in the Caribbean), and you would have the standard chamber of commerce pitch for anywhere. But the next menu selection on their home page breaks with tradition. They have put one of their major independent newspapers online. The *Post* is hardly a government lackey, and giving them access to the electronic public takes some real courage. Consider one article, titled "Plot to Kill Former President Kauda Exposed," from 23 June 1995:

> Secret Intelligence correspondence has revealed that an MMD
> official has offered to arrange for the assassination of former President
> Kenneth Kaunda. A letter from the Mansa office of the Zambia
> Intelligence Security Service (ZISS) dated May 29, 1995 and
> addressed to the director general for the attention of the director
> "B" branch reveals that a National Campaign Committee for the
> re-election of President Frederick Chiluba has been formed and is
> prepared to assassinate the former president. The letter which
> identifies one of the campaign committee members as Ernest
> Chiwama, a former Member of Parliament in the Second Republic,
> says he is ready to arrange the assassination.

Not exactly an advertisement for the country, and certainly not an ad for the ruling party. Our first reaction might be to write off Zambia as just another African country with a bad government. But give some thought to what they have done.

Consider, if you will, the odds of some American corporation creating a home page in which sales literature was presented, but so was their latest OSHA inspection results, or a listing of the current complaints coming in from consumers.

Try to find a U.S. university that would post data on student attrition or the campus crime rate. Find one state home page that has one word critical of the governor. Isn't it odd that we have to go to Africa to find an example of freedom of information?

The People's Lobby

As we saw in the chapter on organizational communication, whether the organization is the Tobacco Institute, AT&T, or the local university, organizations yield honest information grudgingly, if at all. But that doesn't mean they can't be forced into closer proximity to the truth. Within the past few years there have been two great examples of people taking on large organizations and winning. E-mail was a major player both times.

The best known example came at the close of 1994, when Intel was forced to respond to problems with its Pentium microprocessor. In the course of doing some mathematics using the new Pentium chip and its math coprocessor, Thomas Nicely of Lynchburg College in West Virginia came up with some numbers that seemed wrong to him. He spent four months reworking his calculations, using not only his own computer but also one belonging to a colleague and even one at a local computer store. Each time, the answer came out wrong. In October 1994 he called Intel to see if they knew anything about the problem. They would not respond. So he got on the Internet and asked others if they were having the same problems with the chip.

Getting on the Internet was the magic key. Six days later Intel suddenly started returning Nicely's calls and agreed that, yes, there was a problem with the chip. But, according to them, the problem was minor, nothing to take seriously, it just made errors after the first ten digits, a problem that few people would ever encounter. Nicely felt a little differently about the problem: "For it to give you only 10 is utterly atrocious. To get a result that poor from that coprocessor is like having the transmission fall out of your Ford" (BAKER 1994:A5). So it was back onto the Internet with discussions of the problem.

While discussions rippled across the Internet (along with endless Intel jokes: "Why did Intel call the chip the Pentium instead of the 586? Because they added 100 to 486 and came up with 585.999999"), reporters began to pick up the story. Suddenly the reliability of Pentium processors and computers in general was a public issue. Technology stocks began to drop in value. One major investor looked at the situation this way:

> I really believe we're getting an Internet correction of technology
> stocks, the strongest group. I'm old enough to have lived through
> many things—including the 386 and 486 introductions by Intel, both

of which had problems similar to what's going on with the Pentium. But in those days, you didn't have the Internet; you didn't have a bunch of reporters getting into the conversation groups on the Internet, trying to find stories. We're seeing the playing out of a new phenomenon in the information age: reporters using chat groups to write stories. And companies like Intel, not quite understanding— even though they are champions of technology—all the implications of how the new information technology affects human behavior.

(SAMBURG 1994:1–2)

If Intel didn't understand the implications initially, they learned quickly enough. By December they were replacing all Pentium chips free of charge. They also offered Nicely a consulting job.

The ability of the Internet to get the attention of large organizations shows that there is a new forum for people. The opportunity to present ideas and information to millions now exists for people who might have been largely ignored before. Professor Nicely may have been right, but he is from Lynchburg College, a place that isn't usually on the media Rolodex. Without the Internet, the problem might have been fixed, but probably not until someone at Harvard or Yale noticed there was an error.

But while we enjoy the opportunity of the People's Forum, we should also recognize there are limits to what it can do. These limits were first identified, ironically enough, in another one of the Internet's success stories—the stoppage of Lotus MarketPlace, the CD-ROM database of 120 million consumer financial records.

Lotus MarketPlace began as a partnership between Equifax and Lotus. Equifax had data to sell and Lotus had marketing avenues to small-business buyers. They had a great new product: Lotus Marketplace. This product seemed ideal for small businesses. It had a database on 120 million Americans with combined records on consumer financial information and census information. It had a new way of analyzing consumer decisions. Its "Shopping Psychographics" put consumers into nine different categories based on brand, quality, and price preferences, all based on what Equifax had learned by processing "hundreds of millions of consumer transactions with thousands of businesses every month" (U.S. CONGRESS 1991:33). Furthermore, this product had Microvision, a way of targeting marketing efforts down to neighborhoods as small as ten to fifteen households using the new Zip + 4 addressing system. All this could be put on a CD-ROM disk and run off a Macintosh personal computer.

As their April 1990 press release put it, "This is a natural extension of Equifax Marketing's commitment to make our information systems widely accessible to a broad range of business users for all targeting applications." There was only one problem—the targetees. Americans were decidedly unhappy about having their credit information and buying habits put on a CD and sold to anyone who might have an interest. Congressional hearings in April 1991 made the problem clear:

> MR. WISE [Robert E. Wise, chairman of the Government Information, Justice, and Agriculture Subcommittee of the Committee on Government Operations, U.S. House of Representatives]: Wasn't all the information that was contained in Lotus MarketPlace otherwise routinely bought and sold by businesses that market goods and services to consumers?
>
> MR. BAKER [John Baker, senior vice president, Equifax, Inc.]: Yes. I think that's a fair statement, that really the name and address and segmentation capabilities of the service is available from a number of sources today but not—it's not available in such a widely distributed format.
>
> I think the main consumer fear, if I had to sum up all the fears, is that as extensive as our privacy protection mechanisms were, we would not be successful in controlling access to the product because it could be used out there on a personal computer with compact discs.
>
> There might be users out there who are really not legitimate businesses or were individuals portraying themselves as businesses that would somehow use that information for nefarious purposes. I think that was the major concern.　　　(U.S. CONGRESS 1991:75)

These concerns were voiced widely on the Internet and even involved sending so much e-mail to the head of Lotus that his e-mail system became buried. Ultimately, the use of the Internet as a protest mechanism worked. Again, we have congressional testimony to describe the reaction at Lotus:

> MR. WISE: Yes. The consumer concerns about Lotus MarketPlace were widely publicized through electronic mail networks. Is this one reason for increased consumer activism?
>
> MR. BAKER: I'm not sure if it's a reason for increased consumer activism, but it's clear that there is a much wider awareness by consumers of marketing uses of information. In fact, the networks were used extensively to communicate by computer-literate people about this product, giving both their concerns and, in many cases, their misconceptions about the product.
>
> Electronic mail was used a lot. I think, in fact, that they tied up

the chairman of Lotus' electronic mailbox pretty heavily with quite
a few messages. So it was a mechanism for people to express their
concern. Groups of people have called that a new form of grassroots
opinion. So that was widely used, yes.

So far, so good. Another victory for the Internet. But the testimony continues
with Alan Westin, a paid consultant to Equifax, adding his interpretation of the
impact of e-mail:

> DR. WESTIN [Alan F. Westin, professor of public law and government,
> Columbia University]: If I could add something to that, I think
> what you saw was the response from the particular people who, as
> advanced users of technology, feel a special interest in the way in
> which computers are used in areas that affect privacy. But I think it
> helps to put in perspective the claim that thirty thousand people
> communicated through the e-mail system.
>
> When the National Rifle Association pushes a button, it can get
> 5 million people to write in or to deluge you with their views. So I
> don't quite view the e-mail response as a great breakthrough
> necessarily in expressing the will of the people, especially in the
> perspective of what we know to be the letter-writing campaigns and
> telephone campaigns that groups that are interested in an issue are
> capable of mounting. I think we shouldn't overestimate the
> response to this.   (U.S. CONGRESS 1991:71–72)

Westin may well have a point. Presumably with time the number of messages
that can be sent about a problem can grow from thirty thousand to something
approaching the NRA's five million. But what topics will generate that kind of
response? Personal privacy? Computer malfunctions? What about issues that aren't
connected to technology? Will the homeless be sending e-mail? Will battered
women? The Internet provides an expanded forum, but not a universal forum.
Our victory celebrations should probably also include a moment to observe who
is not at the party.

There is one more caveat we should remember before declaring the Internet an invincible weapon of democracy. Laura Gurak traced the Lotus MarketPlace
fight as part of her doctoral dissertation. What she discovered was that the availability of the Internet didn't instantly result in opposition to Lotus. According
to her chronology, very little was said on the Internet, or anywhere else, when
Lotus first announced the product in April 1990. The first response came in May,
when Mary Culnan of Computer Professionals for Social Responsibility saw an
article about the Lotus product. She described the product to Marc Rotenberg,

also of CPSR, and he chose to mention the product in testimony he soon gave before a House subcommittee. CPSR began raising privacy concerns with other advocacy groups.

On 30 August CPSR asked for, and received, a demonstration of the product by Lotus representatives. Rotenberg became more concerned and began sending press releases to major newspapers. Finally, on 13 November, the *Wall Street Journal* printed an article on the product mentioning the privacy concerns. The next day the electronic discussion began. The Electronic Frontier Foundation made Lotus MarketPlace the topic of the day for the fourteenth, and regular postings began on other discussion groups as well.

From 14 November on, Internet traffic exploded. Here's where the thousands of messages took over and began the process of overwhelming Lotus. The discussions on the Net built a solid opposition and gave participants a communication process to use to pressure Lotus. And it worked. Privacy advocates were able to force a major corporation to back away from a product.

But as Gurak's chronology reminds us, the Internet has yet to become a magic vehicle. It still needs to be put into motion. In this case it took two advocates at CPSR and the power of the *Wall Street Journal* to get the ball rolling. Without someone to start the process, the Internet is just another phone line.

The National Suggestion Box

In May 1995 the Office of Management and Budget (OMB) created a National Electronic Open Meeting. The point of the meeting was to collect "comments from all interested parties on the topic of the respective roles of the Federal government, state, local, and Tribal governments, industry, the public interest and library communities, academia, and the general public in creating an electronic government." The two-week-long electronic discussion hardly prepared the world for an electronic government, but there was healthy and open discussion around five main themes: services, benefits, information, participatory democracy, and technology.

Initially discussion took some very bizarre and disappointing turns. The very first message received on information issues involved UFOs: "Seems to me the whole area of UFOs is in dire need of some honesty on the part of our beloved gummint. If there is nothing to it, prove it by telling us all you know." Other requests for government information included repeated demands to know what Bill Clinton did in Moscow while a college student. An anonymous person in Topeka used the opportunity to state, "Our presidents and congress have caved in to the Luciferian New World Orderand [*sic*] their global 2000 plan, which includes, among other horrors, killing 2 BILLION humans by the year 2050, using

wars, chemical and baacteriological warfare, which is happening now, and by
famine and starvation—or THE BOMB. The globalists then will have the
power to divest the entire planet of it s [sic] resources. EVERY thinking American is angry, and fearful. Every American and the entire earth population
SHOULD be angry and fearful."

There were enough similar comments to make the electronic town meeting feel much like a block party in which we discovered many of our neighbors
make bombs in their basements and spend much of the day in desperate need
of medication. But the discussion wasn't all noise and nonsense. A number of
thoughtful people stepped forward to make suggestions for both government
policies and procedures. Carl Hage of Sunnyvale, California, offered a series of
suggestions for improved access to government materials:

1. Include electronic locations in major announcements.
2. Convert public affairs offices to use electronic distribution.
3. Establish a common "storefront" (similar government e-mail
   addresses) in cyberspace.
4. Establish common e-mail conventions.
5. Establish a convention to map a document ID to a URL.
6. Use URLs in references.
7. Use URLs for a document in the document itself.
8. Use subdirectories for publications, and so on.
9. Use multiple indexes.
10. Include road maps of the information.
11. Use table of contents–style World Wide Web directories.
12. Add simple searches over small collections.
13. Use FAQs as guides to information.
14. Promote agency information with outside resources (send
    announcements to newsgroups, and so on).
15. Create data files for Internet robots.

Each of his suggestions presents a very practical (and usually cost-free) way of
making government information more available to citizens. All answer the question, How do I know what is out there? Hage wasn't the only person able and
willing to provide useful suggestions to the OMB. In the process, all of us logged
on to the electronic suggestion box learned about problems and solutions
from our peers. In many ways the two-week comment period was a short
course in information access. There were dozens of instructors and lively class
discussion. The noise coming from the demented in the back of the room was
a small price to pay for the chance to listen to the sound advice of experts. The
discussion also provided a model other government agencies (and private
groups) might use to solicit advice.

Community Computer Centers

Giving more people access to information and to electronic communication will not be easy. As was noted earlier, there are portions of America where barely 50 percent of the population has a phone. Unable to reach emergency services, they are also unable to download information services. Making access to information egalitarian will not be easy, but at least several places are making an attempt.

In a ruling before the Ohio Public Utilities Commission in 1994, Ameritech (a "baby Bell") agreed to pay $2.2 million to create fourteen community computer centers throughout Ohio. Each center will have hardware, software, network access, tutors, and workshops. They will be open evenings and will be located in places that are in proximity to low-income areas. To help low-income individuals get home phone service, the agreement also called for a reduction of $8 in fees charged and the opportunity to establish new service without a deposit or connection fee. Estimates are that six hundred thousand Ohio families will qualify, one hundred thousand of whom don't currently have phone service (JACOBS 1994).

Across Canada a grass-roots effort to build "freenets" has already established community networks in three hundred cities. These networks offer free access to community information and usually have limited connectivity to the Internet. With access points in public libraries and other buildings, these freenets allow even the poorest to learn about their community and to voice their opinions.

The importance of providing means of access to the poor was most dramatically demonstrated in Santa Monica, California, where several homeless people used public-access network terminals to talk about their lives and their problems. When asked, Why don't you get a job? they described difficulties in taking showers (who would hire a smelly applicant?) and problems guarding their few possessions while they were away at work. These were major barriers, barriers unknown by the luckier members of the community. But once the barriers were understood, the community responded with SHWASHLOCK, a facility to provide showers, washers, and lockers. Funded by the city and run by the Salvation Army, SHWASHLOCK is a simple solution to a problem that had been unknown until the city made a few computer terminals available where even the city's poorest could find them.

Cultures of Learning

Earlier we looked extensively at the need for education in the information age and the problems of the Third World. As concerned as we may be about the preparation of American children, it is clear children in the developing world have far greater problems. But there are communities that have responded to the situation. One example comes to us from the Andes Mountains of Ecuador.

The Andes Mountains are one of the poorest places on Earth. But among the terraced farm fields a culture of education has emerged—a culture involving considerable—and lasting—sacrifice. To the peasant communities of the Andes, education is a means to an end. First, to gain literacy, for with literacy comes full citizenship and the right to vote. Second, with completion of schooling comes the chance to find a job in the formal economy and move away from subsistence farming. The odds of achieving this second goal are poor, with one researcher finding only 4 percent of primary school graduates able to find permanent, formal-economy employment (PRESTON 1984:129).

But to give their children a chance for those jobs, parents will make multiple sacrifices. The first is financial. Parents need to pay for books, lunches, boarding fees, and the usual odds and ends of schooling. One researcher observed Ecuadorian women selling chickens so they could buy fabric for costumes their children would wear just once in a festival parade. At the same time that families encounter these additional educational expenses, children are out of the labor pool so the family has less income. Children aren't tending animals or working the fields.

The biggest sacrifice, though, may be the alienation of their children. Preston describes the situation this way:

> Boarders, returning home for holidays, see with new eyes the
> domestic poverty which they attribute to the limitations of their
> parents, rather than to the social and economic positions in which
> they are trapped. Parents do not know how to reincorporate their
> visiting offspring into farming and domestic activities because they
> cannot overcome their awareness of the child's shifted value
> orientations, which are no longer consonant with their own.
> Sibling friction may occur in cases where an older child has been
> deprived of the opportunity to continue education, in order to work
> for the family to provide this opportunity for younger siblings.
>
> (1984:126)

So a lifetime of parental sacrifice often ends up in estrangement from their own children. Why do they do it? Because they value education and love their children. The culture of education is firmly in place. Fortunately, it is firmly in place in much of the world.

MISANet

We have already looked at the problems facing journalists in developing countries. With no budget, limited readership, and an often-hostile government, getting a newspaper out is a huge problem. The problem is compounded by the vagaries of international communication. International calls in developing countries can be far more expensive than in the United States, and are more likely to end up with a dead phone line as equipment along the line goes down. Then there is the growing concentration of news bureaus in London, New York, and Atlanta. What Zambia learns about Zimbabwe is likely to be whatever an editor in London finds interesting and puts out on the wire.

This is the kind of situation that calls out for distributed technology, and that is exactly what is happening in at least one place—southern Africa. With funding from a Swedish foundation, representatives of major news organizations in southern Africa first got together in 1992 and formed the Media Institute for Southern Africa (MISA). The organization decided it would perform two tasks: champion the rights of a free press and improve information flow between newspapers in the region.

To help support a free press, it has created a bimonthly newsletter which highlights problems journalists and newspapers face. Every violation is fully described and members both in Africa and abroad are told to whom to write in order to bring pressure on offending governments. This tactic has already helped reverse some obvious government interference, such as placing a heavy tax on imported printing equipment—a tax that helps maintain the government's monopoly ownership of presses.

To achieve their end of helping each other know more about news in their local region, they are developing MISANet, an e-mail system located in Windhoek, Namibia. So far this is a simple text-only bulletin board where editors can send local stories. They also want to add imaging capability so that pictures can be transferred. Another feature will be a "source" database, listing names of those to call for information on numerous topics in all the local countries. For instance, if a reporter in Botswana wanted to know football scores in Malawi, the database would show him whom to call.

MISA believes its network will have two immediate advantages. First, editors around the region will have access to all the news that's being published by their peers, not just the stories selected in London by Reuters and put back on the wire. For the first time, African journalists would have access to and control of African news. Second, MISA is already saving significantly on communications costs. By its calculations, an e-mail message to Dar es Salaam costs $.05 versus $18.75 for a phone call. Such significant savings should enable cash-strapped newspapers to better stay in touch.

Meet Your Neighbor

While looking at modems and faxes and all the marvelous sources of information available to us, we don't want to forget that much of what we know comes directly from people. It is the conversations we have, the dinners we attend, the people we visit that shape much of our knowledge of the world. How unfortunate then, that much of the world is off limits to us. The other side of the tracks may simply be too dangerous for us to visit, whether that other side is the poor section of town or whole countries where violence rules. The people there have views we will never hear, dreams we will never know.

But there are responses, as has been demonstrated by Jimmy Ntintili of Johannesburg, South Africa. His "Meet Your Neighbors" tour takes people from around the world to the heart of Soweto. They visit an open-air market, have a drink in a shebeen, and visit a typical home—his. They cover the entire township, from squatter camps to the "Beverly Hills" of Soweto, where the better homes are. They see the famous house of Winnie Mandela, and the home of Desmond Tutu—complete with electrical wire on top of a high wall. Through it all they get a nonstop lecture on the world according to Ntintili—comments on the drunks standing on the corners, the BMWs parked outside slums, the violence associated with the single men's quarters. In short, they see it all.

He even has them confront some of their fears by forcing them to get out of his van and walk around a taxi rank that is known for running gun battles. They walk through a squatter camp, smell the smells and hear the sounds. In the end, they all have a drink in a shebeen and talk. He takes questions on any subject and gives straight answers. In the course of an afternoon tourists don't become experts, but they know far more about this part of the world than they are likely to see by watching TV or taking a short drive on their own. He says that far more people from outside South Africa take the tour than South Africans, but at least he has found a way to get willing visitors into a part of South Africa they would normally miss.

The weakness of the tour, of course, is that the learning is all happening in one direction—middle-class foreigners are learning about poor South Africans while the poor are learning nothing about the tourists. But it is a start, and seems far superior to driving rapidly past on the interstate with car doors locked and one hand on the cellular phone in case of an emergency.

Final Thoughts

As we think more about information—where it comes from, where it goes, where it can't go, who gets it, who doesn't—we find a situation that is far more complicated than is usually described in the "gee whiz" articles on the wonders of the World Wide Web. If we are in a new age, this is an age that is still connected to the old age and still has many of its flaws. Yes, technology is producing some benefits and some freedoms. We know the threat of satellite dishes was enough to scare South Africa into creating a television network. Unfortunately, we also know the threat of satellite dishes has been enough to cause governments across the Middle East to ban their use. We know libraries across the world are now accessible electronically. We also know books around the world are still being burned. We know that at this moment hundreds of gigabytes of information are being bounced from satellite to satellite across the sky. We also know that many of those gigabytes are lies. We know that some children can learn about the world by linking their classroom to thousands across the world. Other children wait for their classroom to get a roof, a light bulb, a qualified teacher.

Like most things, it is unlikely the information age will be as good as we hope or as bad as we fear. It will certainly be far different than we imagine. We may shape it, and it certainly will shape us. If we are to influence it, we must first know what it is. At the moment our grasp of this "thing" is far too much like the blind men examining the elephant. We find one thing—usually something hooked to a wire and traveling at blazing speed—and decide that's what the age is. The wire is part of it, but so is the gun and the muffled scream and the obvious lie and the plot hatched online. The point of this book is to shine a light on a few of those other parts of the elephant.

References

Abbott, A. 1988. *The System of Professions: An Essay on the Division of Expert Labor*. Chicago: University of Chicago Press.

Altbach, P., R. Arnov, and G. Kelly. 1982. *Comparative Education*. New York: Macmillan.

Amukugo, E. 1993. *Education and Politics in Namibia: Past Trends and Future Prospects*. Windhoek, Namibia: New Namibia Books.

Anderson, R. C. 1977. "Schema-Directed Processes in Language Comprehension." In *Cognitive Psychology and Instruction*, edited by J. W. Pellegrino, S. D. Fokkema, and R. Glaser. New York: Plenum Press.

Anderson, R. C., R. E. Reynolds, D. L. Schallert, and E. T. Goetz. 1977. "Frameworks for Comprehending Discourse." *American Educational Research Journal*.

Andrews, E. L. 1991. "AT&T Admits Alarms Failed in Cutoff." *New York Times*, 20 September, p. C1.

Armes, R. 1987. *Third World Film Making and the West*. Berkeley and Los Angeles: University of California Press.

"At Least 75 Newsmen Died on Duty in '93." 1993. *Citizen*, 29 December, p. 16.

Baker, P. 1994. "Math Scholar Finds Fame in Flawed Chip." *Milwaukee Journal*, 17 November, p. A5.

Bayles, F., and D. Foster. 1995. "Conspiracy Theories Abound in Bombing." *Stevens Point Journal*, 8 May, p. 9.

Becker, G. 1994. "How the Homeless Crisis was Hyped." *Business Week*, 12 September, 22.

Beder, H. 1986. *Marketing Continuing Education*, San Francisco: Jossey-Bass.

Benoit, W. L., and S. L. Brinson. 1994. "AT&T: 'Apologies are not enough.'" *Communication Quarterly* 42:75–88.

Beresford, D. 1994. "Dogged by Haunting Images of Misery." *Weekly Mail and Guardian*, 26 August, p. 21.

Berners-Lee, T., R. Cailliau, A. Loutonen, H. Frystyk Nielsen, and A. Secret. 1994. "The World-Wide Web." *Communications of the ACM* 37:76–82.

Bernstein, A. 1994. "Inequality: How the Gap between Rich and Poor Hurts the Economy." *Business Week*, 15 August, 78–83.

Bertalanffy, L. 1968. *General System Theory: Foundations, Development, Applications*. New York: George Braziller.

Bester, G. 1993. "Brave New World of the White Militants." *Weekly Mail and Guardian*, 30 December, p. 15.

Bleek, D. 1922. "Report on Anthropological Research among the Bushmen in the South West Africa Protectorate." State Archives, Windhoek, Namibia.

Bloombecker, J. 1994. "Viewpoint." *Communications of the ACM*, November, 15–16.

Bloomfield, M. H. 1988. "Law: The Development of a Profession." In *The Professions in American History*, edited by N. Hatch, 33–50. Notre Dame, Ind.: University of Notre Dame Press.

Blunt, P., and M. L. Jones. 1992. *Managing Organizations in Africa*. Berlin: Walter de Guyter.

Borman, S. 1993. "Benefits of Electronic Conferences Cited by Online Meeting Attendees." *Chemical and Engineering News* 71:26–27.

Borrus, A. 1994. "Will China Scuttle Its Pirates?" *Business Week*, 15 August, 40.

Bowker Annual Library and Book Trade Almanac. 1993. New Providence, N.J.: R. R. Bowker.

Brown, K. 1994. "France Sets Out to Buy Friendship on U.S. Campuses." *International Herald Tribune*, 24 February, p. 2.

Browne, J. 1994. "Distortions Feed our Fears." *Milwaukee Journal*, 23 October, pp. 1, 14.

Buckland, M. K. 1991. "Information as Thing." *Journal of the American Society for Information Science* 42:351–360.

Burress, L. 1989. *Battle of the Books: Literary Censorship in the Public Schools, 1950–1985*. Metuchen, N.J.: Scarecrow Press.

Byers, J. 1984. "The Prediction of Commitment to the Teaching Profession." Paper presented at the annual meeting of the American Educational Research Association, 23–27 April, New Orleans.

Byrne, J. 1994a. "The Craze for Consultants." *Business Week*, 25 July, 60–65.

————. 1994b. "Hired Guns Packing High-powered Knowhow." *Business Week*, 21st Century Capitalism (Special issue), 92–96.

Cage, M. C. 1994. "The Fate of South Asian Studies." *Chronicle of Higher Education*, 3 August, A13.

Calhoun C., and P. DeLargy. 1992. "Computerization, Aid-Dependency, and Administrative Capacity: A Sudanese Case Study." In *Microcomputers in African Development: Critical Perspectives*, edited by S. Grant Lewis and J. Samoff, 25–63. Boulder, Colo.: Westview Press.

Chang, Jung. 1991. *Wild Swans: Three Daughters of China*. London: Flamingo.

Chirandu, G. 1993. "Southern African Film Producers Cry for Help." *Southern Africa Political and Economic Monthly* 7:10–11.

Christie, P. 1985. *The Right to Learn: The Struggle for Education in South Africa*. Johannesburg: Raven Press.

Cole, R. E. 1971. *Japanese Blue Collar: The Changing Tradition*. Berkeley and Los Angeles: University of California Press.

Cornwall, H. 1987. *Data Theft: Computer Fraud, Industrial Espionage, and Information Crime*. London: Heinemann.

Cortese, A. 1995. "Looking for the Next Netscape." *Business Week*, 23 October, 110–114.

Curwen, P. 1986. *The World Book Industry*. New York: Facts on File.

Dagenais, T. 1993. "The IT Interest Group, One Year Later." *CA Magazine* 126:44–45.

Davie, K. 1994. "No Money, No Work, No Land and Little Hope." *Sunday Times*, 20 March, p. 12.

Davis, R. 1995. "Computer Technology Comes to the Aid of Crime Victims." *USA Today*, 15 September, p. 9A.

Delfattore, J. 1992. *What Johnny Shouldn't Read: Textbook Censorship in America*. New Haven, Conn.: Yale University Press.

DeLoughry, T. 1994. "Gatekeeping at the Internet." *Chronicle of Higher Education*, 23 November, A21–22.

Dickey, C. 1994. "We Interrupt This Program." *Newsweek*, 28 March, 46.

"Disillusionment and No Discipline Are the Lasting Legacy." 1994. *Weekly Mail and Guardian*, 6 May, p. 44.

Drucker, P. 1995. "The Information Executives Truly Need." *Harvard Business Review*, January, 54–62.

Dube, P. 1993. "No Fun on the License Trail." *Weekly Mail and Guardian*, 10 December, p. 11.

Duke, B. 1986. *The Japanese School: Lessons for Industrial America*. New York: Praeger.

Eaton, A. E., and P. B. Voos. 1991. "Unions and Contemporary Innovations in Work Organization, Compensation, and Employee Participation." In *Unions and Economic Competitiveness*, edited by L. Mishel and P. B. Voos, 173–215. Armonk, N.Y.: M. E. Sharpe.

Edelstein, A., Y. Ito, and H. Kipplinger. 1989. *Communication and Culture: A Comparative Approach*. New York: Longman.

Edupage. An Online Information Service of EDUCOM, Washington, D.C.

Eltahawy, M. 1994. "Bold and Beautiful in Egyptian Soapie Row." *Citizen*, 6 January, 6.

Faludi, S. 1991. *Backlash: The Undeclared War against American Women*. New York: Crown Publishers.

Farley, C. 1994. "Please, Mr. Postman." *Time*, 1 August, 26.

Festinger, L. 1957. *Cognitive Dissonance*. Stanford, Calif.: Stanford University Press.

Fialka, J. 1995. "Pentagon Studies Art of 'Information Warfare' to Reduce Its Systems' Vulnerability to Hackers." *Wall Street Journal*, 3 July, p. A12.

Fitzgerald, M. 1993. "Truth Commission Report on El Salvador." *Editor and Publisher*, 29 March, 18–20.

Fixses, R. 1994. "Holocaust Hero Died Alone and in Poverty." *Citizen*, 11 February, p. 6.

Flaherty, F. 1994. "Scams Advance through Technology." *Stevens Point Journal*, 22 July, p. 16.

"Foreign Papers May Not Publish in India." 1994. *Citizen*, 3 February, p. 12.

Freeland, N. 1994. "SADC Regional Early Warning System." Paper presented at the African Information Technology Conference, Cambridge, England, September.

Friszman, T. 1982. "Education in Poland." In Altbach, Arnov, and Kelly, *Comparative Education*, 390–406. New York: Macmillan.

Frum, D. 1993. "Lawyers in Cyberspace." *Forbes* 152:56.

Frye, C. 1994. "Expect Federal Directive to Create EDI Hub-bub." *Software Magazine* 14:87–93.

Fussell, P. 1975. *The Great War and Modern Memory*. London: Oxford University Press.

Gibbs, N. 1994. "Cry the Forsaken Country." *Time*, 1 August, 32–37.

Gibbs, W. W. 1995. "Lost Science in the Third World." *Scientific American*, August, 92–99.

Gilbert, J. 1994. "The Best Jobs in America." *Money*, March, 70–73.

Glastris, P., and J. Thornton. 1994. "A New Civil Rights Frontier." *U.S. News and World Report*, 17 January, 38–39.

Glenn, J. 1994. News release. Opening Statement of Senator John Glenn, Chairman, Government Affairs committee on High Risk and Emerging Fraud: IRS, Student Loans and HUD, 19 July.

Glennon, G. 1994. Sales Manager, Journal Printing Company. Interview by author. Stevens Point, Wisconsin, August.

Goldhaber, G. M. 1990. *Organizational Communication*. Dubuque, Iowa: W. C. Brown.

Goldstuck, A. 1994. "SA's 'Net Surfers Have to Learn to Swim Right." *Weekly Guardian and Mail*, 24 September, pp. 30, 26.

Gordon, R. 1992. *The Bushman Myth: The Making of a Namibian Underclass*. Boulder, Colo.: Westview Press.

Gram, D. 1994. "Securities Regulators Warn of I-way Robbery." *Stevens Point Journal*, 30 June, 24.

Grant Lewis, S. 1992. "Microcomputer Adoption in Tanzania and the Rise of a Professional Elite." In *Microcomputers in African Development: Critical Perspectives*, edited by S. Grant Lewis, S. and J. Samoff, 65–118. Boulder, Colo.: Westview Press.

Gurak, L. J. 1994. "The Rhetorical Dynamics of a Community Protest in Cyberspace:

The case of Lotus MarketPlace." Ph.D. diss., Rensselaer Polytechnic Institute.

Haffejee, F. 1993. "Cosatus's Thought Industry." *Weekly Mail and Guardian*, 17 December, 18.

Hall, R. H. 1991. *Organizations, Structures, Processes, and Outcomes*. Englewood Cliffs, N.J.: Prentice-Hall.

Halls, W. 1982. "The French Secondary School Today." In Altbach, Arnov, and Kelly, *Comparative Education*, 47–71. New York: Macmillan.

Hedlund, M. 1994. Electronic communication (march@europa.com).

Hentoff, N. 1992. *Free Speech for Me—But Not for Thee*. New York: HarperCollins.

Hertling, J. 1995. "Internet Growth Challenges China's Authoritarian Ways." *Chronicle of Higher Education*, 9 June, A22.

Hinchman, J. 1994. IRS Automation: Controlling electronic filing fraud and improper access to taxpayer data, Testimony before the Committee on Governmental Affairs, United States Senate, 19 July.

House, D. 1991. *Continuing Liberal Education*. New York: Macmillan.

Hruska, J. 1990. *Computer Viruses and Anti-Virus Warfare*. New York: Ellis Horwood.

Huband, M. 1994. "Kenyan Politicians Stoke Tribal Violence." *Weekly Mail and Guardian*, 29 July, p. 18.

Huckshorn, K. 1995. "TV Invasion." *Milwaukee Journal Sentinel*, 24 September, p. 10A.

Huey, J. 1994. "The New Post-Heroic Leadership." *Fortune*, 21 February, 18–22.

Hull, J. 1993. "Have We Gone Mad?" *Time*, 20 December, 33–34.

Ibrahim, Y. 1993. "16 Are Shot in Attack on Tourists in Cairo." *International Herald-Tribune*, 28 December, p. 2.

Inkeles, A. 1982. "National Differences in Scholastic Performance." In Altbach, Arnov, and Kelly, *Comparative Education*, 210–231. New York: Macmillan.

Jackson, S. 1993. "Experiment in Columbia." *Editor and Publisher*, 20 March, 12–15.

Jacobs, E. 1994. Making the Information Superhighway Accessible to Low Income Communities: A New Approach in Ohio. Legal Aid Society of Dayton, Handsnet email posting.

Janis, I. 1982. *Groupthink*. New York: Houghton Mifflin.

Jarvis, P. 1988. *Britain: Policy and Practice of Continuing Education*. San Francisco: Jossey-Bass.

Jixiang, L., and Z. Maosheng. 1988. "Cadre Education." In *China: Lessons from Practice*, edited by M. Wang, W. Lin, S. Sun, and J. Fang. San Francisco: Jossey-Bass.

Jones, W. 1994. "Humanist Scholar's Use of Computers in Libraries and Writing." In *Literacy and Computers*, edited by C. Selfe and S. Hilligoss, 157–170. New York: Modern Library Association.

Jules-Rosette, B. 1992. "Fragile and Progressive Computer Contracts in Kenya and the Ivory Coast: New Social Forums in the Workplace." In *Microcomputers in African Development: Critical Perspectives*, edited by S. Grant Lewis and J. Samoff, 119–145. Boulder, Colo.: Westview Press.

Kadi, M. 1995. "Welcome to Cyberbia." *Utne Reader*, March–April, 57–59.

Kantor, A., and E. Berlin. 1994. "The SurfBoard." *Internet World*, November, 15.

Keming, G. 1988. "Distance Education." In *China: Lessons from Practice*, edited by M. Wang, W. Lin, S. Sun, and J. Fang. San Francisco: Jossey-Bass.

Kuhn, T. S. 1962. *The Structure of Scientific Revolutions*. Chicago: University of Chicago Press.

Kurtz, H. 1995. "Newspaper Industry Going through a Rough Year." *Milwaukee Journal Sentinel*, 5 November, pp. 1D, 4D.

Lapides, G. 1982. "Sexual Equality through Educational Reform: The Case of the USSR." In Altbach, Arnov, and Kelly, *Comparative Education*, 252–268. New York: Macmillan.

Larson, E. 1992. *The Naked Consumer: How Our Private Lives Become Public Commodities*. New York: Henry Holt.

Larson, M. 1977. *The Rise of Professionalism: a Sociological Analysis*. Berkeley and Los Angeles: University of California Press.

Lawson, R. F. 1988. *Changing Patterns in Secondary Education: An International Comparison*. Calgary, Alberta: University of Calgary Press.

Lee, J., and J. Merisotis. 1990. *Proprietary Schools: Programs, Policies, and Prospects*. ASHE-ERIC Higher Education Report No. 5, Washington D.C.: George Washington University.

Leepile. M. 1994. Editor-in-chief, *Mmegi*. Interview by author. Gabarone, Botswana, 7 April.

Lent, J. 1993. "Four Conundrums of Third World Communications: A Generational Analysis." In *Beyond National Sovereignty: International Communication in the 1990s*, edited by K. Nordenstregn and H. Schiller, 235–255. Norwood, N.J.: Ablex Publishing.

Levins, H. 1994a. "Prime Time Crime: TV Coverage Heavy." *St. Louis Post-Dispatch*, 14 August, pp. 1, 6.

———. 1994b. "Rural Views See Chaos, Mayhem Here." *St. Louis Post-Dispatch*, 14 August, pp. 1, 7.

Levinson, M. 1994. "Write if You Find Work." *Newsweek*, 14 March, 44–49.

Levitt, T. 1975. "Marketing Myopia." *Harvard Business Review*, September.

Levy, F., and R. Murname. 1992. "U.S. Earnings Levels and Earnings Inequality: A Review of Recent Trends and Proposed Explanations." Paper presented at a public policy seminar at Columbia University, New York.

Levy, S. 1994. "E-Money (That's What I Want)." *Wired*, December, 174–179, 213–215, 218–219.

Lewin, K., and A. Little. 1984. "Examination Reform and Educational Change in Sri Lanka, 1972–1982: Modernization or Dependent Underdevelopment." In Watson, *Dependence and Interdependence in Education*, 47–94. London: Cromm Helm.

Loban, W. 1976. *Language Development: Kindergarten through Grade Twelve*. Urbana, Ill.: National Council of Teachers of English.

Lush, D. 1994. President, Media Institute of Southern Africa. Interview by author. Windhoek, Namibia, March.

Lutz, W. 1989. *Double-Speak*. New York: Harper and Row.

MacBride, S. 1980. *Many Voices, One World*. Report by the International Commission for the Study of Communication Problems. New York: UNESCO.

Mandell, M. 1994. "The Real Truth about the Economy." *Business Week*, 7 November, 110–118.

Maranto, G. 1995. "Delayed Childbearing." *Atlantic Monthly* 275:55–66.

Marcaccio, K. 1992. *Computer Readable Databases*. Detroit: Gale Research.

Marchand, D., and F. Horton. 1986. *Infrotrends: Profiting from your Information Resources*. New York: John Wiley.

Margolis, M. 1994. "Wrong Number, Please Try Again." *Newsweek*, 28 February, 19.

Matkin, G. 1990. *Technology Transfer and the University*. New York: Macmillan.

Mbaso, C. 1993. "Zimbabwe's Fledgling Film Industry." *Southern Africa Political and Economic Monthly* 7:16–18.

McClough, L. 1993. "HealthNet Information Service." *SatelLife News*, 1 February.

McIvor, G., and A. Mahmood. 1994. "Feminist Author Nasreen Finds Asylum in Sweden." *Weekly Mail and Guardian*, 12 August, p. 13.

McKeown, K. 1991. "Social Norms and Implications of Santa Monica's PEN (Public Electronic Network)." Paper presented at the annual convention of the American Psychological Association, San Francisco, August.

Meek, J. 1995. "Dubbing of American Soap into Ukrainian Enrages Crimea." *Milwaukee*

Journal Sentinel, 24 September, p. 10A.

Meyer, M. 1994. "Keeping the Cybercops out of Cyberspace." *Newsweek*, 14 March, 52.

"Militants Raid Paper in Algiers: Two Killed." 1994. *Citizen*, 22 March, p. 7.

Miller, J. 1982. "The German Secondary School." In Altbach, Arnov, and Kelly, *Comparative Education*, 91–106. New York: Macmillan.

Miner Brook, Scott. 1994. "The New Civil Rights Frontier." *U.S. News and World Report*, 17 January, 38–39.

Morgan, B. 1992. *Information Industry Directory*. Detroit: Gale Research.

Moroke, Montishiwa, 1994. "Telkom Is under Fire in Reef Townships." *Star*, 18 March, p. 5.

Murdock, G., and P. Golding. 1989. "Information Poverty and Political Inequality: Citizenship in the Age of Privatized Communications." *Journal of Communications* 39:180–195.

Naisbitt, J. 1982. *Megatrends: Ten New Directions Transforming Our Lives*. New York: Warner Books.

"The Nation." 1994. *Chronicle of Higher Education Almanac*, 1 September, 6.

Ndivanga, C. 1994. "Africa—'Just another BAD NEWS story.' " *Namibian Weekender*, 27 May, p. 8.

Nicholls, P. 1991. *CD-ROM Collection Builder's Toolkit: 1992 Edition*. Weston, Conn.: Eight Bit Books.

Ngongo, A. S. 1995. "Zaire's Public Schools Go Public." *Weekly Mail and Guardian*, 3 March, p. 21.

Noack, D. 1994. "Supernatural, Strange, and Sinister." *Internet World*, November, 88–92.

Nyakunu, T. 1994. "An Examination of WHO's Budget." *Southern Africa Political and Economic Monthly* 7:22–26.

Ogbu, J. 1982. "Equalization of Educational Opportunity and Racial/Ethnic Inequality." In Altbach, Arnov, and Kelly, *Comparative Education*, 269–289. New York: Macmillan.

Oliveira, O. 1993. "Brazilian Soaps Outshine Hollywood: Is Cultural Imperialism Fading Out?" In *Beyond National Sovereignty: International Communication in the 1990s*, edited by K. Nordenstregn and H. Schiller, 116–131. Norwood, N.J.: Ablex Publishing.

O'Neill, S., K. Marks, and H. Muir. 1994. "Head Sorry for Ban on Romeo and Juliet." *Weekly Mail*, 24 January, p. 7.

"Online Fraud Case Settled." 1994. *Wall Street Journal*, 17 November, p. A4.

"Paedophiles Now Use Computers to Snare Their Victims." 1994. *Citizen*, 5 April, p. 12.

Palmer, M. 1994. "The Singing Dustman." *Weekly Telegraph*, April, p. viii–ix.

Paton, L. 1994. "Movers and Shakers." *Namibian Weekender*, 25 March, p. 3.

Pearce, J. 1995. "More Local Content Will Be Even More Lekker." *Weekly Mail and Guardian*, 1 September, p. B5.

Penberthy, J. 1994. "State of Siege Downtown." *Time*, 31 January, p. 54.

"Politically Incorrect Students Start Fight for Free Thinking on American Campuses." 1994. *Sunday Times*, 1 May, p. 20.

Pope, N. W. 1979. "Mickey Mouse Marketing." *American Banker*, July, 25.

Port, O. 1994. "Halting Highway Robbery on the Internet." *Business Week*, 17 October, 212.

Porter, T. M. 1995. *Trust in Numbers: The Pursuit of Objectivity in Science and Public Life*. Princeton, N.J.: Princeton University Press.

"Power and Control." Pamphlet of the Domestic Abuse Intervention Project, Duluth, Minnesota.

Presidential Commission. 1986. *Report to the President on the Space Shuttle Challenger Accident*. Washington, D.C.: Government Printing Office.

Preston, R. 1984. "Dependency Perspectives on the Impact of Education on Family Livelihood Strategies in Rural Areas of Andean America." In Watson, *Dependence and Interdependence in Education,* 119–140. London: Cromm Helm.

Putnam, R. D. 1995. "Bowling Alone: America's Declining Social Capital." *Journal of Democracy* 6:65–78.

Quindlen, A. 1994. "Child's Book Offers Two World Views." *Stevens Point Journal,* 30 July, p. 4.

Ramirez, A. 1991. "More Errors Admitted by AT&T." *New York Times,* 19 September, pp. 15, 27.

Ramirez, R., and J. Boli-Bennett. 1982. "Global Patterns of Educational Institutionalization." In Altbach, Arnov, and Kelly, *Comparative Education,* 15–38. New York: Macmillan.

Rappaport, A., and S. Halevi. 1991. "The Computerless Computer Company." *Harvard Business Review,* July, 69–80.

Realizing the Potential. 1995. The National Report of the National Center on Postsecondary Teaching, Learning, and Assessment. University Park, Pa.: NCPTLA.

Reason, J. T. 1990. *Human Error.* Cambridge: Cambridge University Press.

Reiss, S. 1994. "Taxes: Hands Up, I've Got a Joystick." *Newsweek,* 14 February, 28.

Rettle, J. 1993. "Bangladeshi Feminist Writer Gets 'Death Sentence.'" *Weekly Mail and Guardian,* 30 December, p. 26.

Ricchiardi, S. 1994. "Under the Gun." *American Journalism Review,* July/August, 19–25.

Richards, W. 1976. "Using G-Network Analysis in Research." Paper presented at a meeting of the International Communication Association, Portland, Oregon.

Rickard, C. 1993. "Man Wins His Battle to Get Off Secret List." *Sunday Times,* 19 December, p. 12.

Rizzo, K. 1994. "IRS Snooping through Files is a Problem." *Stevens Point Journal,* 19 July, p. 16.

Roberts, K., and C. O'Reilly. 1975. Communication Roles in Organizations. Some Potential Antecedents and Consequences. Technical Report No. 11, Contract No. N000314-69a1054. Washington, D.C.: Office of Naval Research.

Rosen, N. 1994. "Film: UK Fails to Make the World Ratings." *Sunday Telegraph,* 27 March, p. 6.

Rottenberg, D. 1994. "And That's the Way It Is." *American Journalism Review,* May, 35–37.

"Rural Pupils Outshine Urban Kids." 1994. *Weekly Mail and Guardian,* 14 January, p. 6.

"Rushdie 'Death Sentence' No Respite after 5 Years." 1994. *Citizen,* 14 February, p. 11.

Salia-Bao, K. 1991. *The Namibian Educational System under the Colonialists.* Randberg, S.A.: Hodder and Stoughton.

Samburg, A. 1994. "Online Ripple Effect." Edupage, 27 December.

"Schindler's Draws 100,000 in 4 Days." 1994. *Citizen,* 9 March, p. 16.

"Schindler's List May Be Stopped in Thailand." 1994. *Citizen,* 10 May, p. 13.

Schlesinger, L., and Heskett, J. 1991. "Breaking the Cycle of Failure in Services." *Sloan Management Review* 32 (Spring): 17–28.

Shieh, J., and R. Ballard. 1994. "E-Mail Privacy." *Educom Review,* March, 59–61.

Sidley, P. 1994. "Face to Face—Then Vote." *Weekly Mail and Guardian,* 4 March, p. 15.

Snyder, J. 1994. "Internet: Going South." *Internet World,* November, 94–95.

Starr, M., P. King, and F. Washington. 1994. "Thin Ice." *Newsweek,* 24 January, p. 40.

"State Collects Over 8,000 Types of Personal Records." 1994. *Stevens Point Journal,* 28 November, 19.

Stevenson, R. W. 1994. "U.S. Shines in European TV." *International Herald Tribune,* 7 February, p. 9.

Stewart, T. 1994a. "Managing in a Wired Company." *Fortune,* 11 July, 44–56.

———. 1994b. "The Netplex: It's a New Silicon Valley." *Fortune,* 7 March, 62–68.

Stix, G. 1994. "The Speed of Write." *Scientific American,* December, 106–111.

Stoll, C. 1990. *Cuckoo's Egg: Tracking a Spy through the Maze of Computer Espionage*. New York: Pocket Books.

Sullum, J. 1994. "Passive Reporting on Passive Smoke." *Forbes Mediacritic*.

Suskind, R. "Tormented for Learning." 1994. *Reader's Digest*, September, 49–53.

Szczesny, J. 1993. "Back on the Fast Track." *Time*, 13 December, 58–63.

"Talk of the Streets." 1994. *Time*, 30 May, 12.

Taylor, F. W. 1947. *The Principles of Scientific Management*. New York, N.Y.: Harper and Row.

Tetzeli, R. 1994. "The Infobog, by the Numbers." *Fortune*, 11 July, 62.

Theil, S. 1994. "Inside the Neo-Nazi Movement." *Newsweek*, 28 March, 54.

"There's Smoke in Ads . . . but Is There Fire?" 1994. *Milwaukee Journal*, 3 July, p. A11.

Thomas, E. 1988. *The Harmless People*. Cape Town, S.A.: Africasouth Paperbacks.

Tincher, W. 1986. "Attitudes toward Teaching of High Aptitude High School Seniors." Paper presented at the annual meeting of American Association of Colleges for teacher education. 26 February 26–1 March, Chicago.

Toffler, A. 1990. *Powershift: Knowledge, Wealth, and Violence at the Edge of the 21st Century*. New York: Bantam Books.

Tomaselli, R., K. Tomaselli, and J. Muller, J. 1989. *Broadcasting in South Africa*. New York: St. Martin's Press.

"Top U.S. Author's Book Labelled Anti-Religious." 1994. *Citizen*, 21 February, p. 17.

"Tried to Ban Mixed-Race Dates: Suspended." 1994. *Citizen*, 16 March, p. 17.

Tully, S. 1994. "Teens, the Most Global Market of All." *Fortune*, 16 May, 34–41.

UNESCO. *Statistical Yearbook*. 1992. Geneva: UNESCO.

"Uniform Crime Reports." 1993. *World Almanac and Book of Facts, 1994*. Mahwah, N.J.: Funk and Wagnalls.

"UN: Keeping the Peace by Keeping Reporters Out." 1994. *Time*, 23 May, 17.

U.S. Bureau of the Census. 1990. *100 Years of Data Processing: The Punchcard Century*. Washington, D.C.

———. 1993. *Statistical Abstracts of the United States*. Washington, D.C.

U.S. Congress. House of Representatives. 1987. *NASA's Response to the Committee's Investigation of the Challenger Accident. Hearings before the Committee on Space, Science, and Technology*.

———. 1991. *Hearings before the Government Information, Justice, and Agriculture Subcommittee of the Committee on Government Operations*, 10 April. Washington, D.C.

U.S. Department of Education (DOE). 1992a. *Digest of Educational Statistics*. Washington, D.C.

———. 1992b. *International Education Comparisons*. Washington, D.C.

U.S. Department of Housing and Urban Development, Office of the Assistant Secretary for Administration (HUD). 1992. *Strategic Plan for Electronic Data Interchange*. Washington, D.C.

Vandewater, B. 1994. "State Ranks High in Households without Phones." *Daily Oklahoman*, 17 August, p. 14.

Voronov, A. 1994. *Newsweek*, 21 March, p. 9.

Wald, M. L. 1995. "Is Internet a Baud Thing?" *Stevens Point Journal*, 5 May, 4.

Walden, G. 1994. "All the World's a Screen—and We Should Aim to Fill It." *Weekly Telegraph*, 5 January, p. x.

Walker, M. 1994a. "All On-Line for a Town Meeting with the Planet." *Weekly Mail and Guardian*, 6 May, p. 27.

———. 1994b. "American Review." *Weekly Mail and Guardian*, 21 January, p. 22.

———. 1994c. "A Tragi-Comedy of Modern Manners." *Weekly Mail and Guardian*, 20 May, p. 18.

Walsh, J. 1994. "Death to the Author." *Time*, 15 August, 26.

Wang, M., W. Lin, S. Sun, and J. Fang, eds. 1988. *China: Lessons from Practice*. San Francisco: Jossey-Bass.

Watson, K. 1984. *Dependence and Interdependence in Education: International Perspectives*. London: Cromm Helm.

White, M. 1987. *The Japanese Educational Challenge: A Commitment to Children*. London: Free Press.

Wildstrom, S. 1994. "Data Privacy: A Win for Business." *Business Week*, 8 August, 11.

Williams, M. 1992. "The State of Databases Today." In *Computer Readable Databases*, edited by K. Marcaccio. Detroit: Gale Research.

World Bank. 1995. "Improving African Transport Corridors." Project Report Number 84.

Wurman, R. S. 1989. *Information Anxiety: What to Do When Information Doesn't Tell You What You Need to Know*. New York: Bantam Books.

Zuboff, S. 1988. *In the Age of the Smart Machine*. New York: Basic Books.

Index

About the Author

BILL WRESCH chairs the Department of Mathematics and Computing at the University of Wisconsin—Stevens Point. He is the author of five other books, three textbooks and two books published by the National Council of Teachers of English on classroom uses of computers. He is best known for Writer's Helper, a computer program used widely in high schools and colleges. In September 1993 he was named a Fulbright Senior Scholar for the University of Namibia. He taught computer science at the university and helped get UNAM connected to the Internet. He began the research for this book during his nine months in Southern Africa.